CONSCIOUS MANAGEMENT
Managing and Leading Happily at the Workplace and at Home

CONSCIOUS MANAGEMENT

Managing and Leading Happily at the Workplace and at Home

> What all is Not Taught at any Campus
> or
> Training Centre

Siddhartha Ganguli, Ph.D.

ALLIED PUBLISHERS PVT. LTD.

New Delhi • Mumbai • Kolkata • Lucknow • Chennai
Nagpur • Bangalore • Hyderabad • Ahmedabad

ALLIED PUBLISHERS PRIVATE LIMITED

1/13-14 Asaf Ali Road, **New Delhi**–110002
Ph.: 011-23239001 • E-mail: delhi.books@alliedpublishers.com

47/9 Prag Narain Road, Near Kalyan Bhawan, **Lucknow**–226001
Ph.: 0522-2209942 • E-mail: lko.books@alliedpublishers.com

17 Chittaranjan Avenue, **Kolkata**–700072
Ph.: 033-22129618 • E-mail: cal.books@alliedpublishers.com

15 J.N. Heredia Marg, Ballard Estate, **Mumbai**—400001
Ph.: 022-42126969 • E-mail: mumbai.books@alliedpublishers.com

60 Shiv Sunder Apartments (Ground Floor), Central Bazar Road, Bajaj Nagar, **Nagpur**–440010
Ph.: 0712-2234210 • E-mail: ngp.books@alliedpublishers.com

F-1 Sun House (First Floor), C.G. Road, Navrangpura, Ellisbridge P.O., **Ahmedabad**–380006
Ph.: 079-26465916 • E-mail: ahmbd.books@alliedpublishers.com

751 Anna Salai, **Chennai**–600002
Ph.: 044-28523938 • E-mail: chennai.books@alliedpublishers.com

5th Main Road, Gandhinagar, **Bangalore**–560009
Ph.: 080-22262081 • E-mail: bngl.books@alliedpublishers.com

3-2-844/6 & 7 Kachiguda Station Road, **Hyderabad**–500027
Ph.: 040-24619079 • E-mail: hyd.books@alliedpublishers.com

Website: www.alliedpublishers.com

© 2011, Siddhartha Ganguli

No part of the material protected by this copyright notice may be reproduced or utilized in any form or by any means, electronic or mechanical including photocopying, recording or by any information storage and retrieval system, without prior written permission from the copyright owners.

ISBN: 978-81-8424-658-2

Published by Sunil Sachdev and printed by Ravi Sachdev at Allied Publishers Pvt. Ltd. (Printing Division), A-104 Mayapuri Phase II, New Delhi-110064

Acknowledgements

Live Happily, Work Happily, published in 2009, received a fabulous response. The appreciation of my enquiry into the *Science of Happiness* was visible as requests started pouring into our body-brain management and development boutique *Learning Club* from the corporate world as well as academic institutions for conducting workshops on this topic for their employees at all levels who had been performing *unhappily* under *stress* for different reasons. Besides, people from all backgrounds and age groups started calling at our *Happiness*, *Planned Success* and *Winning Child* clinics to get their problems solved and dreams come true.

We have been, for the last few years, conducting a very effective workshop module on *Conscious Management* called *The Conscious Manager*, *The Conscious Supervisor*, *Conscious Management*, and *The Conscious Teacher* (shall we say, the *Consciousness* series) for different types and levels of participants. After the success of *Live Happily, Work Happily*, we decided to include inputs on the science of *happiness* in the *'consciousness'*-related workshop contents and the participants found those extremely practical and useful. Life being a mix of family, social and work roles, we shared practical case studies on family management and good parenting practices also. This enriched the quality of our workshops.

The present work, *Conscious Management* is a well thought-out and expanded treatise based on our *'Consciousness'* series workshops which are still being highly appreciated by our customers—the workshop participants. In writing this book, I have been encouraged tremendously by my thousands of participants, my *Learning Club* team members Ravi Verma, Niranjan Das, Pervez Alam and Prabir Roy and, of course, my wife Utpala. Especially, Pervez and Ravi were excellent in technical assistance and Niranjan was always ready with marketing ideas. My daughter Ishita, a senior HR manager and her husband Anand Krishnan a senior IT professional, while they were staying abroad, had helped me with latest books on *brain science* which had not reached the Indian market still. I could glance through the most up-to-date findings.

I greatly appreciate the active help of Sharad Gupta and his editorial and production team of Allied Publishers Pvt. Ltd., New Delhi who took up the *Conscious Management* project readily after publishing two of my works *Live Happily, Work Happily* and *SUCCESS: Can be Planned and Earned* in quick succession. I shall never forget the co-operation of Jayant Manaktala, Samir Dey and the entire marketing team of Allied Publishers, Kolkata in ensuring that copies of my books reach every corner of the country.

Finally, genuine greetings to Dr. Marshall Goldsmith who is considered one of the topmost management thinkers in the world today and whose concept of *MOJO* (which is his very personal way of representing motivation and happiness) has crossed the shores of America and reached different corners of the world, for agreeing to write the Foreword of *Conscious Management*. His contribution has been one of my greatest motivators to continue my journey into the depths of *happiness* which, somehow, coincides with Dr Goldsmith's concept of *MOJO*. Thank you very much Marshall!

Foreword

When I first read Siddhartha Ganguli's *Conscious Management,* I was thrilled at how intricately its message is tied to what I call Mojo. Without knowledge of my definition of Mojo, my foreword might not make sense. So, I define *Mojo* as that positive spirit towards what we are doing now, which starts from the inside and radiates to the outside.

In *Conscious Management,* Siddhartha deftly explains how we can identify and develop the right levels of consciousness so that we may manage, lead, and produce "winners" who will create other "winners". In other words, how we can develop that positive spirit towards what we are doing now, be it with our families or at work, and allow it to spread out to our families, friends, and co-workers. The idea is for them to learn to do the same thing thus managing a higher level of consciousness and a greater awareness of Mojo and its opposite Nojo (that negative spirit toward what you are doing now that starts from the inside and radiates to the outside).

Not too long ago, I put a dent in the rear fender of my car. The dealership told me it could not be fixed, but needed to be replaced for $2000. A nearby bodyshop quoted nearly the same price. A neighbor referred me to a new bodyshop near my house. I drove there and was greeted by a young man. He said that while he couldn't guarantee a fix, he had an idea that might work. He told me to come back in 30 minutes. After 30 minutes I went back. "He's just finished. It's $63.75," said the receptionist. Surprised, I gave her my credit card. When I stepped outside, the young mechanic was standing at my car, beaming, and pointing to where the dent had been. It looked just like new! (And for less than $100). I thanked the young man, we shook hands, and he said, "Isn't it nice to meet a repairman who is trying to *save* you money?" This young man was the epitome of someone with Mojo. He took time out from his own work to experiment on my fender in order to save me time and money. This man, who takes more delight in doing his job well, even at the expense of some easy profit, is rich in Mojo. He will never starve.

To attain this level of consciousness and pass it on to others is what Siddhartha Ganguli's *Conscious Management* is all about. Read it, enjoy it, practice it, and you will learn the right kinds and levels of consciousness, which will lead you to Mojo both at work and at home.

Life is good.

Marshall Goldsmith
World renowned executive coach and author of the New York Times best sellers, MOJO and *What Got You Here Won't Get You There*

Contents

Acknowledgements .... *iii*
Foreword .... *v*
Introduction: How the Idea of Conscious Management Dawned 1
CHAPTER 1: Scenario Review: Where are We Today 11
CHAPTER 2: Conscious Management: The Need of the Day 22
CHAPTER 3: The Conscious Manager: Managing and 39
                     Leading *Happily*
CHAPTER 4: The Shortest Route to Conscious Self-Management.... 52
CHAPTER 5: Delving into the Depths of Consciousness 59
CHAPTER 6: Two Organisational Scenarios 75
CHAPTER 7: Your Work Role under a Microscope 85
CHAPTER 8: Your Personality Development 95
CHAPTER 9: Conscious Right Brain Management 104
CHAPTER 10: Developing Self-Consciousness 112
CHAPTER 11: Conscious Change within Yourself 120
CHAPTER 12: Conscious Brain Skills Management: Conscious 131
                      Intuition
CHAPTER 13: Lateral Thinking and Other Approaches 144
                      to Conscious Brain Skills Management
CHAPTER 14: Conscious Communication 156
                      for Relationship-Building
CHAPTER 15: Conscious Time Management 174
CHAPTER 16: Conscious Work-Life Balance 182

CHAPTER 17: Unconscious Motivation and Motivation 193
for Performance in the Work Role
CHAPTER 18: Conscious Motivation for Peak Performance 203
CHAPTER 19: Unconscious Leadership Styles 213
CHAPTER 20: Conscious Strategic Leadership (CSL)........................... 220
CHAPTER 21: Conscious Choice of Addiction which 230
will Make You Proud
Appendix I: 10 Key Result Factors (KRFs) for Self-Appraisal 247
and Discovery
Appendix II: Another UBP of Many Conscious Strategic 253
Leaders (CSLs)

INTRODUCTION

How the Idea of Conscious Management Dawned

BOOKS HAVE MINDS

Each book has a mind of its own. The thousands of books that are arranged in a systematic fashion on the racks of the library where I am a regular visitor have thousands of minds. I cannot be totally right when I say this. Because where a book has two authors, it's a product of two minds. When the authors are three in number, it is a mixture of three minds; where it is a collection of articles or serious papers by many contributors, it is a collage of many minds.

However, the mind of a book cannot be accessed into unless you go through the volume. Even a quick browsing through by avid readers like us can reveal a lot. Moreover, the innards of a book's mind cannot be fathomed by looking at its body—the outside cover, the jacket.

I believe in the quality of both—the contents presented inside and the covers on the outside. These together represent the book's personality.

FRESH-FROM-THE-OVEN

During a recent visit to the library, I picked up two glossy volumes. The packaging attracted me and a rapid flip through the pages of both the books developed a temptation in me to come close to the authors' minds. And, both were brand new additions to the world of non-fictions; absolutely fresh-from-the-oven! There was a second reason for the choice: both had unusually smart titles.

The title of the first book was *Profit with Honor* authored by the well-known social scientist and thinker Daniel Yankelovich [1]. It had an endorsement by Ged Davis of the World Economic Forum on the lacquered surface of the front cover: 'The one book that every Chairman and CEO must read this year'. That increased my reading curiosity.

The second one was called: *Firms of Endearment* with a flowing subtitle: *How World-Class Companies Profit from Passion and Purpose* authored by Raj Sisodia and Jag Sheth, both top marketing professors and David B. Wolfe, the internationally recognised customer behaviour expert in middle-age and older markets [2]. It had a foreword by Warren Bennis, distinguished Professor of Business Administration, University of Southern California. As I have always been an ardent admirer of Prof. Bennis, it was certainly a special drawing feature for me.

Both the volumes exuding strong print chemicals (the stimulus somehow attracts me a lot I'm not a bookworm in its true sense though!) dealt with *'profit-making'* in different than normal ways. Value-addition to the human capital being one of my prime areas of interest and having been preoccupied, over the last few years, with sculpting and shaping up a concept which I call *Human Resource Economics (HRE)*, this 'profit-making' focus attracted me readily.

CONGRATULATIONS, DANIEL YANKELOVICH!

As I was flipping through the first volume, I got totally absorbed with interest. I wanted to convey my heartiest congratulations to Yankelovich for his guts and upright spirit: how unhesitatingly he was exposing the truth of what has been going on in the American corporate world in the name of corporate governance.

Corporate Wrongdoing

In the *Introduction: How to Profit from the Scandal*, Yankelovich has asked a powerful probing question: Why is our culture suddenly confronted with so much corporate wrongdoing?

By 'corporate wrongdoing' Yankelovich means: many of the corporate custodians (managers, executives and supervisors at all levels) and gate-keepers (auditors and other regulatory professional bodies) today are sacrificing the principles of their profession for their own selfish economic gain; tying executive incentives to the price of the company's stock tempting them to take questionable shortcuts; shifting from the deepest tradition rooted in the ethic of *'enlightened' self-interest* to *'unenlightened' self-interest*—celebrating an ethic of *'winning for oneself'*. According to him, it is a 'zero-sum social Darwinian conception of winning' manifesting the 'I win, you lose' attitude.

'Fear of the consequences of losing is part of this outlook, as is an offhand attitude toward *'gaming the system'*. Many of today's business executives consider it a challenge—and fun—to find ways to manipulate the system for their own personal benefit'.

The Regulatory Medicine is Not Enough

However, in the midst of the darkness with which the corporate sky is overcast today, Yankelovich sees a ray of hope when he says: 'It would be a great relief to say that now, in the light of our experience with so many scandals, our business sector is finally taking the right medicine to cure itself. But unfortunately, this is far from the case. The medicine we are taking—a heavy dose of legal and regulatory actions—may be necessary, but it is far from sufficient' [3].

The Right Therapy

Yankelovich is absolutely right. We'll go a step farther to claim that the legal and regulatory actions do not really constitute the right medicine. Scope for the right therapy is within one's own self—in one's own *consciousness*. *Consciousness* is the right thing to be analysed and attacked.

The father of modern capitalism in the 18th century, Adam Smith, a professor at the University of Glasgow, was a moral philosopher, with a mind as fresh and high as the Scottish Highlands. He attributed to human nature an inborn empathy for others. It was this presupposition that gave credibility to his master concept of 'the invisible hand', which made the economic pursuit of *self-interest* compatible with the interests of the larger society in what Smith called 'a society of perfect liberty'. Capitalism, to follow the Adam Smith ideology, has always aligned itself with this concept of *'enlightened' self-interest*, arising from a different type and level of *consciousness*. But, in the real society, in the real business world, how many operate from the level of *consciousness* that Smith was operating from and he was perhaps expecting all others to operate from?

What an Octogenarian Indian Industrialist Says

I had penned up to here. Then, suddenly a flash of memory appeared on my mind's screen. I remembered how Indian industrialist Basant Kumar Birla, the illustrious son of one of the founder-fathers of modern Indian business and industry, the Late G D Birla, had shared his thoughts in his memoirs, where he had said: 'The main thing is the quality of life—how has one lived one's life, whether one's activities have been fruitful and beneficial to society or whether one could achieve success in life... these questions matter. The most significant criterion is whether one has upheld high moral values. During the last few decades, the importance of such ideals has been severely undermined. The world no longer seems to care for ethical principles. Indeed crass materialism has become the order of the day' [4]. Birla was talking about the same universal reality which Yankelovich is harping on today in the second decade of the 21st century, highlighting the need for a special level of *consciousness* which provides a value-based quality of life.

THE SOUL OF CAPITALISM

In the Wharton School publication *Firms of Endearment*, the three accomplished marketing experts are unified in their minds with a bright spark of hope when they claim that: '......we have entered a new era, the *Age of Transcendence*. This term signifies a fact supported by numerous consumer surveys showing that people are increasingly looking for higher meaning in their lives, rather than simply looking to add to the store of things they own. This is a signature trait of people in midlife and beyond who are not battling basic survival issues, either materially or emotionally. The search for meaning is changing expectations in the marketplace, and in the workplace. Indeed, we believe it is changing the very soul of capitalism'.

Sisodia, Wolfe and Sheth have come up with the idea of a *humanistic company* which is run in such a way that its stakeholders—customers, employees, suppliers, business partners, society, and many investors—develop an emotional connection and a *happy* association with it. They have chosen to call such humanistic companies *firms of endearment (FoEs)* as these organisations seek to maximise their value—emotional, experiential, social and financial, to society as a whole, not just to their shareholders. In suggesting the concept of a *humanistic company* or a *FoE*, are they not hinting at a certain higher level of *consciousness*?

Television producer and writer Norman Lear once told Warren Bennis, Professor of Business Administration, University of Southern California, 'When I've been most effective, I've listened to my inner voice'...'. Is Professor Bennis, by any chance, referring to the right kind of *consciousness* when he cites the example of the 'inner voice'? [5].

THE EMERGING VOICE OF INDIA

India's (₹ 6,000 Crores) ($60-billion) IT industry is getting ready to come out of the last few year's recessive phase and prepares to aim for the (₹ 10,000 Crores) ($100-billion) goal. Nevertheless, its current top threats are rising attrition, commoditisation of workforce and wage inflation. According to Vineet Nayar, the CEO of HCL Technologies, these threats would not have turned out to be such pressing worries for Indian managers, if they had worked according to the 'employee first, customer second' principle. In his own words: 'Today, we have four stakeholders—shareholders, employees, customers and society. Unfortunately, we are in the stranglehold of only one stakeholder, the shareholder. There are many CEOs across industries, who are at the edge of a building on fire, because the employees' trust in the management is at its lowest; their management models have become obsolete' [6].

Nayar, no doubt, is vouching for the right kind of *consciousness* while managing an industry.

FAMILY MANAGEMENT

We have looked at the economic front and talked only about the business and industrial segments of the society so far. Our concern extends equally to all non-government, quasi-, semi-, and government organisations which constitute the framework of any state or the nation as well as educational and human development and care systems like schools, colleges, universities and health care institutions which provide the foundation for any developing country.

Family: The Basic Social Unit

However, the basic social unit is indeed the family comprising the life partners and their dependents, particularly the children. Let us look at it now.

Cases of traditional joint and even modern nuclear families burning, breaking and falling apart and children approaching and growing up in their teens turning into rapists, raggers, murderers and indulgent in other forms of delinquent and sub-normal behaviour are on the rise. Very few of these juvenile characters, nevertheless, hit the headlines and get exposed through the media—both print and audio-visual. Many such cases do not get projected through the mass communication channels except for the most sensational ones.

Potential Assets Turning into Non-performing Assets

From the angle of *Human Resource Economics (HRE)*, a newborn child is equipped with potential assets by way of the diverse powers of its body and brain. We call them 'potential assets' as the child's body and brain have inherent capabilities which had evolved, bit by bit, over millions of years in our prehistoric predecessors and handed down through generations until the present.

However, small children in today's modern nuclear families are being either over-protected and over-pampered or handled most unkindly with physical or mental torture or both—the two extreme parenting styles known to elders rearing them [7]. The same handling styles are being cloned and carried into the educational units as the teachers and other care-givers, whether they are already playing parent roles or not in their families, have been exposed to nothing much different from and better than these when they were being brought up by their respective parents, elders and teachers. The human brain tends to conserve energy by repeating what it has seen, heard and been told rather than thinking and innovating something of an improved nature. It is not progressive, fast and forward-looking in that sense. It wants to act *unconsciously* most of the time as *conscious* neural processes (which obviously have to be fresh and potent with risks) would be energy-costly. Its natural propensity is to stay in the comfort zone.

Due to the over-protection or intimidation that the young human resources are subjected to, many of their potential assets turn into junk 'Non-Performing Assets (NPAs)' by the time they reach their adolescence. And, since all living cells follow one simple biological law: 'Use it or lose it'., sometimes, some kids unconsciously use some of those powers negatively or wrongly (in order to retain and not lose them for ever)—against social interests (such as while bullying other youngsters) or do not

Introduction: How the Idea of Conscious Management Dawned 7

use some of them (like it happens when the kid takes a bus or a car ride to school when it is just a walking distance away). As a consequence, those powers do not conform to this basic law of Nature. So, by the time the adolescent gets qualified and gets employed, self-employed or starts his own enterprise, the organisational system and the society—the market, get, as their human resource, individuals who have been handled wrongly and being non-performing assets want to get into a very restricted 'comfort zone' as otherwise they would be under *stress* and their body and brain attributes will further turn into liabilities (see Figure 1). All this happen due to the wrong kind of *consciousness*. The right kind of *consciousness* would call for the potential assets to be positively utilised to the extent possible in day-to-day life [8].

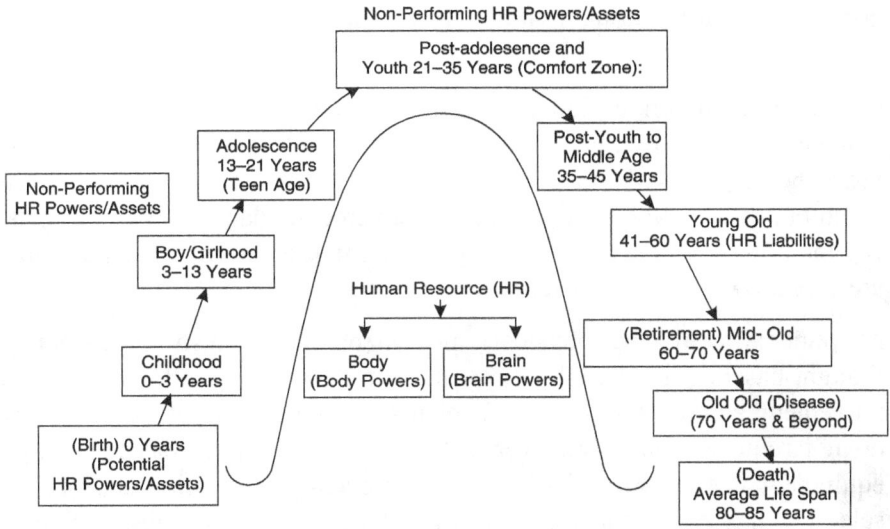

Fig. 1: Biological Life Cycle: What Happens Today: Potential Powers are Wasted due to Non-performance

Thus, the issue of the right kind and level of *consciousness* has become an urgent and important one even for management within the family—for creating *happy* members including *happy* life partners and their *happy* children.

WINNERS AND LOSERS

Happy managers produce people who feel being happily managed. Happy leaders produce happy followers. Happy husbands produce happy wives and *vice versa*. And happy parents produce happy children. Happy children make their parents happy too.

Happy individuals are *winners* and unhappy ones are *losers*. This book is meant to see how we can produce *winners* by making others *winners* too (and certainly not *losers* as it normally happens in cut-throat competition when living creatures including humans are overpowered by their 'selfish genes'), right from the beginning of a child's life and by conversion of grown-ups with the help of the right kind of *consciousness*.

HAVE THE KEY TO OPEN THE BLACK BOX

You and I are all being guided by our respective *consciousnesses*. And, our consciousness is like the Dark Continent. It is stored inside the black box—in the interior domain of our brain which neither can we see, nor can others pay a visit to.

Charles Sherrington, a pioneer British physiologist of the first half of the 20th century, had highlighted the contribution of 'movement' in our lives. From the subtleties of non-verbal expressions to the precision of our verbal communication, everything relies on movement. Plants, unlike animals, cannot move from one place to another. Animals are animals because they are *animated*; and, in Latin, *animus* means *consciousness*.

Movements could be physical; movements could also be mental—thought-based, idea-based or even attitude-based. And, for mental movement, a brain is necessary. As plants do not perform locomotion, they do not require brains; but even a tiny fish or a reptile has navigation equipment in the form of a brain. The process of evolution and natural selection has given us, the members of the human species, the most developed and versatile brain machinery where the left half of the *cerebrum* or the upper brain ('neo-cortex' is the bioligical term) represents the intelligent and rational thinking and planning mind, while the right half stands for the emotional, feeling and human relations mind. The left brain is the driver—manager for systematic performance-delivering results and the right brain is responsible for leading and motivating for results. Switching on and off only one or both the brains produces the right kind of *consciousness* required for a particular situation or set of circumstances.

Nevertheless, while the *cerebrum* envelopes the inner and lower brain jutting out from the brain stem on top of the spinal cord physically, and is supposed to keep its wrongdoings under control, it still feels the throb, at every instant, of the old primitive neural unit which has passed through billions and billions of years of evolution as fish brain, reptilian brain and mammalian brain. The primitive brain has a primitive kind of *consciousness* where it tries to cope with every perceived threat using its characteristic survival mechanism—the 'fight-or-flight' strategy.

OUR GUIDING CONSCIOUSNESSES

The question to be asked is: am I, are you, being guided by the right level, the right type of *consciousness* as appropriate for the situation at the workplace and in the family?

Do we ask ourselves this question? We don't have the 'key' to open the black box (which stores the question as well as its right answer), wherefrom our *consciousnesses* are operated. *Conscious Management* is an attempt to provide such a 'key'. Read on to get an insight into all facets—right and wrong, of that 'key.

I will devote more space and words to organisational issues and provide some to family issues wherever relevant. However, the *conscious management* principles being the same while their practices and application grounds are different—that is at the workplace and at home, they will be discussed in common chapters with citing of examples from both the scenarios of our life's revolving stage.

I shall end the introduction by quoting the inimitable philosopher Bertrand Russell who had exposed his heart when he expressed with utmost honesty: 'It has been said that man is a rational animal. All my life I have been searching for evidence which could support this' [9].

REFERENCES

[1] Yankelovich, Daniel, *Profit with Honor: The New Stage of Market Capitalism,* Yale University Press, New Haven, 2006, p. 1.
[2] Sisodia, Rajendra S., David B. Wolfe and Jagdish N. Sheth, *Firms of Endearment: How World-Class Companies Profit from Passion and Purpose*, Wharton School Publishing (Pearson Education), New Jersey, Fifth Printing, June 2008.
[3] Yankelovich, Daniel, *loc. cit.* p. 5.
[4] Birla, Basant Kumar, *A Rare Legacy: Memoirs of B. K. Birla*, Image Incorporated, Bombay, First Paper Back Edition, 1994.
[5] Bennis, Warren, In: Foreword of *Firms of Endearment, loc. cit.*, p. xiii.

[6] Mishra, Pankaj, 'Firms must enthuse employees, says Nayar', *The Economic Times, Kolkata*, 14 July 2010, p. 9.
[7] Mathai, Gita, 'Catch them early', *The Telegraph, Kolkata*, 12 July 2010, p. 12.
[8] Ganguli, Siddhartha, *Live Happily, Work Happily*, Allied Publishers, New Delhi, 2009.
[9] Marcus, Gary, *KLUGE: The Haphazard Evolution of the Human Mind*, Mariner Books: Houghton Mifflin Harcourt, New York, 2009, p. 1.

KEY TAKE-HOMES

- The arenas, where we perform our 'work roles' and 'family roles'—both are blistered and potholed with wrongdoings arising from the wrong kinds of *consciousness* or, shall we say, from the dark depths of gross *unconsciousness*.
- There is thus a very strong case for identifying the right kinds and levels of *consciousness* which will make us manage and lead *happily* at the workplace and in the family.
- This book is meant to see how we can produce *winners* who will make others *winners* (and not *losers* as it normally happens in cut-throat competition) too—right from the beginning of life in the case of children and by conversion of grown-ups with the right kind of *consciousness*.

CHAPTER 1

Scenario Review: Where are We Today

LOOK AT THE PRESENT

The phenomenon of organisational slow-poisoning has not been something unseen in the third world. As a matter of fact, it has been always present in diverse forms posing a threat to organisational well-being despite strong vigilance measures, particularly in the government and public sectors. However, the fact that such incidents are equally eroding the value-base of the private sector has started coming to public limelight after the wide media exposure of the Satyam corporate scam and the most recent Union Carbide India's Bhopal tragedy judgement. Now, scanning through the media, even on a single day, will make you meet a few such cases for example, on 17th February 2010 the two most striking press reports were:

Case 1: Private Sector

'*Wipro staff siphons off $4 million:* A WIPRO employee embezzled crores of rupees over the past three years, sending India's third-biggest software exporter scrambling to tighten internal controls in the finance division where the fraud took place. The employee has been working with the company for the past three years in the 'controllership' division within the finance department. This cell is responsible for keeping the company's financial books and also has powers to authorise payments whenever needed. The employee is believed to have embezzled about $4 million of

Wipro's money and used it for his own personal purpose.... Wipro has since disbanded the controllership unit' [1].

Case 2: Govt./Public Sector

'Day, after, ministers face kin's ire': '...The relatives of the jawans who died in the attack did not allow the ministers..........to even get down from their vehicles for an hour, and then they were confined in a building at the barrack.... The relatives alleged that the jawans had to pay bribe to senior officials to get postings and those who could not afford to pay were sent to Maoist-dominated areas' [2].

Another interesting case from a more recent press coverage is cited below.

Case 3: Mackintosh Burn Ltd.

Mackintosh Burn Ltd. (MBL) was a Calcutta-headquartered (now Kolkata) British construction company, specialising in the construction of buildings, factories and bridges. When the British management left the country and the company became sick, the West Bengal government acquired a 48.5 per cent stake to save the jobs of hundreds who were employed in the company. Under company law, MBL thus remained a private company as the WB govt.'s stake was just about 2 per cent short of the controlling stake.

However, strangely enough, by a WB govt. order in 1990, it had been conferred special status, with preferential terms for getting government tenders. For instance, the company was given a 10 per cent rate preference, exempted from paying earnest money in government tenders, allowed to place hugely reduced security deposits in jobs awarded to it and granted other facilities. Most recently, the office of the principal accountant general (audit), West Bengal has queried the state government about preferential treatment being extended to MBL. The government has also been asked why it has not acquired 2 per cent of the equity necessary to make it a public enterprise, and thus subject to government audit [3].

A retired senior bureaucrat, Ms. Kalyani Chaudhuri, had revealed in her recent book *When the Pendulum Stops* that MBL has for years claimed the privileges of a government company while retaining its status as a private enterprise, sometimes even filing cases against the state's public works department [4]. Is it not interesting? Would you call it a case of *conscious mis-management*?

CONSCIOUSNESS: DIVERSE FORMS

Most interestingly, *consciousness* could be of different types; and all types are not appropriate for all situations. What may be wrong for one situation would be right for another. For instance, when one is being attacked in a strange unknown, perhaps enemy territory, he has to 'fight' it out, or 'flee'. But, this 'fight-or-flight' type of reactive *consciousness* may not generally be the right kind in a social or corporate situation.

There is another new dimension of *consciousness* on which light has been thrown in some recent research. Organisational employees, placed at any level, who indulge in misgovernance through unethical practices, are obviously taking big risks. It is negative risk-taking whereas any entrepreneur or a change-maker takes positive risks. In a way, the behaviour of negative and socially unacceptable risk-takers can be compared to that of gamblers.

The new research has shown that the brains of people who risk everything when gambling may be wired up differently than those of the naturally cautious. People were far more gullible to high-risk gambling when a small but distinct part of their inner or lower brain—the primitive *amygdala*, had been damaged as a result of a genetic disorder. A fully functioning *amygdala* appears to make us more cautious as it is involved in processing fear. It is responsible for making us afraid of any loss. Dr Benedetto De Martinoa, a researcher of the California Institute of Technology, Pasadena and the University College, London and his colleagues carried out the research and published the findings in the *Proceedings of the National Academy of Sciences* in early 2010. Their study offers insight into economic behaviour and suggests that humans evolved to be cautious about the prospects of losing food or other valued possessions [5, 6]. The study could also possibly explain why some people are more willing to take risks than others. Perhaps genetic differences in the DNA activated in the *amygdala* explain it, according to the same researchers.

WHAT A COINCIDENCE

The General Manager Mr G's Dilemma

During my few days' endeavour to tune my mind with that of Yankelovich, a very senior manager Mr. G dropped in for a desperate consultation in our '*Happiness*' clinic. He had changed his job recently to move into the higher position of 'General Manager' of a medium-sized enterprise owned by a trader-entrepreneur belonging to the traditional Indian business community. The director Mr A expected the General Manager to run the organisation profitably by indulging in all kinds of corrupt practices—an attitude which was not matching with the G.M.'s who had been schooled by us.

What step would G take? He has the following few choices:

- *First*, he being the second in command, can try and change the attitude of A and bring him round to accept the impeccable value system that he has been schooled by us to follow. (This would simply be a stupendous task for G as A's value system is a product of his nature as well as nurture. He belongs to a business community where people, for generations together, have been engaged in commerce, trade, business and industry, which would be responsible for genetic propensities as well as impact of family and community culture. A will simply not accept this "A's loss-G's win" situation).
- *Second*, he can attempt to bring about a change in his own attitude and value system by making a compromise and align himself with A. (This also would be difficult for him as his values are strong and deeply embedded. Besides, he is in his mid-forties—an age where any rapid change in in-grained values is almost impossible. And, any compromise would mean he will have to do it unwillingly by suppressing his negative emotions arising out of the "A's win-G's loss" situation, resulting in *stress*, which if became a recurrent condition, would affect his physical and mental health adversely).
- *Third*, he can become most practical and situational to convince himself that to run a business or an industry profitably in a stiff competitive environment, there is nothing wrong in making a compromise in some of his values (not at the cost of his 'personal dignity', nevertheless) as leaving aside some 'core values'* in business all other values, which stand as 'mental blocks', are just relative and can be changed, as necessary. It leads to a "A's win-also G's win" situation.

---

*There are some values which are universal in corporate transactions whereas there are others where people differ in their opinions about morality. To give an example related to the first category of values, taken from a different field, one can talk of 'cleanliness' in medical operations.

Similarly, in business and industry, some such 'musts' are: maintenance of time, quality, quantity, cost and safety. These are of utmost importance because of their relationship with customer satisfaction. Every customer is keen to have timely

- *Fourth and last*, he would not forsake any of his solid values leading to a "G's loss-A's win" situation; instead he must look for a change, without wait, where he would not have to face such value conflicts and the consequent mental turmoil. If he gets a working environment which suits his value system, he would be able to perform happily.

Strongly in favour of the fourth and last alternative, G was thus frantically looking for an alternative place where he would not be expected to compromise the good values that he had been protecting and living with so far. There was no dilemma in him; he was quite clear that he needed a change. I was not only delighted but also incredibly proud that this young friend of ours was determined not to subscribe to the culture of corporate misgovernance.

We have till now considered only Mr G's points of view, out of the two involved in the employer-employee relationship. Mr A, on his part, can also have the following choices:

- *First*, he pays attention to G and *consciously* (without any prejudice) listens to what he has to say and seriously consider reorienting his attitude and some of his values in line with G's (to create a 'win-win' situation for both).
- *Second*, he can use tact and try to influence G to adopt some of A's values (creating a 'win-win' situation for both) and work accordingly in the best interest of the organisation and its profitable business operations.
- *Third*, he leaves out G from getting involved in the corrupt practices and takes up the implementation in his own hands so that G remains clean. It will also lead to a 'win-win' situation for both.

---

delivery or ready availability of the product or service in the right quantity whenever he has the need for its consumption or utilisation. He is interested in the best quality, assured safety and guaranteed defect-free service after sale, at a reasonable cost so that he feels that it is the best value for money. In other words, he has to feel that his money has been well-spent; he has no regrets. These values are all tangible and, therefore, they conform to certain prescribed quantitative standards.

However, in order to achieve conformity to and compliance with these tangible and measurable values, what intangible values every supervisor, executive and manager ought to follow, are not prescribed so systematically and specifically in the performance standards. These are the values related to the supervisor, executive or manager himself and a few others related to his attitude towards and style of interacting with and handling people who are responsible for mobilising performance.

- *Fourth and final choice:* he would ask G to leave the job/look for another job/put in his papers. (It is a "A's win-G's loss" situation).

G and A, like you and me, represent the most invaluable of all resources—the *human resource (HR)* or, we would rather describe it as *human capital*. Every member of the human species has body and brain powers to perform activities to 'add value' to other resources including other humans. And, such performance is possible at its peak or maximum level if the individual exerted himself *willingly* and *happily* opening the floodgates for the positive biological chemistry to flow and positive bio-electricity to stimulate the cells. That would be the best utilisation of human capital to obtain maximum 'Return on Investment (ROI)' of its inherent powers. This condition has to be achieved in the practice of human work performance, to the extent feasible, *consciously*. This, in principle, is one of the most important aspects of *conscious management*.

Which of the options, in your opinion, would represent *conscious management* and will be in tune with its principle, for G and A?

THE FAMILY SEGMENT: DILEMMAS AND PROBLEMS

The Husband, Mr C's Predicament

While our sessions with Mr G were going on, another senior but much younger executive came to our '*Happiness*' clinic by appointment. This executive, Mr C had completed his MBA in Human Resource Management from an institute in Delhi and, thereafter, having worked in a Noida-based company for six years had come to Kolkata as Head of HR in the corporate office of the Indian subsidiary of an European multinational company two years ago. Immediately on his taking up this assignment in Kolkata, his marriage was arranged with an eligible girl who was academically inclined and had a first class MA degree in English from Calcutta University. She was keeping herself busy at home giving private tuitions to school and college students in small batches and had six batches in hand when her marriage was fixed with Mr C. She was quite assertive that she was committed to her students and could not give up her tuitions in the middle of the session and was willing to marry Mr C provided he and his parents could wait until all her students' exams were over. Mr C and his parents agreed and the marriage took place once she had done with all her students' exams.

Within two months of their marriage, Mr C. had to take a new rented apartment as his newly wed wife could not adjust with the mother-in-law.

That was not too bad, but the real bolt from the blue came when she said: 'I cannot stay without my tuitions because of two reasons—first, I love teaching young boys and girls and preparing them really well to get good scores in their class terminal and also board exams; and, second, I need money to make me feel economically independent. Since I used to earn around ₹ 25,000/- a month from my tuitions, if you give me the same amount every month I'll stay on, otherwise I am going back to my parents' place to resume my tuition activities'. Mr C tried to convince his wife in every possible way that she is being unfair with him, but she was adamant and one day only recently she left Mr C's apartment and went back to her parents' place. And, most surprisingly, her parents stood by her in her impulsive decision. Incidentally, Mr C. had come to know that his wife had intimacy with one Mr Jayant Sood, a young merchant banker from Chandigarh, presently located in New Delhi—whom she came to know through the Internet. She used to talk about him in her dreams and repeat some of their conversations in that dreaming state.

Faced with this problem which had converted him into an emotional wreck, Mr C. came to us for consultation.

We told Mr C. that he has the following choices: (i) to start a divorce case on the ground of mental torture provided she could be persuaded to part with him (which she was apparently unwilling to) and start everything afresh; (ii) to work through a neutral third party, somebody like an arbitrator, and try to come to a compromising situation; (iii) to continue as it is and persuade her to live together once in a while when her tuition load was light; (iv) he can take up another equally good job or try for a transfer to a sister company in Mumbai and start a new relationship. Mr C was asked to evaluate each alternative choice—its plus points (PP), minus points (MP) and most interesting/important points (MIP) in the short- (1 to 2 years), medium- (2 to 5 years) and long-terms (beyond 5 years) and try out the best alternative. It took three months for Mr C to choose alternative (i) as his best choice and he has started working on it most earnestly.

This is a case where mismatch of *consciousness* between the husband and the wife did upset a family relationship.

The Parents, Mrs and Mr R's Dilemma

Around the same period, Mrs and Mr R dropped into our *'Winning Child'* clinic with a pressing problem. Their second child, the 11-year, old son Ronit, who was a student of Class VI in a good Kolkata school had suddenly stopped studying at home. He was attending school but most reluctantly? On asking, he would say: 'What good will happen to me if I study? I should rather fail in the examination and denied promotion to the next higher class'. Ronit was behaving like a depressed 'loser' child who had given up all hopes for progressing in life happily.

When such cases visit our clinic, we ask the parents to bring some samples of things in which the child was good at. Ronit's parents had brought his latest drawing book but were most reluctant to show it to me as they thought that the theme of all of Ronit's sketches and paintings was inauspicious according to our social values.

However, I forced them to show me the drawings and I was amazed. Ronit was a high-class artist and he specialised in drawing pictures of snakes, serpents and reptiles which, in a way, are not looked at with reverence as they were dangerous and big threats to our lives. When I asked Ronit what he wanted to be, prompt came his answer. He said he wanted to be a herpetologist—one who specialises in snakes. His parents got excited and said: 'Certainly not! We would make Ronit a doctor, an engineer, an accountant, a lawyer or a manager'.—all 'me too' career choices, nothing unique. But the young boy wanted to be a unique person and if he had really gone into herpetology and took it up seriously, the chances of his becoming one of the very few experts in the country and may also be in the whole world would have been possible.

Herpetology was the field which motivated Ronit and made him happy. The parents were pressing him in the opposite direction, imposing their choice on to him—thus making him frustrated and depressed, so much so that he had decided to give up studies at home although he continued to attend school unwillingly.

I counselled and convinced Mrs and Mr R. not to force Ronit to give up the idea of being a herpetologist but let his ideas flow freely so that he became happy and motivated. He was too young to apply his intelligence to choose the right profession for himself which will have enough value in the market when he became a young adult. Let the thought process take its own course. The parents' excitement subsided and they went back home. In two days' time, I got a call from Mrs R. that Ronit had resumed his studies at home and he had regained his happy spirits. If Mrs and Mr R. would have stuck to their stand and forced Ronit to study, it could have led to dire consequences as you will see from the next case study.

Mrs and Mr B's Problem

I had never expected that the famous film director Mr B and his wife would contact me and request me to come to their rescue. How much do we, who stay outside the boundaries of the film world, get exposed to the film professionals' personal and family problems?

Mrs and Mr B wanted to speak to me on the phone. Then they dropped in by appointment. I came to know that their twelve year old son Pracheta was not attending school for seven days although he was dressing up every morning in his school uniform, having his breakfast and leaving for school by public transport. When the school reported about his absence to Mrs B, on enquiry it was found that Pracheta was climbing up to the roof of their multi-storeyed apartment building and spending the whole day there. He would not open up to his parents to share the reason for his behaviour.

I took him aside, away from his parents, talked to him and found out that seven days ago he was watching the TV at home, when his dad unexpectedly appeared on the scene and started shouting at him for not having sat for his studies although it was already 8 pm and his half-yearly exam dates were drawing close. In a strong voice, he poured out his frustration on his son: 'Do you think you'll be spared by the school authorities if you fail in the exam, being the son of a celebrity?' It had hurt Pracheta deeply and he decided to bunk school from the very next day.

We could make him cool down but could not persuade him to go back to the same school as he felt that he really would not pass the school being of a very high standard and one of the bests in Kolkata. He was admitted in another school not comparable to his previous school in all respects. Only then he resumed his regular studies.

Celebrities are thus no exceptions to behaving from a wrong level of *consciousness* with their young kids. In fact, some of them are even worse than common family people.

Families are the most important social units where husbands and wives, who are lifetime partners, must have a reasonably good understanding leading to some amount of sacrificing personal interests for the sake of each other. In families having young children, the parents and elders must have a positive attitude towards the young ones that they are dealing with day-to-day and try to understand their feelings by giving them attention, listening to and empathising with them. Only this style will help them to convert their kids into valuable human capitals.

A DIFFERENT PERSPECTIVE

Did you ever notice that on the back of the US dollar bill there is an unfinished pyramid with a brilliant glowing eye at the top?

It was the idea of President Roosevelt in 1935, in the middle of the Great depression, when America's wealth was in sharp decline. The pyramid symbolises economic strength and durability.

Today, when we're just about to embark our journey into the second decade of the 21st century, in order to keep afloat amidst the turbulent tidal waves of fast change that is typical of modern times, every individual engaged in the management of resources must keep his eyes and ears open and be conscious and alert.

Thus the glowing eye at the top of the wealth pyramid would represent the main character of the story that we're about to tell you—the *Conscious Manager* who practises *conscious management* whether he is a supervisor, an executive or a parent [7].

NO GENDER BIAS

My adoption of the male gender in this book does not reflect any gender bias that I may have. It stands for both the male and female genders but only the former has been chosen to keep things simple. Being a male member of the human society, I have not been guided by the *unconscious* propensity of the male brain advocating dominance over the females.

References

[1] Ramsurya, M.V. and Pankaj Mishra, 'Wipro staff siphons off $4 million', *The Economic Times, Kolkata,* pp. 1, 17.
[2] 'Day after, ministers face kin's ire', *The Statesman, Kolkata,* 17 February 2010, p. 1.
[3] Chowdhury, Anindita, 'AG posers on Mackintosh Burn', *The Statesman, Kolkata,* 11 July 2010, p. 1.
[4] Chaudhuri, K., *When the Pendulum Stops*, Nachiketa Publications, Kolkata, 2010.
[5] Connor, Steve, 'From being wary to risking it all', *The Statesman, Kolkata,* 10 February 2010, p. 10.
[6] 'Here's why it is scary to lose money', *The Economic Times, Kolkata,* 10 February 2010, p. 24.

[7] Lester C. Thurow, *Building Wealth: The New Rules for Individuals, Companies, and Nations in a Knowledge-Based Economy*; HarperCollins Publishers, New York, 1999.

KEY TAKE-HOMES

- There are different types of *consciousnesses* but not all are suitable for all situations. For example, the 'fight-or-flight' type which had evolved over billions and billions of years and served us extremely well in our primitive, prehistoric days when every moment was potent with threats to our lives, is certainly not the most appropriate one today when we are well protected by the products and services of science and technology and are existing in our own created respective 'comfort zones'.
- For indulging in unethical and immoral practices, one has to take raw risks. And people with the impulsive 'fight-or-flight' propensities are unrefined risk-takers.
- Right kind of *consciousness* is balanced. It gives you patience and nurtures calculated risk-taking. It is soft and loose and, at the same time, tight and tough also as necessary according to the circumstances. This is what is called for in the work, social and family roles so that you are free from hassles and lead your waking and sleeping hours *happily*.

CHAPTER 2

Conscious Management: The Need of the Day

PEOPLE: THE MOST IMPORTANT LEVER IN VALUE CREATION

The Business and Industry Segment

In any business, accounting and banking professionals have always given thrust on tangible physical assets like buildings, factory sheds, plants and machineries, tools and tackles, and stocks. *People* had never been regarded by these hard core financial specialists as 'assets' despite the fact that they constituted the most valuable intangible asset group.

Managing people was considered 'most important' from the business results calculation point of view, solely because people represented the greatest current period cost. And, for the past few years, the shift from industrial to a services economy has made the control of 'people costs' more important than ever before because of the obvious reason that the tangible assets in a service industry are almost nothing compared to those of the manufacturing sector.

However, what is required is to look at the worth of the knowledge, skills, intelligences, talents, habits and attitudes of the employees as having value at present as well as in the future, not just as costs in the current period. It has to be realised that people, not 'tangible' but even as 'intangible' assets, have become the most important invisible lever in value creation through the 'tangible' assets. Remember how Vineet Nayar, the CEO of HCL

Technologies had highlighted the priority of a value shift from the so far prevailing 'customer first, employee second' to the 'employee first, customer second' principle for fast revival and rapid growth of the IT industry after it was hit by the blow of recession over the last few years [1].

The Family Segment

On the family front too, from the dawn of human civilisation, common man has been putting more thrust on acquiring and building fixed and movable assets. Ancient and traditional men (even today it is the trend in the rural society of the third world countries) used to concentrate on owning land and buildings, farmhouses, livestock and ponds full of fishes and hoarding gold and silver and even commodities like grains, pulses, roots and tubers as valuable inventories.

Modern men has changed somewhat to attach more value to bungalows and apartments, automobiles and household gadgets for entertainment and also for saving manual labour in a conscious attempt to enter more and more into a restricted 'comfort zone' where his body powers and brain powers would not have to be exerted for his survival and secure existence unlike his prehistoric predecessors whose in-built physical and mental capabilities were not only being utilised but got exposed to unexpected challenges almost everyday during a nomadic life, which led to the development of those capabilities into powers.

Today, in the modern era of technological breakthroughs, nobody that we know of ever thinks of and recognises the critical importance of the potential assets available in the form of the members of the family—the *human capital* without the effort and investment of which acquisition and building up of material assets and wealth would have been unthinkable. The only step taken has been limited to educate the younger family members to acquire qualifications and training recognised by the concerned authorities for employment and self-employment as professionals as practicing doctors, architects, consulting engineers, accountants, management consultants, interior and fashion designers and so on. Entering into a trade or setting up a business or an industry never required any qualifications or professional training as such as the main attributes needed were the business sense for identification of the gap between demand and supply of one or more commodities or services, the enterprise and risk-taking attitude, the street-smartness to adapt oneself with the tides of change in the market and capacity for hard work.

INFLEXIBILITY OF THE CURRENT ACCOUNTING APPROACH

Even today, in the sphere of organised work, the tools of the accounting profession (such as the *balance sheet* and the *profit-and-loss statement*) are not sufficiently flexible to shed light on any 'intangible asset' investment decision largely because there is currently no mechanism available to account for the knowledge, skills, intelligences, talents, habits and attitudes of the people available as 'assets' of the organisation.

The criteria for accounting classification as an 'asset' are:
- It is well-defined and tangible and separate from other assets.
- The firm has total control over it and can transfer that control if required.
- The future economic benefits it will provide can be predicted.
- Any impairment of its economic value can be determined.

The second criterion in the above list distinguishes *human capital* from being considered an asset by accountants. The organisation does not have total control over humans and cannot transfer that control to others [2].

RESOURCE ALLOCATION IN HUMAN RESOURCE MANAGEMENT AND DEVELOPMENT

The challenge of today's global economy is to equip practising supervisors, executives and managers with the methods and tools to improve resource allocation in 'intangible assets' wherefrom 92 per cent of the productivity growth is originating and, to make the organisation more cost-effective and competitive.

For example, the 'cost-benefit' technique may be a handy tool for managerial decision-makers regarding investment decision in the human resource by way of *training and development* as outlined below.

Costs

(a) *Direct:* training partners' charges and other costs; venue hiring and infrastructural arrangements; training stationeries; food, refreshments and beverages; cost of power; cost of programme coordinator and attendants; pre-training costs; participants' travel, board, lodging, local transportation, etc.
(b) *Indirect:* releasing the programme participants from their work schedule (their proportionate costs for the programme duration period; loss of performance during the programme period).

Benefits

(a) *Direct*: updating of knowledge/know-how (even many of the human resource management concepts and practices of five years ago are almost obsolete today); expansion/widening of knowledge as knowledge is doubling every five years [3]; readiness for application in self-improvement and team performance improvement (measuring sticks: *Ten 'Key Result Factors (KRFs)'* developed through our years of organisational research is presented in Appendix I); getting to know the participants' present status of Knowledge (K)-Attitude (A)- Skills (S)-and-Habits (H); and, getting the participants' commitments regarding practical applications of the lessons learnt.

(b) *Indirect:* confidence development; proper motivational tuning and toning up; realisation of the importance of *inter-dependence* and the *principle of diversity* in 'strengths' and 'weaknesses'; attitudinal reorientation to a certain extent.

You may consider the following methods for calculating the *'Return on the Investment (ROI)'* that you have made by going in for the human resource training and development project:

- Testing the HRD programme participant *before* and *after* the learning activity; namely, the training programme.
- Evaluating the 'self-managed' work performance pattern of the programme participant before and after attending the training event where the individual takes all the initiative to undertake the assignment and complete it in proper coordination with his controlling manager and all other departmental representatives with whom he shares the inter-dependent roles of 'internal customers' and 'internal suppliers'.
- The performance ratings of the 'self-managed' portion suggested by us are: good/fair (51 to 60% of the overall performance standards which are fixed with the highest and most outstanding performer's performance pattern being taken as the benchmark); very good/just satisfactory (61 to 70%); very very good/satisfactory (71 to 85%); excellent/more than satisfactory (86 to 95%); great/extraordinary (beyond 96%, even exceeding 100% of the performance standards thus reaching the 'peak performance' level).
- Examining to what extent the learning outcomes are being converted into business outcomes (in terms of: time-saving, quality-enhancement, productivity improvement, cost control, revenue growth, improvement in cash-inflow and profitability, improvement in health and safety

maintenance of employees, faster and defect-free information flow, better reporting and feedback process; and so on).

The task of converting simple and naive human resource in the form of a youngster into a great or an extraordinary human capital as he grows is equally if not more important for parents. Although nearly all parents possess the same ambition, set goals and start acting to reach those goals, they stumble as they do not possess the knack for such conversion, which essentially is a *leadership* quality. The youngsters pursue their goals with passion and their parents keep a track of their performance and progress. Since very few are willing to take risks and go beyond the norms that they copy from their counterparts around them I consider it as most challenging for them today when they are hard pressed for time and live a stressful life. It is equally applicable to the youngsters and their parents and elders.

TODAY'S LEADER

What is the role of today's *leaders* in dealing with people for maximum value creation for them (as 'personal worth') as well as for the organisation (as 'organisational assets' or 'human capital')?*

Historically, the role of leaders and the concept of leadership were confined to the very highest executive positions in the organisation. Leadership, traditionally, has been most directly related to the 'command and control' organisational structure of the military. Today, leadership has a more dynamic meaning. The modern-day discussion on leadership qualities is largely about: critical thinking skills; people-reading, inspiring, motivating and communication skills; and proficiency in how to organise, analyse and synthesise the exploding pool of information.

Nevertheless, it's not fully clear whether 'managing performance' which is the prime responsibility of a 'supervisor' (who supervises the work of one, two, or a few persons), an 'executive' (who is responsible for execution of tasks according to plans and programmes), and a 'manager' (who is expected to manage the performance of the employees reporting to him) is integrated into the leadership concept. Although the leadership role and the roles of a supervisor, an executive or a manager are not in conflict with each other, to what extent they are complementary to each other and

---

*Please do remember that the family is the most basic and the smallest social organisational unit.

which of the two is integrated into which other is still clouded as would be seen from the discussion that follows, under the title: 'Leader *versus* Manager: Going to the Roots'.

I want to highlight here the most striking feature in this context. It is that *leadership* is a capability that is required throughout the length and breadth of the organisation, even where one does not have anyone reporting to him but he has to influence his 'internal suppliers' (who are supplying a semi-finished product or service to him for him to accomplish his part of the processing work) and 'internal customers' (to whom he supplies the part of the product or service that was his responsibility to complete), vertically, horizontally, diagonally as well as angularly, to produce the desired outcomes which would all combine and add up to the organisation's performance.

Leaders, in that sense and spirit, are required at every level and in every corner of the organisation today as critical decisions are being delegated downward. Every member of the organisation is expected to be 'street-smart'. There is no alternative, as critical information is flooding into organisations at all levels from internal as well as external sources (namely, the external suppliers and customers who might require interacting with the organisational employees at different levels), not merely overcrowding the senior and top managers' desks.

For instance, the field force sales staff are getting first-hand information about the competitors' products, services and practices from the organisation's trading and channel partners as well as directly from the end-users visiting the same market and, the shop-floor. And, office-floor grassroots personnel are becoming the organisation's receptor organs for collecting information from one-time suppliers and enlisted vendors who are also suppliers and vendors to its competitors. You cannot compel any of them to serve you solely unless you strike a big deal which they will consider attractive and will commit to be your sole suppliers.

Leadership is also indisputably a skill which is equally essential for effective family management and maintaining a happy forward-moving family. There is always a demand on the leadership potential of every member of the family—young, middle-aged and old to influence others and get convinced by others, as relevant to maintain a reasonably steady state of equilibrium—in other words, a good balance in the family's activities.

LEADER *VERSUS* MANAGER: GOING TO THE ROOTS

Case Study 1

A two-day sales training workshop for the middle to senior level marketing and sales managers of the Indian subsidiary of a multinational company was about to start. The corporate senior vice-president (sales) walked into the banquet hall at 9.30 am sharp. Six feet two inches tall, stoutly built with a big belly, he looked like an amateur version of a North Indian wrestler—who was expensively dressed in modern executive attire.

The top business honcho started his inaugural address by saying that he had to literally fight with his boss, the director (marketing), to prepone the training from the month of January next year to November of the current year as he thought that from January onwards the battle in the market between the few front-runner players in the industry was going to take a fiercer turn. The key ideas that he wanted the participating highly paid executives to internalise were: intrinsic motivation, sales growth, increasing the market share by 15–20 per cent more than the rate at which it had risen during the last operating year, aggressive marketing, management of uncertainties, anticipation of the shape of things to come, selecting the difficult and most critical channel partners and trying not only to win them over and woo them away from competitors but also to influence them to grow by strategically increasing the business volume, and so on.

The senior vice-president's voice was commanding. Most of the time, he had both his hands placed at the waist level in a challenging posture. From time to time, to reinforce his commanding tone, he was shaking his right index finger displaying the baton signal—representative of a forceful and autocratic direction.

He concluded his stormy talk by saying that after the workshop ended at six in the evening, he would sit with the participants as long as it needed to formulate practical plans and strategies for reaching the ambitious goals that he had already talked about.

When the workshop faculty took over from him, he sat through for half-an-hour; then suddenly he left the banquet hall with his lady secretary. Within a few minutes, the workshop coordinator from the company's HR department got a message from him most unexpectedly to conclude the workshop at 4.00 pm and not to continue with the workshop proceedings on the second day (it was meant to be a two whole-day workshop) so that the marketing second-in-command could have the whole late afternoon and evening of the first day and the entire second day at his disposal to drive his points home and get the senior executives to make some realistic commitments.

In this case study that has just been shared with you, did you think that the senior vice president behaved like a leader or an autocratic manager who does not spare anything to get those managed by him to produce performance?

Case Study 2

The location of this case study is the plant of a private limited company which is the joint venture between two Fortune 500 companies—one is a foreign giant organisation, world leader in its own field, and the other is an Indian market leader in the field of essential products.

The plant manager Mr X is a qualified electrical engineer who has come on deputation to the JV Company and has stepped into his seventh year here after having spent more than thirty years with the Indian JV partner. He is in charge of the entire operations of the plant and, as one would expect, is given a tough production target to make the entire plant operations most cost-effective. He gets up every morning very early so that he is available at the plant by 6 am. He jogs in the campus; then has his light breakfast and lunch in the office; continues up to 8.30 or 9 pm, then calls it a day and retires to his apartment. His wife and son stay in the nearby metro city which is nearly 200 km away from Mr X's plant location.

He gets performance from a work force of nearly 60 people from deputy manager downwards up to junior executives which is the lowest cadre. However, he is unable to involve his next level of executives and mobilise performance from them. One of them is a senior manager and the other one is a manager both of whom are just passing their time.

In this case study also, do you think the plant head is operating as a manager or a leader?

Case Study 3

There is an Indian Company—which is amongst the world leaders in respect of a particular type of engineering product. Our case study is based on its plant where finished items are rolled out from semi-finished products manufactured in another plant located in the same state but around 100 km away from the plant that we're talking about.

The senior vice-president (manufacturing) who is in charge of this plant is very young, in his early 40s. He mixes well with his deputies and also with people below them but he is highly task and performance-oriented. However, most of the time, he is out of his spacious office and available with his people in various shops and different ongoing project sites inside the plant campus. He uses a lot of wit and humour in his communication, has a very confident and attractive voice and is also an excellent listener.

This gentleman, Mr X had joined the Company immediately after his graduation in mechanical engineering as a graduate engineering trainee at the age of 22 and has had a meteoric rise to the position of senior vice-president within 12 years.

Do you feel Mr X is only a good manager or a good leader or a combination of both?

You'll be in a position to answer the questions related to all the three case studies, once you go through the information on leadership that will follow soon.

Case Study 4

During my daily morning walk, I meet one Mr B who used to be a cricketer during his younger days. A Calcutta University Blue, he had played regularly for the Bengal team and, as far I could gather, he had also led his team a few times.

I had a very interesting discussion with B most recently. He shared the perceptions prevailing about 'leadership' in the cricketing parlance. B said that according to cricket-lovers and players a good captain is one who can mobilise performance from his team and lead it to success—winning in a game.

Our contention is: is Mr B talking about 'managing' or 'leading' or a combination of both? What do you think?

I, never having been a cricketing buff, felt like a stranger to such perceptions. I'll also have to join you in the brainstorming.

Definitions of Leadership Through Decades

We put below the definitions of leadership through various periods since the 1920s, a dateline from when business and industry started gaining ground. A microscopic look at these definitions would reveal that, in all of them, the main role and responsibility of a manager (which is mobilising performance through, by and from people) have been implied and included in the roles of leaders (the comments within brackets are mine) [4, 5]:

- *1920s:* Leadership is the ability to impress the will of the leader on those led and induce obedience, respect, loyalty and cooperation [For what? Obviously, to mobilise performance. Isn't it?].
- *1930s:* Leadership is a process in which the activities of many are organised to move in a specific direction by one [What is the big purpose? Obviously, to produce certain targeted results].
- *1940s:* Leadership is the result of an ability to persuade or direct men, apart from the prestige or power that comes from office or external circumstance [Why persuasion or direction? To give the desired outcomes, of course].
- *1950s:* Leadership is what leaders do in groups. The leader's authority is spontaneously accorded to him by his fellow group members [Authority for what? Certainly for mobilising performance].
- *1960s:* Leadership constitutes acts by a person, which influence other persons in a shared direction* [Direction to reach the performance goals].
- *1970s:* Leadership is defined in terms of discretionary influence. Discretionary influence refers to those leader behaviours under control of the leader, which he may vary from individual to individual [Influencing others to produce performance].
- *1980s:* Regardless of the complexities involved in the study of leadership, its meaning is relatively simple. Leadership means to inspire others to undertake some form of purposeful action as determined by the leader [During this decade, we find one definite exception in the perception of leadership when Drucker noted that 'leadership is performance' [6].
- *1990s:* Leadership is an influence relationship between leaders and followers who intend real changes that reflect their mutual purposes [What are the mutual purposes? Of course, to produce performance].
- *Early 2000s:* According to much of the recent literature, a leader is one who inspires and motivates, not just resolves or 'manages' [A change in the treatment of the concept of 'management' today may be a result of the recent focus on the search for leadership].

It is one of our prime objectives in this book to remove a common confusion which has invaded the 21st century management domain regarding whether leadership is integrated into a manager's role. This was not so in the Druckerian era (1970–90s) as management theorists used to include 'leading', 'motivating' and 'directing' as vital parts of a manager's job.

Today, there is a difference. Leadership is a hot favourite word in corporate corridors and management institutions. Scores of lines, paragraphs and volumes are being written on *leadership* and thousands of HRD programmes are being conducted the entire world over. Many authors also put leadership in the title of books on traditional management subjects. The questions that arise from the whirlpool of the prevailing confusion include (here the term 'manager' also covers the supervisory and executive cadres of personnel):

- Are leadership qualities totally different from or integrated into the qualities of an effective manager?
- Or, is leadership an essential quality to have, to emerge as an effective manager?
- Is there a different place for leaders from managers in an organisation?
- If that be so, then why designations and job titles do not carry the word 'leader' whereas all managerial positions carry the word 'manager'?

Perceptions of Leadership: Modern

Amongst the prevailing confusion, there have been a few genuine attempts to identify some rays of clarity. Like, Warren Bennis and Burt Nanus were amongst the rare few who had posed to think straight but still could not come straight to the facts of life when they said: 'The manager does things right and the leader does the right thing' [7]. But that was more than two decades ago.

We have another, rather unusual (and, most interestingly, biological) very recent view of leadership offered by Taleb, who holds an MBA degree from the Wharton School and a Ph.D. from the University of Paris, and currently is the Dean's Professor in the Sciences of Uncertainty at the Isenberg School of Management of the University of Massachusetts at Amherst. A hardcore practical thinker having an uninterrupted two-decade career as a quantitative trader in New York and London, Taleb brings us much closer to reality about leadership when he states in two paragraphs:

> Scientists found out that *serotonin* (italics ours), a neurotransmitter, seems to command a large share of our human behavior. It sets a positive feedback, the virtuous cycle, but, owing to an external kick from randomness, can start a reverse motion and cause a vicious cycle.

It has been shown that monkeys injected with *serotonin* will rise in the pecking order*, which in turn causes an increase of the *serotonin* level in their blood—until the virtuous cycle breaks and starts a vicious one (during the vicious cycle failure will cause one to slide in the pecking order, causing a behavior that will bring further drops in the pecking order). Likewise, an increase in personal performance... induces a rise of *serotonin* in the subject, itself causing an increase in what is commonly called 'leadership' ability. One is 'on a roll'. Some imperceptible changes in deportment**, like an ability to express oneself with serenity and confidence, make the subject look credible—as if he truly deserved the shekels***....'

A word on the display of emotions. Almost no one can conceal his emotions. Behavioural scientists believe that one of the main reasons why people become leaders is not from what skills they seem to possess, but rather from what extremely superficial impression they make on others through hardly perceptible physical signals—what we call today 'charisma', for example. The biology of the phenomenon is now well studied under the subject heading 'social emotions'. Meanwhile some historian will 'explain' the success in terms of, perhaps, tactical skills, the right education, or some other theoretical reason seen in hindsight. In addition, there seems to be curious evidence of a link between leadership and a form of psychopathology (the sociopath) that encourages the non-blinking, self-confident, insensitive person to rally followers [8].

'Leaders' and 'Managers': Going to the Roots

Let us now analyse the formal positions of leaders and managers by going to the roots of both the terms.

In an organisation, any employee belonging to a section, department, unit, or division—who has one, two or more people reporting to, has a leadership role to play. The leadership role centres around one or a set of 'visions' which requires a broader perspective on the organisation's operational processes and on their impact on the stakeholders, located in the organisation's internal as well as external environments. A true leader

---
* 'The pecking order' means the order of importance in relation to one another among the members of a group.

** 'Deportment' represents the way in which a person stands and moves.

*** 'Shekel' is the unit of money in Israel/or an ancient silver coin used by the Jews.

is very much concerned with the moral and ethical aspects of all policies and strategies.

Once the leader's vision is set, his target is clear; and there is clarity of purpose, it means he has already made some progress. An effective leader can foresee tomorrow and plans to make a difference. Wangchuk [9] illustrates by citing a beautiful story: 'Two persons offered to supply water to a village hit by water shortage. While the stronger one used buckets, the other supplied water through a pipeline from the source. The former got tired soon and gave up, but the latter could relax and yet earn a lot of money'.

The concept of leadership is very broad, both in context and content. The manager's perspective is considered to be narrower. A manager's job is to ensure that people perform what all they are expected to perform. A manager thus has to play primarily a performance-oriented role. You can 'manage' and get performance without communicating effectively but in order to 'lead' you have to communicate effectively. You 'mislead' with wrong communication.

Let us look at performance-orientation, once again, through the eyes of Taleb who gave up his successful trader's career to become an essayist and a teacher. He paints the picture through the case study of a character called Nero who was, by nature, not suited to do any administrative and managerial work. Taleb writes:

> Nero spent a couple of years shuttling between the two cities, attending important 'meetings' and wearing expensive suits. But soon Nero went into hiding; he rapidly pulled back to anonymity—the Wall Street stardom track did not quite fit his temperament. To stay a 'hot trader' requires some organisational ambitions and a power hunger that he feels lucky not to possess. He was only in it for the fun—and his idea of fun does not include administrative and managerial work. He is susceptible to conference room boredom and is incapable of talking to businesses, particularly the run-of-the-mill variety. Nero is allergic to the vocabulary of business talk, not just on plain aesthetic grounds. Phrases like 'game plan', 'bottom line', 'how to get there from here', 'we provide our clients with solutions', 'our mission' and other hackneyed expressions that dominate meetings lack both the precision and the coloration that he prefers to hear. Whether people populate silence with hotter sentences, or if such meetings present any true merit, he does not know; at any rate he did not want to be a part of it [10].

When you merely 'manage', you act *unconsciously* (using your auto-pilot system) or *subconsciously* (guided by the 'hidden agenda' based on your past experience) as you will have to mobilise performance at any cost. When you 'lead', you are managing *consciously*. A manager behaves like a leader when he thinks what moral and ethical impact such performance is going to have in the short, medium and longer terms on the organisation's operations and its stakeholders. This is the sort of managerial behaviour that we want to emphasise the importance of for success in the domain of management as the 21st century steps into its second decade, when the environment is full of stiff competition and there are enough temptations present for winning using unfair practices. We would like to call the owner of such managerial behaviour, the *conscious manager* and what he practices—*conscious management*. So, *effective leading* is *conscious management* and *conscious management* is *effective leadership*. Let us now try to develop the concept.

ONE MORE POINT IN FAVOUR OF *CONSCIOUS MANAGEMENT*

"A natural science deals with the behaviour of *objects*. But a social discipline such as management deals with the behaviour of *people* and *human institutions*. Practitioners will therefore tend to act and to behave as the discipline's assumptions tell them to. Even more important—the reality of a natural science, the physical universe and its laws, do not change (or if they do only over eons rather than over centuries, let alone over decades). The social universe has no 'natural laws' of this kind. It is thus subject to continuous change. And this means that assumptions that were valid yesterday can become invalid and, indeed, totally misleading in no time at all" [11].

Environmental Consciousness Is a Must

The laws of nature related to light, sound, heat, electricity, magnetism and the like will go on working following the same set of principles and rules, even if you do not have time, opportunity or care to pay heed to them. However, if you happen to be in management and happen not to be *conscious* about what all are happening around you and how all the people in relationship with you—your boss and other seniors, your peers and colleagues, your subordinates and juniors, your internal and external customers and suppliers and other stakeholders in your organisation, respond to those environmental stimuli, it may result in mismanagement, quarter-management, half- or three-quarter management as it happens normally in a manager's day-to-day management practice.

It is equally true for family management. In a modern family where the husband and wife may both be working or the homemaker wife is overburdened with all domestic and family operational chores including going for daily shopping, getting the child ready and reaching him to and bringing him back from school, preparing food for all, care-giving to him in every other respect that neither she nor her corporate executive husband has the opportunity, time and energy for the study of the nature of all the individuals with whom they interact in the family context—the milkman, the newspaper vendor, the sweeper, the part-time maid, the launderer, the LPG gas cylinder delivery man, the shopkeepers, sales persons and vendors in the local market and, above all, each other and the child. The vague idea that they have of each other is unorganised—it is a gestalt effect—the point of view of whole perceptual structures rather than in detail. The gestalt impression does not help much in 'relationship management'.

Modern brain research has, as one of its priority areas, the plasticity of the human brain. Just try to understand your brain's plastic behavioural nature from two simple analogies that I give you. If you place your body weight on a foam rubber mattress only two or three times, the rubber will get depressed in response to your body weight only temporarily and will regain its original shape once you raise your body from it. But, if you do it again and again and for quite some time, the configuration of the foam will change permanently.

Similarly, continuous fall of water on a stone base or rock makes a dent in the solid which, if it happened only a few times, will not have the same effect. The same principle holds true for the human brain. The behavioural response of an individual may change to a certain extent if the same stimulus is repeated over a period of time as the brain cells will form new clusters and networks by erasing the old and original ones. Unless you maintain awareness and watch everything meticulously *consciously*, you'll never be able to alter your expectations about and from the same individual and your earlier dealing strategies may not give you the desired results under the same circumstances. Although the stimuli might have remained the same, the neural networks and processing software would have changed leading to different outcome which you had never expected.

In dealing with people—individuals, pairs and teams, you must not hold on to the same basic assumptions. In order to *lead* people and manage them for results, if you do have to change your basic assumptions, you ought to be prepared to do it. It strengthens the cause of *conscious management*.

REFERENCES

[1] Mishra, Pankaj, 'Firms must enthuse employees, says Nayar', *The Economic Times, Kolkata*, 14 July 2010, p. 9.

[2] Blair, Margaret M. and Steven M. Wallman, *Unseen Wealth: Report of the Brookings Task Force on Intangibles,* The Brookings Institution, New York, 2001, p. 52.

[3] Echols, Michael E., *Competitive Advantage for Human Capital Investment*, Tapestry Press, Arlington, Texas, 2006, p. 101.

[4] Rost, Joseph, *Leadership for the Twenty-First Century*, Praeger, Westport, Connecticut, 1991.

[5] Ciulla, Joanne B., 'Leadership Ethics: Mapping the Territory', In: Joanne B. Ciulla (ed.) *Ethics, the Heart of Leadership*, Praeger, Westport, Connecticut, 2004, pp. 3–24.

[6] Drucker, Peter F., 'Leadership: More doing than dash', *Wall Street Journal*, 6 January 1988, p. 14.

[7] Bennis, Warren and Burt Nanus, *Leader: the Strategies for Taking Charge*, HarperCollins, New York, 1985, p. 45.

[8] Taleb, Nassim Nicholas, *Fooled by Randomness: The Hidden Role of Chance in Life and in the Markets,* Penguin Books, London, 2nd edition, 2007, pp. 18–19.

[9] Wangchuk, P.P., 'A visionary wins', *Hindustan Times, Kolkata,* 16 February 2010, p. 5.

[10] Taleb, Nassim Nicholas, *loc. cit.*, p. 8.

[11] Drucker, Peter F. *Management Challenges for the 21st Century*, HarperCollins Publishers, New York, 1999, pp. 3–4.

KEY TAKE-HOMES

- The concept of 'assets' in finance, banking and accounting as well as in personal and family resource and wealth management has been, most narrowly, related to 'hard' assets like buildings, plants and machineries, vehicles, tools and tackles. People, constituting 'soft' assets, who play the most important role in value creation by mobilising and properly utilising those 'hard' assets, had been kept away from the limelight in economics and business management.
- One of today's main challenges in the 'work' as well as 'family' roles is to convert the flimsy and variable 'soft' assets into strong *human capital* and, to evaluate the '*Return on Investment (ROI)*' on education and other human resource development initiatives.
- In business and industry as well as in the family, an effective manager manages performance to meet or exceed the performance standards. But, an effective leader's main attribute is people-orientation and management of performance is integrated into his leadership role.
- Effective leading is *conscious management* and *conscious management* is effective leading.

CHAPTER 3

The Conscious Manager: Managing and Leading *Happily*

BEING CONSCIOUS: IN GENERALLY

'Being conscious' means transcending the usual, day-to-day level of your mind which makes you to unconsciously 'react' to some situations and be influenced by your attitudes and outcomes of your past experiences.

If you look a little deeper, you can see how you are completely responsible for what is happening in your life! We do many things unconsciously because we do not live every moment with awareness and take responsibility for our words and actions. Remaining in consciousness is enough to break free from the past conditioning and act intelligently. This consciousness will simply kindle the spark of intelligence that has always been a part of you. The whole key lies in being conscious so that your intelligence can function. When you're consciously taking any decision or interpreting any event or a situation, you're using your intelligence. When you're conscious, you do not normally make mistakes as you do not rely on the past conditioning that has gone inside you for many years. With deep consciousness, you're in the present moment, alive and alert.

BEING CONSCIOUS: IN AN ORGANISATION

In an organisation, any individual's job is divided into two distinctly different types of tasks and assignments (See Figure 3.1). One of the two can be described as 'Technical (T)' consisting of activities which can be

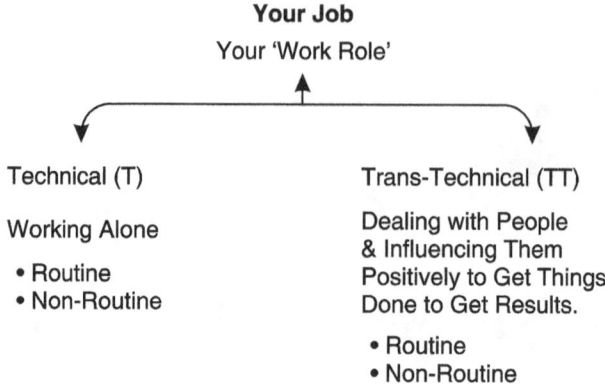

You are playing the role of an 'Internal Supplier' to all your 'Internal Customers'. Your immediate boss happens to be your 'Chief Internal Customer'

Fig. 3.1: Your Job/Work Role and its Two Parts

performed by the performer, by and large alone with minimum assistance from others, by following some standard rules, methods, systems and procedures. The individual performs these activities by drawing outputs from the storehouse of his own knowledge and experience. Most of the time for most people, these are routine jobs; non-routine activities come up on very rare occasions. Whatever may be the content or context of the 'T' type activities, the performer has to perform them *happily.*

The other part of the performer's job is 'Trans-Technical (TT)' where he has to interact with others—both inside and outside the organisation to get things done to meet the performance standards set for him, leading to the targeted results. Here also the trans-technical transactions could be 'routine' and 'non-routine'. In any case, such mobilisation of performance has to be achieved *happily* on his part and he also has to ensure *happiness* prevailing in all others with whom he interacted. This *happy managing* and *leading* must be done at least eighty to ninety percent of the time in all his transactions.

To what extent he achieves performance in the 'T' part of his job by putting into practice as 'output' whatever 'input' he has stored in himself determines his 'Efficiency (E)'. On the other hand, how he handles the 'TT' part of his job with *happiness* prevailing in him as well as also in others with whom he deals determines his 'Effectiveness (Eff)'. Being conscious about his 'E' and 'Eff' demands is a part of one's *conscious management* responsibility.

Let us see, through a case study, how important the 'TT' part of your role is in determining your 'Effectiveness (Eff)' with regard to others.

Case 4

This case study is not from our own stock of case materials. Instead, we have collected it from a press report with the lead line: "Govt. officer wins fight against 'quarrelsome' tag, but rewarded with ninth transfer" [1].

Mr Y, a finance and accounts officer with a Govt. of India organisation has paid for his arguments—in other words, his 'reactive' behaviour with a transfer—his ninth in nine years.

He had moved the central administrative tribunal after being labelled 'argumentative' and 'quarrelsome' in his 2003–04 annual performance appraisal, which had, otherwise, found his performance to be satisfactory. He won his quarrel with the tribunal quashing his annual confidential report. But, as if to prove all that the 'Argumentative Indian'—which is what Amartya Sen called his book on the country's argumentative tradition—deserved was an official swat, his organisational authorities struck back with another transfer.

Mr. X was rated 'satisfactory' in logical and analytical abilities and 'extremely honest' in the general assessment category, his honesty and straightforwardness in communication (that is, calling a spade a spade) had never been appreciated by any of the bosses under whom he worked ever since he joined the organisation as a bright, young officer fresh from the campus in 2001. Every senior had opined that he needed to be more positive and helpful and ought to improve his human relations skills.

This case clearly highlights the importance of the trans-technical abilities of any responsible employee.

The same thing may happen in a family and it really did happen in one case that we know of. A young man chose a young lady as his wife for her culinary talent as he was fond of tasty food. However, although she was really fantastic in her cooking skill, her behaviour with the husband, his parents and her own son (when the son reached 3–4 years age) was extremely rude. So although on the 'T' side of her job she was superb, her 'TT' side deserved a lot of improvement. She was efficient but not effective at all.

SELF-MANAGED *VIS-À-VIS* BOSS-MANAGED PERFORMANCE

Another thing is there about an employee's performance: it is important for him to be aware as to what extent he is 'self-managed' and to what extent 'boss-managed' (Figure 3.2). There may be an 'others-managed' portion also where he is being managed by his peers, internal or external suppliers or customers, or even by his juniors and subordinates.

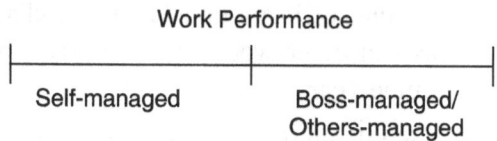

Work Performance

| Self-managed | Boss-managed/ Others-managed |

Your conscious goal should be to increase the 'self-managed' portion by reducing the 'boss-managed'/'others-managed' portion

Fig. 3.2: The Self-managed and 'Boss-managed/ Others-managed Portions of Work Performance

To be *conscious* about his performance management pattern from this angle and to try and maximise the self-managed portion *happily* is also a part of his *conscious management* requirement. On the family front, the boss-managed portion is replaced by spouse-managed and the others-managed by parents-managed, in-laws-managed or child-managed. As a matter of fact, those whose self-managed portion of work performance is significantly low than the others-managed portion as a young boy or girl grows up to have the same performance pattern as an employee or as a self-employed professional.

IMPORTANT: TO BE CONSCIOUS ABOUT BODY AND BRAIN POWERS

The term 'conscious manager' is thus being proposed for every individual in the organisation and in the family from a specific point of view which we feel is most scientific and concrete and thus justified. The qualifier 'conscious' is being highlighted as every such individual has to be fully aware of his two entirely personal inherent resource components—the *body* and the *brain* and their power potentials, which is hardly a part of the consciousness of our day-to-day living and working. He has to *manage* and *lead* these powers 'properly' in the interest of the society, in the macro sense, and his family and his work organisation, in the micro sense. What does such proper 'managing and leading' signify? Let us discuss and analyse a very simple example from our daily life.

An Example from Our Daily Life

Any individual can behave 'reactively' (rudely, harshly, aggressively, refusing cooperation—instead arguing and finding fault; or, avoiding eye contact and communication, withdrawing himself into a shell, suppressing emotions normally manifested through the orchestrated non-verbal and verbal channels of his expression) which is a natural outcome of 'stress' (arising out of frustration or dissatisfaction due to 'losing' instead of 'winning' in a specific situation), 'managing and leading' his body and brain powers negatively resulting in wastage of energy and effort.

Under 'stress', such behaviour will originate from the 'fight-or-flight' department located in the lower primitive structures of his brain (responsible for all our basic survival-oriented instincts) which we have inherited from our animal ancestors. This is improper 'managing and leading' as there is 'no thinking or feeling before acting'.

On the contrary, he can behave, without any 'stress' (free from any frustration or dissatisfaction by realising and accepting that 'loss' and 'win' are nothing but the two opposite sides of the same coin representing life's processes), most happily 'proactively' (which is 'thinking or feeling before acting'). This behaviour is supposed to originate from the outer and upper structures of our brain which is the seat of our 'thinking' and 'feeling' minds and is most pronounced and uniquely designed, in the human species, with a lot of versatility. This is proper 'managing and leading' as he is using his body and brain powers positively. Moreover, he is doing it mindfully and thus *consciously*.

A Simple Model for Your Easy Visualisation

It is not difficult for anyone to develop such *consciousness*. One has to use a very simple model to visualise his own brain to be a two-storied structure without going into any of its complexities.

The ground floor (which we will describe as the *creaturely brain* and its consciousness as the *creaturely consciousness*), whose structures are primitive, representing all basic instincts for survival and which is responsible for all stereotyped behaviour, has the 'fight-or-flight' switch. This switch is triggered when there is a spontaneous 'threat' reflex or an automatic apprehension of 'loss', leading to 'reactive' behaviour where there is 'no conscious thinking or feeling before acting' as the ground floor does not have such powers.

The New York University psychologist Gary Marcus refers to the system followed by our brain's ground floor, the *ancestral* or the *reflexive* system [2].

Incidentally, 'reactive' behaviour was necessary for the human species, as its members evolved over millions of years, to be developed as a tool and strategy for coping with threats posed by predating animals and enemies from alien human tribes and also from aggressive leaders and team mates. Even in the long course of evolution, this propensity for self-defence [which in many of us works almost like any spontaneous reaction as the knee-jerk reflex] has not left us; thus, it would be necessary for us to be *conscious* about this unwelcome trait which gets switched on all of a sudden. Most probably, but only intensive research can confirm this assumption, this reactivity has remained with us to be sharpened regularly through use as a defensive tool in any human inter-personal encounter.

The upper or first floor has the more mature and intelligent *cerebral consciousness* as it is most developed in humans amongst all species; and, being the seat of the 'thinking' and 'feeling' minds, possesses the ability for 'proactive' behaviour leading to 'conscious thinking or feeling before acting'. The power of *cerebral consciousness* makes an individual 'situational'. The more structured, developed, spacious and extensive and, of course, the more occupied and utilised the first floor is, the more effectively an individual will be able to deal with the situation in a specific fashion in accordance with the dictates of the complex situation. The conscious pro-activity that we are talking about here is a power of the *frontal lobes* (front portion of the brain's upper and outer floor), located precisely in the *Pre-Frontal Cortex (PFC)* area. This has been scientifically established by observing 'patients with damaged *frontal lobes* who are less able to develop novel strategies or plans to tackle a particular problem. They cannot use information from their environment to regulate or change behaviour'; which is what conscious managers are expected to do. In another way, we may say that a conscious manager's speciality is to have a 'blackboard of the mind'

> which has all the current factors noted down very clearly and distinctly (with all their relationships with the past experiences wherever applicable) in a particular situation. Some people describe it as the 'working memory'. And, he takes a decision or handles the situation taking into proper consideration all those factors, in minimum time. [3]
>
> Once you are able to visualise this simple model, you can analyse your every behaviour as to from which level of your brain it is originating. If you pursue this habit of regular analysis, you'll develop the skill of *conscious management* of your body and brain.

MANAGING PERFORMANCE FROM PERSONAL RESOURCES

Apart from 'leading' his personal resources—the body and the brain, an individual has to 'manage' performance from those resources in the best possible manner so that he is not 'stressed' in any way. In a nutshell, he has to be his own leader and manager (Do you know of any writer or practitioner of human resource management who has ever highlighted the importance 'self-leadership' and 'self-management' from such an angle?).

He also has to obtain the best 'performance' from others by ensuring that the power potentials of the body and brain of every other individual that he has to deal with are best utilised. He has people all around him: vertically above and below him, horizontally in the same functional domain as well as in other inter-dependent domains placed in 'internal supplier/internal customer' relationships; even as external suppliers and customers.

It may be that some of these people are in his team under his charge and leadership. It may also not be so; he may not be directly responsible for a team's performance. In any case, he has to lead them and manage 'performance' from everyone with whom he is engaged in any work relationship in a most positive manner, not causing any 'stress' to any one of them.

Such performance management requirements would be equally valid in all kinds of social units—whether it is a small nuclear or a large joint family, or a business or industrial or a non-governmental social service organisation or a set-up representing a particular religious movement.

CONSCIOUS MANAGEMENT: REVISITED AND REDEFINED

So in the concept of *conscious management*, there are primarily two different aspects.

The first one is, to lead and manage 'performance' from your own self ('self-leadership' and 'self-management')—all very consciously. As, of all items of 'knowledge', 'self-knowledge' is most important and, of all aspects of 'management', 'self-management' is most vital and most difficult, conscious self-management is the primary step to be taken by you.

And the second one is to lead others and manage performance from others, whether they are directly reporting to you and are responsible to you for their performance or not, keeping in mind the stress-free utilisation of their two inherent personal resources—the 'body' and the 'brain' which are to be utilised positively and productively in the interest of your organisation and the society. With conscious self-management being effectively accomplished, leading and managing others would automatically fall in place. This consciousness development is essential for managing self as well as others *consciously* in any situation.

The 'self-managed' and the 'boss-managed' or 'others-managed' parts of performance need a little more discussion. In the case of any job or work performance, there is a portion where the performance is managed by the performer himself and there is also another portion where the performer's boss has to chase and interact much with the performer to mobilise performance and get the work done. In general, we find that the performer-managed portion which we will describe as 'self-managed' gets promptly done by the performer himself because he likes it and enjoys performing the tasks and assignments associated. The boss has to chase him for the portion which he does not enjoy performing. As a result, he procrastinates and it gets postponed. We will call it the 'boss-managed' portion.

The concept of *conscious management* is applicable here in two ways. Firstly, if you happen to be the performer, then you will practice conscious management to increase the 'self-managed' portion (including the 'disliked' portion by looking at it from a positive viewpoint) from its present quantum to reduce the 'boss-managed' portion so that your boss is free to do other things which are beyond your domain. Secondly, if you are the boss, you can enthuse, inspire, guide, coach, mentor, train and develop your subordinates making them look at the disliked portions of their job content from a different motivating angle to increase their 'self-managed' portions so that you're free to do more complicated things offering challenges to your body and brain powers, pulling yourself out from your 'comfort zone' existence.

In the family situation also, a young child happily performs the portions of his assignments which he enjoys leaving the parents to chase him to take up and complete the disliked parts. As a parent, you will have to be very conscious about what your child likes and what he dislikes and handle him most tactfully so that he not only performs the liked parts of his job happily but also does not avoid the disliked portions but feels responsible to complete those also willingly.

There could be another interesting application of *conscious management* here in this context. If, as a subordinate, you have been somewhat dependent on your boss for your performance, your goal now should be reversal of the process; that is, to increase your boss's dependence on you. You should try to minimise your boss to be handling tasks and assignments independently of you. And, if you are the boss then your goal should be to be more and more dependent on your subordinates by delegating some of your work activities to them as per their likes; so that you are free to think, plan and do to increase your contribution in areas of development and improvement.

THE SCIENCE BEHIND *CONSCIOUS MANAGEMENT*: UNCOVERING THE LORD OF RESOURCES

Let us now talk a little more about the simple science behind *conscious management*. Mind you, it is not 'science fiction'; it is 'simple and straight natural science'.

People talk about positive behaviour, positive attitude and so on. Management preachers and behavioural science faculties advise that you should be positive towards others. So do the religious scriptures and *gurus*. But, have you come across anybody talking about the science behind it? Your most probable answer would be a 'No'.

We are providing you with the basic alphabets of the underlying science before we go into the details of it in subsequent chapters. For that we are going to uncover the lord of all available resources that we know of, that is **you**—a most valuable Human Resource (HR). You are the owner and lord of your entirely personal resources: your *body* and your *brain*. We are going to uncover you; peel off your skin which does not allow us to see your interiors: your multi-million dollar property.

A VIRTUAL JOURNEY

Come with me on a virtual journey.

A Peep Inside You

Imagine your whole body and brain are encased by glass instead of skin and one can see through as it is transparent. There are trillions of cells of which you are made; and these cells are visible right through your glass cladding.

Your incredible physical structure is your personal asset. It is made of about a hundred million million (10^{14}) human cells together with 10 to 100 million million (10^{13} to 10^{14}) bacterial cells. (In a sense, up to half the cells of your body are bacterial).

Your body has over 500 muscles, 200 bones and 60 miles of veins and arteries to serve you. Yet it tirelessly builds thousands of new cells daily and features a heart which beats over 100,000 times and pumps over 1,600 gallons a day without complaint.

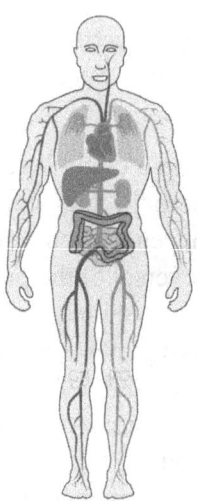

Fig. 3.3: You as a Transparent Living System

An Insight into Your Cell

Your every living cell is a micro-organism. On the one hand, it works like an organic computer as it is an input-processing-output mechanism. It receives stimuli from the external as well as its adjoining internal environments; it processes them by using its built-in software; and then comes out with the resultant response actions. As an input-processing-output mechanism, every cell must minimise the energy cost of every such activity which it manages to achieve only under stress-free conditions.

You should be able to visualise such transactions which others can see through your glassy skin. You can also see it yourself if you stand in front of a mirror. That you are receiving stimulus inputs through your receptor organs (eyes, ears, nose, tongue, skin and mind); that those are being transmitted through your nerves to your brain where every input is being processed (compared with your stored inputs to evaluate whether the input is known, partially familiar or totally new); that a response decision is taken to be translated into action; that the impact of the response action is again going into your system as a 'feedback'—this entire process you are able to witness clearly and consciously.

On the other hand, your every living cell is an electro-chemical device. You are now looking at you brain cells through your glassy skull bone. When a cell is healthy and happy, it gets flushed with positive brain chemicals, amongst which four principal ones are *endorphin* (brain's natural pain-inhibitor belonging to the 'morphine' group), *dopamine* (brain's reward chemical and natural movement balancer—depletion of which eventually leads to *Parkinson's* disease), *serotonin* (a rise in its level produces elatedness whereas its reduction is typical of mental depression—we may describe it as the brain's natural emotional controller), and *oxytocin* (a hormone best known for its role in female reproduction but for our purpose its main role would be as the love and compassion chemical which is produced during warm and intimate physical contact like a warm handshake, or embracing, or giving a pat on the back apart from kissing, hugging and other forms of intimacy without the regular supply of which a child may die of deprivation or an adult may turn a psychological wreck). Imagine, you are able to see the dance of the happy chemicals inside your brain and experience peace and relaxation in your whole body and all body parts. Doesn't it make you consciously happy for the first time?

When a brain cell gets ready for a 'fight' or 'flight' stance under dissatisfaction and frustration, the level of negative brain chemicals (such as *adrenalin* and *cortisol*) rise affecting the cell's structure and functions adversely. You can feel the pinch of such adversity in your brain and body and witness the ups-and-downs of these negative chemicals behind the glass screen protecting your brain. Under the 'fight' stance, your body and mind both become aggressive and you indulge in rude behaviour and jerky movements of your arms, hands and fingers. While, under the 'flight' stance, your body and mind both become defensive and suppressive—you start hiding your true emotions and your body becomes stiff to support the suppression and your hands and fingers hide away from the sight of people in front of you. They disappear behind your back, or enter inside your pant pockets (in males) or underneath your scarf (in females) or your arms get crossed across your chest and your fingers get placed under your armpits.

As regards the electrical characteristics of the cell, good health and happiness generates *beta-positive* (14 to 24 cycles per second) brain waves, whereas bad health and frustration leads to the predominance of *beta-negative* (25 to 32 cycles per second). You can not only feel but also see your brain cells vibrating to form such good or bad brain waves respectively under favourable and adverse circumstances.

Consciousness Development Through Visualisation

With the regular practice of such visualisation, you would develop the fabulous power of *consciousness* which is a very rare but certainly accessible power which common people are totally unaware of.

You can also develop the skill of looking at and analysing the roots of others' behaviour using this 'glass-clad body and brain' visualisation technique.

Our model, the *Conscious Manager* consciously endeavours to remain with a relaxed body and positive brain chemicals and brain waves most of the time (in 80 to 85 per cent of his transactions with 'self' and 'others'). He also consciously tries to generate physical as well as mental relaxation in others, whosoever he interacts with singly, in pairs, and in teams so that there is predominance of positive brain chemicals and brain waves in them too [4]

However, there is a new research finding which may help you in your practice of conscious management. According to Robin Dunbar, a researcher at Oxford University, an average human brain is capable of handling up to a maximum of 150 persons only. This limits us to managing social circles of around 150 people including inside and outside our work organisation, and including the family and social environments [5].

REFERENCES

[1] Sengupta, Ananya, 'Official Swat for Argumentative Indian', *The Telegraph, Kolkata*, 23 January, 2010, pp. 1, 4.
[2] Marcus, Gary, *KLUGE: The Haphazard Evolution of the Human Mind*, Mariner Books: Houghton Mifflin Harcourt, New York, 2009, pp. 51–53.
[3] Greenfield, Susan, *The Human Brain: a Guided Tour*, Phoenix, Sixth Impression, London, 2000, p. 25.

[4] Ganguli, Siddhartha, *Live Happily, Work Happily*: Allied Publishers, New Delhi, 2009.
[5] 'Your Brain can't Handle More Than 150 Facebook Friends', *Hindustan Times, Kolkata*, 25 January 2010, p. 14.

KEY TAKE-HOMES

- 'Being conscious' means really being conscious about the happenings in your environment and not indulging in any impulsive, reflex-type 'reactive' behaviour which had saved us from extinction during our jungle days. Instead, you need to be 'responsive' and 'proactive' to be effective in your interaction with the external environment which includes other people. Being 'effective' and not just 'efficient' technically or professionally is thus everyone's *conscious management* responsibility.
- Your conscious goal should be to increase the 'self-managed' portion by reducing the 'boss-managed'/'others-managed' portion of your team members' work performance.
- Every individual anywhere must be a *conscious manager* by practising self-management of his inherent personal resources—his body and brain powers and *lead* those most appropriately. He must be a 'conscious manager' of others' personal resources too—whosoever he would interact and have relationship with in the 'work', 'social' and 'family' roles.

CHAPTER 4

The Shortest Route to Conscious Self-Management

Before we delve into the depths of 'consciousness' and discuss different routes to 'conscious self-management' and 'conscious management', we are exposing you to the shortest route to 'conscious self-management'.

The best managers everywhere, those who are consciously self-managed, are observed to follow this shortest route. This is our firm conviction, based on our experience of conducting developmental programmes in over 950 organisations in India and overseas.

From now onwards, in the practical portions of this book, we'll address you—the reader, as 'Mr Manager' as your goal would be to manage yourself and others as well, consciously. We would assume that many of you are in that category already or aspiring to be.

Mind you, we have no gender bias. The style of calling someone as 'Mr Manager' and using the pronouns 'he', 'his' and 'him' will cover members of the fair sex as well to highlight importance of the role and not the gender.

Dear Mr Manager, do you realise that, like any other living organism, you too are an automatic S-R ('Stimulus-Response') system? [1]. I have touched upon this concept already in the previous chapter under 'An Insight into Your Cell'. Of course, being a human, your S-R system's hardware and software are of the highest order—the most sophisticated and versatile that Mother Nature has ever produced.

THE STIMULUS-RESPONSE PROCESS

Let us get to understand it better. When you are reading a line in this article, your eyes are receiving visual signals—the words. So, your eyes are the receptors, and the words constitute the stimuli 'S'. The word-based information is sent off, faster than light, to the CPU, the central processing unit, your brain. The brain compares the data with those already stored in the huge data-base inside the millions of cells (neurons) forming the tissue mass, retrieves the correct meaning, makes the most appropriate interpretation, finds the message interesting, and decides to carry on reading. That decision is the response 'R'.

Your Attitude Dictates Your Behaviour

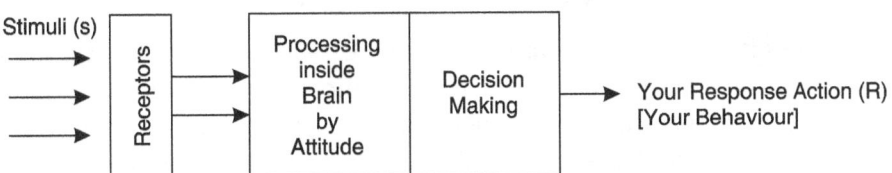

Fig. 4.1: The Stimulus-Response Process

THE IMPACT OF A PAUSE 'P' BETWEEN 'S' AND 'R'

If you ponder for a while, you will easily understand what goes on. In the case of reading (like now), or listening to a lecture, there is an intermediate phase—a pause 'P' in between the 'S' and the 'R'. During 'P', your brain is processing the input 'S' logically, using the consciousness of the left half of your upper brain, the *cerebral cortex* (see chapter five for an exposure to the structure and functions of your brain). In the case of any language-based formal communication—written or oral, the left half of the brain gets involved as it does in the event of any step-by-step planning and programming activity that you may undertake.

However, most interestingly, this does not necessarily happen during informal, social, or organisational communication, between one person and another, within the same group, or between two different groups. Let us get exposed to what really happens.

THE CREATURELY DESIRE TO WIN

When you interact with another person, generally speaking, a *creaturely* feeling pervades your consciousness—your *desire to win*. It emanates from the lower structures of your brain which is the storehouse of your creaturely basic instincts related to your survival and sustenance and continuity of your *selfish genes*.

You want to prove that you are right, and the other person is wrong. This desire is accompanied with your need for *attention* (you want him to establish and maintain positive eye contact and listen to you attentively), *acceptance* or *acknowledgement* and *affiliation* (you want to be acceptable to or acknowledged by the other person and get the feeling of affiliation), and your resistance to direct attack (you hate to be told bluntly and blatantly that you are wrong). Instead, you are hungry for *appreciation* (you want him to appreciate your point of view).

THE PLEASURE-PAIN PRINCIPLE

Why does it happen? For your brain, the CPU—its most prized possession are the *neurons*, the brain cells that are more than 10,000 million in number. And, there are thousands of in-built programmes, which make those neurons process stimuli and take response decisions in different contexts. One such programme by which all stimuli are processed is the 'repeat pleasure, avoid pain' principle. If you *win*, you derive *pleasure*; if you *lose*, you get *pain*.

The 'pleasure-pain' principle is a law, essential for every individual's survival and progress through life's long and arduous journey. The principle is 'self'-oriented and, therefore, it originates from the basic instincts in-grained in the innermost primitive parts of the human brain, inter-linked closely with the feelings-guided imaginative right half of the *cerebral cortex*, your upper brain. So, whenever there is any negative 'S', contrary to your 'desire to win'—not favourable for you, the information is abruptly routed to a very sensitive area of your brain. There is a threat to your biological system. You get the feeling of pain and frustration. The physiological processes inside your body undergo a rapid change, alterations take place in their electro-chemical characteristics, and the 'fight-flight' response centre of the brain is triggered. You are either under the grip of *anger* and start *fighting* verbally (argumentation, adverse criticism, shouting, screaming, and so on) or take all steps to *flee* (withdrawing yourself or keeping yourself mum, to avoid further pain).

CONSEQUENCES OF S-R WITHOUT A 'P'

There is no 'P' in this case, between the 'S' and the 'R'. You lose the power of logical thinking. Your left brain consciousness is switched off. You manage yourself in a most primitive manner, like a lowly creature, and lose your identity as a balanced, mature human being.

Try to think of as many practical situations as you can when you have *reacted* in such a creaturely manner. Instances will certainly include occasions when you were trying to sell a product or a service and your customer had raised an objection, or negotiating a price or a delivery schedule with your vendor and he had expressed his inability to comply, or communicating with somebody—a senior, junior or a peer and he had expressed a point of view totally different from yours. Apart from the inter-personal context, it is a common occurrence between individuals or small groups within the same group, or between two groups. Are you not a witness to the communication gaps (better to avoid the term 'conflict') between sections, departments, divisions, corporate office and the plant or the branches, or between the executive and the unionised cadres and, more commonly, between family members—the husband and the wife or a parent and a child?

When one falls a prey to the working of the automatic S-R mechanism, there is loss of control over the 'self'. When it happens to you, you are not managing yourself properly. But as knowledge starts with self-knowledge, management also should start with *self-management*. Nevertheless, to be a self-managed person or not, is entirely your choice. You can easily attain the self-managed state by simply introducing a 'P' in between your 'S' and 'R'. If you react abruptly, you are operating as a rudimentary S-R device and do not deserve to claim the sophistication and wisdom of a mature human being. In conscious self-management, we have to train our brain to introduce the 'P' after the 'S'. But, how to do it?

TWO PRACTICAL EXAMPLES

Boss Management

Let us first take the case of *boss management*. Imagine a situation, when your high-*adrenaline* boss is shouting and screaming at you, not being happy with the work that you have just completed for him.

He is holding the working paper in one hand; the other hand and the body are engaged in restless, jerky movements representing annoyance. The visual and auditory stimuli enter through your eyes and ears, travel instantaneously via the nervous route to your lower brain structure and, immediately, to the right half of your upper brain which is the seat of your 'feeling mind'. Your right brain takes the situation as a threat to your 'ego' (your 'desire to win'). It may now respond in one of the following ways.

Firstly, it may put into your mouth, a self-protective logic that, since the time given to you was too short, you failed to do a very good job. Secondly, it may make you react by arguing back due to a rush of *adrenaline* into your cells. Thirdly, it may try to persuade your boss to give you some more time so that you can produce something which would satisfy him. Lastly, it may prompt you to disengage eye contact and lower your gaze or look away from the boss, along with which your body becomes stiff. Your hands and fingers escape from his vision and find a shelter behind your back (with the fingers interlocked and hands held hanging in front of your spine) or underneath your armpits. These are typical features when the level of the stress chemical *cortisol* rises.

The first response leads to a clear communication gap, the second to a conflict, the third to an outright rejection and unnecessary argumentation; and the last to your subconscious fear and escapism. Poor self-management indeed! The reason: your response R has been too abrupt in all the four cases. You have failed to insert a P after the S, before the R. These are all *reactive* behaviours.

What would happen if you introduce a 'P' after the 'S' that you receive from your boss? Try not to *react* immediately. Continue to maintain your eye contact with him, or keep your gaze on a lower plane. It will help you to absorb the heat generated by him. Your patient listening, without any interruption, will satisfy his 'ego' and give him the feeling of winning. He is satisfied now; you have gratified his creaturely needs. His cooling down process will manifest through the transformation in his body language, his tone of voice, and choice of words. There is a very big chance that now he will be a little more prepared to listen to your logic (the first alternative 'R') or your persuasive request (the third alternative 'R') and give you another opportunity for reworking on the task. You have now succeeded in creating a 'win-win' ('You win, I also win') situation. For satisfying the other person's ego, whosoever he may be, you have to keep your own 'ego' under control and subdued.

Child Management

Now imagine you are at home and your four-year-old son is throwing up temper tantrums as subconsciously he is hungry for your attention (you are a working person and have been away from home for almost ten hours). He is accusing you of not having brought the chocolate that you had promised to bring for him in the morning. It's really your fault since the commitment had just slipped off from your mind as you had a hectic day at the workplace. You have behavioural choices.

First, you 'react' by shouting and screaming at a rate that his voice is drowned. It will make him angrier and there is every chance that he will throw and break something into pieces or tear off whatever soft he finds in front of him.

Second, you immediately go out to get a bar of chocolate for him. In the midst of heat, when he finds that you're going out, he may in desperate anger ask for more chocolates or a chocolate plus something as he knows this is a weak moment of yours when you can be manipulated.

Third, you remain cool and let the heat flow from his hot head to your cool head. When his excitement has somewhat reduced, you admit your mistake and say that it had simply slipped off your mind and tell him that you'll certainly get for him tomorrow whatever brand of chocolate he wants to have. This 'I lose, you win' strategy is a product of the thinking upper brain and is a *conscious management* act which should work best. Now you bring the child close to you and kiss, hug and embrace him to produce *'oxytocin'*—a happiness hormone in his system.

TIME TO PONDER AND GET INTO THE S-P-R HABIT

Right now, Mr Manager, you are as good as your R's and no better. But your R's might not be very good because you haven't taken a good 'P' as yet. You may say that it's almost impossible to take a good 'P' in human encounters unless someone gives you a good 'S'. But that's thinking immaturely.

Do not expect that all others will always be good to you under all circumstances. 80% of the bad behaviour (negative S's) that you experience in life, you will find, generates from 20% of the people with whom you interact—who are caustic and toxic by nature. Irrespective of whether you get a good or bad 'S', always give yourself a brief 'P' to plan and prepare your 'R'.

Your objective is simple and straight, based on the fundamental pleasure-pain principle. You have to make the other person win and feel good first so that, being now in a happy frame of mind himself (don't forget the *endorphin-dopamine-serotonin-oxytocin* and other happiness chemicals and the *beta-positive* brain wave generation objective), he will be prepared to allow you to win and feel good too. Try out on this basis, in all your human interactions, from right now. This S (Stimulus)-P (Pause)-R (Response) habit will put you firmly on the road leading to *conscious self-management*.

THE IBM 'THINK' PAD

Many years ago, I had been presented with a gift hamper by the IBM Corporation. Tucked in amongst the good amount of sweets, candies, chocolates and savouries that it contained, there was a wee notepad with 'Think' written on top—small enough to be kept in the chest pocket. We consumed the sweets and savouries over the next few days; but I preserved the 'Think' pad with great care. Now, after so many years when I look and think back, I feel that the idea of the pad was not only to serve as a piece of stationery for noting down, but also to serve as a reminder for the individual to 'think' before acting or doing something. The hidden message is: practise 'conscious self-management'.

REFERENCE

[1] Ganguli, Siddhartha, *Human Engineering for Better Management*: Kwality Book Company, Calcutta, 1977, pp. 9–10.

KEY TAKE-HOMES

- In dealing with any 'Stimulus (S)' arising from outside or inside, the practice of *conscious management* calls for the use of a 'Pause (P)' before coming up with a 'Response (R)' abruptly.
- Evaluate your present spontaneous 'Response (R)' strategy and try to get into the 'S (Stimulus) → P (Pause) → R (Response)' habit.
- The practice of *conscious management* recommends the use of a small notepad (plain and unruled) for noting down pertinent points in logical sequence or even writing down something using block letters being conscious about each letter's verticality, and maintaining each line's horizontality on the plain paper. This habit will help you to switch on the frontal intelligence area of the left half of the upper portion of your brain and your lower *creaturely* brain's 'fight-or-flight' propensities would be inhibited.

CHAPTER 5

Delving into the Depths of Consciousness

THE CONSCIOUSNESS FACTOR

Dear Mr Manager, let us explain the *consciousness factor* a little more clearly and in somewhat detail. We suppose, meanwhile, you have already started: number one—looking at your own and others' internal processes through the transparent cladding of the body and brain discussed in chapter three; and, number two, taking the shortest route to *conscious self-management*, shared with you in chapter four and getting positive results as expected.

Let me now share with you a psychological model which says that our mind is like an iceberg where the tip is the layer of *consciousness*.

May I explain, what I mean? In writing every sentence of this book, I have two choices. One choice is that I become really serious and try to write every sentence here from my mind's *conscious* plane with full concentration, keeping all my cognitive doors and windows open for being alert and also for sustaining the alert state of mind. I choose every word to form every sentence consciously. I construct the sentence consciously so that it is not only grammatically correct but also reads well; I check and recheck the spellings.

The other choice is that I do everything casually, not so much consciously. I'm not being alert and attentive. Sometimes, I may be focused, while at other times, I may be semi-conscious or even unconscious of what I am writing. Later on I realise that it was not the right thing to do. The first choice allows me to reach the goals that every organisational as well as family member must have: *First Time Right (FTR)* and *Zero Defect (ZD)*. If I am not fully conscious all through and in all respects, I'll unnecessarily (since I have the choice of *conscious working* also) waste my effort, time, energy, computer time and space which would all add up to the cost of the book's production. Therefore, I should be wise enough to choose the *consciousness* route.

Mr Manager, you're also having two choices while reading it. One choice is to use your *conscious* mind-powers, read it word by word, sentence by sentence and try to understand and interpret properly so that you are able to internalise the learning for ready application whenever and wherever necessary. In this process, wherever you stumble against a word of which the meaning is not known to you, you have a standard dictionary handy to be consulted. Your reading time and energy are thus properly invested to give you the highest return whenever you apply any of the lessons learnt. Your second choice is to read it casually: sometimes *consciously* and mindfully, sometimes *semi-consciously* and unmindfully. In this process, your time, effort, energy and all other personal resources are not being effectively utilised; there is a lot of wastage. In the present era of *lean thinking* and *lean management*, such practices are not worthy of a responsible employee of an organisation or a committed family member.

Let us discuss two examples of how you can use your body *consciously*.

Example 1

Elin Ekblom-Bak of the Swedish School of Sport and Health Sciences has contributed the editorial in an issue of the *British Journal of Sports Medicine* where he has categorically mentioned that after four hours of sitting, the body starts to send harmful signals. The genes regulating the amount of glucose and fat in the body start to shut down. Even for people who exercise, spending long periods sitting at a desk is harmful. According to Tim Armstrong, a physical activity expert of the World Health Organisation, people who exercise every day, but still spend a lot of time sitting, might get more benefit if that exercise were spread across the day, rather than in a single go [1].

Example 2

Running regularly not just helps one shed extra weight, it also does wonders for the brain. According to scientists at Cambridge University led by Timothy Bussey, behavioural specialist, regular jogging leads to growth of new cells in the area of the brain which is responsible for memory power. Why only running or jogging, any aerobic exercise triggers the growth of *neurons* or brain cells (the condition is known as 'neurogenesis'). It may be linked to increased blood flow or higher levels of 'feel good' hormones or happiness chemicals like *'endorphin'* that are released while exercising. Previous studies on people with depression have found that their mental health conditions can improve if they exercised regularly [2].

If we take lessons from these two recent research studies, take the correct steps and incorporate those in our lifestyle, we'd be practising *conscious management*.

BE CONSCIOUS: DO THINGS CONSCIOUSLY

So, the theme of this volume is to drive home the message that: Mr Manager, *be conscious*. And, whatever you do, you must do it *consciously*. In other words, you must utilise your own as well as others' body and brain powers *consciously* so that there is highest positive and productive, *Return on the Investment (ROI)* of the *human assets* being utilised for some activity, having least negative consequences such as non-achievement, wrong achievement, partial achievement, stress and so on. It calls for good planning skill which is available in the human brain in the raw form and needs to be polished and sharpened.

THE ICEBERG MODEL OF THE HUMAN MIND

Let us take a break and refer to the *iceberg* model of the human mind. The tip of the iceberg is the *conscious* mind which is expected to remain alert and active as long as we're awake and focused on some activity. It is meant for recognising, understanding and learning. The learning becomes the base of our explicit short-term memory.

Immediately below the *conscious* layer of the mind, there is a very thick layer of *subconscious* which is the storehouse of our memories of *pleasure* and *pain*. The *subconscious* mind also contains our dreams, wishful thinking, desires, ambitions and aspirations, and future plans of actions about which we may be dead sure or may be in doubt whether we'll achieve those or not. There is a thin layer of *semi-conscious* between the *conscious* and the *subconscious* through which we may be receiving inputs obtained by our sensory receptor organs—the eyes, the ears, the nose, the tongue and the skin but not being within our zone of attention, we may not be fully aware of them as much as we're aware about the *conscious inputs*.

Beneath the *subconscious* is the deep layer of the *unconscious* which is responsible for all the involuntary mechanisms and processes, going inside our body and brain that make us live and grow. According to some mind-watchers, below the *unconscious*, exists the deep layer of *collective unconscious* which is still a 'dark continent' for us.

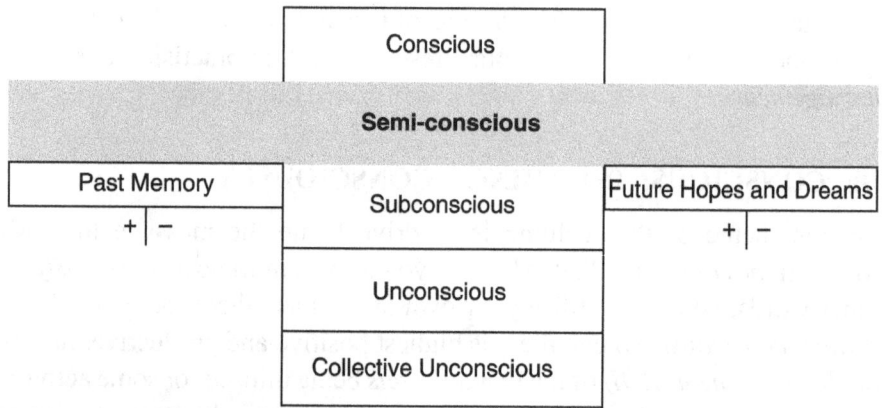

Fig. 5.1: The Iceberg Model of the Human Mind

BIOLOGICAL VERSION OF THE ICEBERG MODEL

Evolution of Your Brain's Structure

If we describe the 'iceberg' model of the mind biologically, we may say that the human brain is comparable to a two-storied structure, where the foundation or base of the ground floor is the *brain stem* which is an extension of the *spinal cord* passing through the spine from which all the peripheral nerves get distributed throughout the body for transmission and reception of signals.

How Did the *Brain Stem* Develop?

When *fish* came into existence on this planet, it developed a tube to carry nerves from the distant parts of its body to a central control station—a bulge on top of the fish-spine or the main fishbone. From the central set of nerves, other nerves started getting spread into specialised nodules. Some of these nodules became the *smell brain* while some developed into *eyes* (which are nothing but extensions of the brain itself), and some came to control movement—the *cerebellum*. All these important parts collectively formed the *reptilian brain*, purely *mechanical* and *unconscious* in its operations. Today, this collection happens to be the lowest and most primitive portion of the ground floor of the two-storied human brain structure.

Subsequently, *thalamus* developed allowing sight, smell and hearing to be used together. *Amygdala* and *hippocampus* came along on the way creating a crude memory system. They were joined up by the *hypothalamus*, making it possible for the organism to react to more stimuli. All together, known as the *limbic system*, is a typical feature of the *mammalian brain*. Emotions like *pleasure* (joy, delight, and any 'feel-good' feeling) and *pain* (unhappiness, anger, anxiety, fear and any other 'feel-bad' feeling) are generated here but not experienced as these structures are still *unconscious* on their own.

The *reptilian brain* and the *limbic system*, typical of the *mammalian brain* together thus may be said to constitute the *unconscious layers* of your 'iceberg' mind—the ground floor of the two-storied *human brain*. In our intellectual drama, we will give it the role of *creaturely brain*.

With evolution of the *mammals*, the *mammalian brain* also evolved in the process so as to trigger the development of the brain's first floor—a layer consisting of a thin matrix of cells whose shape allowed for a multitude of neural connections to be formed between them. This 'skin' became the *cerebral cortex*, which is most pronounced in humans amongst the mammals. It is this *cerebral cortex* which became responsible for our *consciousness*—the 'conscious' layers of the 'iceberg' model of the human mind. It is going to play the role of the *cerebral brain* in our discussion [3].

How Your Brain Works

Mr Manager, when you learn something by understanding, you are using your *cortex* or the conscious mind. After repeated practice (or 'conditioning'), its memory gets stored into the subconscious part of your mind. Whenever you become reminiscent of your past and remember some good or bad experience, you are bringing that information from your subconscious mind (that is *cortex-limbic system* interface) to the conscious mind-plane. The subconscious stores all your beliefs and values that you have imbibed from the environment during the socialisation process of your growing up from the kid-stage.

The subconscious also contains your future dreams, desires, hopes, ambitions and aspirations in the form of good or bad emotions and sensory perceptions. And again, whenever you are pondering over your future, you are making your *cortex-limbic system* interface. In other words, bringing something from your subconscious to the conscious plane is comparable to your climbing up from the ground floor to the first floor of your two-storied *brain-house*.

The *brain stem* is enveloped by some vital tissue structures which we have inherited from our closest mammalian ancestors like chimpanzees. This inner and lower brain contains all the brain components responsible for our metabolic processes, basic survival systems and functions like circulation, respiration, digestion, excretion, reproduction, immunisation, emotions and so on. The outer and upper floor of our brain is the *cortex* which contains departments for all higher mental functions.

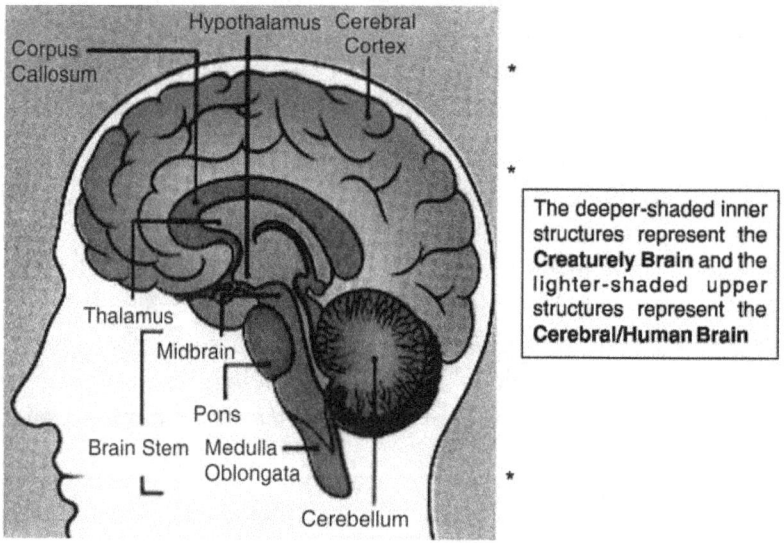

Fig. 5.2: Cross-section of the Human Brain

'For activities that are performed with attention or conscious effort, there needs to be a constant referral to the *cortex*, which is known to play a key role in conscious attention' [4].

Once a movement can become automated, either by internalised triggers in the basic structures of the inner and lower floor of the brain, or from sensory inputs fed through the *cerebellum* (which is a vital part of the brain's ground floor and responsible, amongst many functions for balance,

Delving into the Depths of Consciousness

equilibrium, synchronised movements and so on), the *cerebral cortex* is free for other functions, such as explicit memory, the remembering of facts and events.

In a nutshell, therefore, we would insist on your using the *cerebral cortex*, the outer and upper floor of your brain consciously in everything that you do, keeping the switching on of the inner and lower floor to the bare minimum.

Unfortunately, the *cerebral brain*, which is a subsequent addition to the primitive *creaturely brain*, does not remain as ready and conscious as the latter. The reason is simple. The creaturely brain is responsible for our survival. It has to mobilise resources for our subsistence, for our day-to-day living. It is also ready with the 'fight-or-flight' strategy to face any kind of opposition and negative forces which threaten our existence and survival, values and opinions. Such negative forces may include other people's non-harmonious behaviour. When the creaturely brain feels that it is under threat, it comes up with 'reactive' (that is 'fight-or flight') behaviour.

What is *Conscious Management*

Conscious management is, first and foremost, to be aware of this spontaneous propensity and mechanism inherent in us and, secondly, to rise above it to use 'proactive' behaviour which is a function of the cerebral brain.

Most of the time, or rather nearly all the time, we are guided by some fixed operating system and software, stored in our creaturely brain. Some of these are inherent while a few others are acquired during the phases of our primary and secondary socialisations. The creaturely brain prompts us to function as plain, simple, ordinary data entry operators. The keyboard and mouse which are the entry devices are represented by our sensory organs—the eyes, ears, nose, tongue, skin and our unconscious mind (of course, the portion related to the creaturely brain). We do not develop any special neural software as long as we are operating from our creaturely brain unconsciously. The moment we become conscious and start using our conscious mind (that is, the cerebral brain), we start developing customised neural software, to suit the situation and the person or people involved, we use our cerebral brain.

Three Levels of Consciousness

Consciousness can thus be of three different levels, related to three different planes of the brain. The first of these is the *creaturely brain*, where the mind is preoccupied with thought processes typical of the creaturely existence. At some other time or for some of us, consciousness can be related to the *cerebral brain*'s left side having a logical mind-set whereas at some other time or for some others amongst us, it could be related to the *cerebral brain*'s right side, filled with feelings and imaginative propensities.

Your goal should be to remain, as much as possible, in the cerebral consciousness and even if your consciousness tends to slide down to the creaturely level, it ought to be pulled up to the cerebral level by a proven technique like noting down points or starting to write relevant ideas on a piece of paper using big, clearly legible script or, if no paper or pencil is available with you, just thinking about what to write and beginning 'virtual' or 'imaginary' writing.

CONSCIOUSNESS: A LIFETIME SEARCH

On the shore of the Pacific Ocean, overlooking the vast expanse of marine beauty, in La Jolla, California, Francis Crick lived like a recluse. Crick is one of the famous duos who, in 1953, discovered the double helix structure of DNA, and not only shared the Nobel Prize with James Watson but also made history by engineering the 20th century biology's biggest breakthrough.

Even at a ripe old age when he should have had nothing to do with the complexities of cut and dry science, instead would have enjoyed his retirement, Crick remained passionately engaged in solving the ultimate riddle of our existence—*consciousness* and, that too, taking the help of his most favourite tool, biology.

Crick and his research partner computation expert Christof Koch claimed that the seat of free will, or *soul,* is deep inside your brain, in the *anterior cingulate sulcus*. Neither religion nor philosophy, nor psychology can help us to locate the soul's whereabouts, as its existence is very much in the vast assembly of brain cells or *neurons* [5].

CONSCIOUSNESS AS A CONCEPT: A REVIEW OF DIFFERENT SCHOOLS OF THINKERS

Consciousness has always remained a concept, shrouded in philosophical mystery. Spiritually inclined philosophers have linked all kinds of consciousness to their perceived supreme source of energy and power, the cosmic consciousness. Cognitive psychologists, on the other hand, are

Delving into the Depths of Consciousness

guided more by inductive or deductive logic than by faith. Since their domain is the human mind and its unknown facts, they claim that there are different kinds of mind. The design of the receptacle of the mental processes—the brain, is by and large the same. So, one major reason behind individual differences in human beings is the fact that different people have different levels of *consciousness*. One important factor responsible is the difference in the manner in which the electro-chemical processes differ in one from the other.

Going back to the earliest stage of psychology, we find in the 1890s, in the U.S., William James described five properties of what he called 'thought':

- Every thought tends to be a part of personal *consciousness*.
- Thought, based on *consciousness*, is always changing; but the thinking process is sensibly continuous.
- Thought focuses on some objects to the exclusion of others. In other words, it involves 'attention'.
- 'Attention' is the taking possession by the mind, in clear and vivid form, of one out of what seem several simultaneously possible objects or trains of thought.
- 'Attention' implies withdrawal from some things in order to deal effectively with others.

Around the same period, in Europe, French psychologist Charles Richet's perception of *consciousness* was related specifically to 'attention'. The least attention span that would generate consciousness was, in his opinion, a hundredth of a second. Sometimes, he would jokingly say that he was ready to undergo a pain, however acute and intense it might be, provided it lasted only a hundredth of a second, and leave after it neither reverberation nor recall.

In the late 19th and early 20th century, there were other schools of psychological thought which suggested an additional feature of *consciousness* that, it involved some form of memory, probably a very short-term one. Latest researchers from the field of cognitive psychology, share a loose consensus on the following points:

- All plants and animals do possess consciousness.
- Consciousness correlates with the degree of complexity of any nervous system.
- There are many forms of consciousness such as those associated with seeing, thinking, emotion, pain, and so on. Self-consciousness is possibly a special case of consciousness. There are various other rather

semi-conscious and unconscious states, such as the hypnotic state, lucid-dreaming, and sleep-walking.

Psychological interpretations of consciousness, although relatively more comprehensive than philosophical explanations, are still not so concrete in every respect that you can make an ordinary man comprehend easily and accept them without any doubt. From that point of view, the biological route that Crick has adopted is much more convincing as it deals with something really tangible—the brain. Earlier, of course, there was a serious limitation as it called for brain research through invasive surgical interventions. Now, with the advent of non-invasive imaging techniques (like CT scan, MRI, fMRI, PET), brain research has become much easier. Nevertheless, their applications are still very expensive [6, 7].

BIOLOGICAL BASIS OF CONSCIOUSNESS IN HUMANS

Path-breaking human brain research began with Nobel-laureate neurosurgeon Roger Sperry and his school at California, in the 1960s and 70s, when he established through split-brain surgery that the left and the right halves of the outer or upper brain (connected by a thick bridging tissue called *corpus callosum*, shown in Figure 5.3) represented two altogether different types of minds [8–14].

Quite contrary to our two hands, two legs, two eyes, two ears, two lungs, and two kidneys, which perform the same functions, the two brains have two distinctly different identities. In the case of the former parts, the impairment of one of the pairs did not take away the whole function, whereas in the case of brain, if one half was damaged, the functions contributed by the portions affected would be totally gone. Brain was an exception to the principle of duplicate or spare parts.

It is well-known that the two halves of the brain are crossly wired up by means of nerves with the opposite sides of the body—the left controls the right and *vice versa*. Sperry proved that, for right-handed persons, brain's left hemispheric cortex (the upper layers enveloping the inner brains) represents the logical, analytical, and rational mind, whereas the right half was responsible for all the intuitive, imaginative, emotional thought-processes. So, the two halves of the brain possessed two distinctly different streams of *consciousness*.

In the last 30 years, modern bio-psychological research, the foundation of which was led by Sperry, has come up with the following observations regarding the *cerebral cortex* [15–20].

Left Brain-Right Brain Functional Job Distribution

(For right-handed persons; for left-handed persons, it is just the opposite)

- The left brain contains specific areas responsible for language and its application in terms of expression or speaking, comprehension, reading and writing (Brewer [17] held an extreme hypothesis that deficiency in performing all tasks showing left-brain dominance is due to an underlying linguistic deficit. Thus proficiency in language would, understandably, lead to efficiency in intelligent and logical thinking [both abstract and concrete], planning, problem solving and calculations).
- The left brain, since it accommodates the 'speech area', is the 'talking brain', while the mute right brain has better access to emotions. The right brain provides the contextual inputs, the intonation (voice modulation) typical of a natural conversation, and the appropriate emotional contents such as humour.
- While facial recognition is accomplished by the right brain, its association with a verbal identity (for example, the name) is the function of the left side.
- Verbal memory (names, addresses, telephone numbers, and all such facts and figures) are stored in the left whereas the non-verbal data (both visual and auditory) are preserved in the right.
- The left brain's strength is the verbal skill; the right brain's proficiency is in its visual-spatial skill.
- The right brain is dominant for 'attention' that is a complex concept, embracing increased physiological responsiveness (that is, alertness of the body's senses), preparation for action (that is, preparedness of the motor parts of the body), and, response selectivity.
- The left brain's frontal lobe programmes the order of things, and plays a major role in judging the relative recency of the events; so, it has got the sense of time and timing.
- The right brain, as it codes sensory inputs in terms of images, perceives the form and notes visual similarities, whereas the left, takes the sensory information in terms of linguistic descriptions, grasps the conceptual similarities and notes the detail. The right is thus artistic and aesthetic, the left intelligent.
- Speech sounds are processed by the left brain and non-linguistic sound stimuli by the right.

System of Working of the Two Sides of the Brain

- There is a switch, which allows either the left or the right brain to be dominant during different mental tasks, with the two sides constantly taking turns. (In people suffering from manic depression, one half becomes locked into a dominant position in periods of depression while the mute right hemisphere has better access to emotions).
- One half of the brain can be more immature than the other, and that imbalance leads to dominance of one brain's consciousness—logical or emotional.
- Since the two sides of the brain get along so well with each other, people simply have the illusion of one mind whereas, in reality, there are two minds.
- Because each individual brain is a complex system that evolves in response to a unique environment, many brain functions do not end up in the same physical place.
- Often, the two sides of the brain appear to struggle against or sabotage each other. The troubled part seems stuck in a traumatic past, whereas the other part seems more mature and in control.

A HIERARCHY OF CONSCIOUSNESS

One main finding emerging from the bio-psychological research conducted so far is that there are primarily two main streams of higher order of consciousness, originating from your *cerebral cortex*, the upper portion enveloping your inner brain, which is man's own property. One of them is logical, related to the left half of the cortex, and the other is intuitive, emotional, related to the right half, in right-handed persons. The former signifies the 'head', and the latter, the 'heart', as we normally say in common parlance.

However, the lower orders of consciousness emanate from the inner and lower portion, that is, the ground floor of your brain. The lowest level of consciousness amongst them relates to the body. This mainstream of consciousness itself has various constituent sub-streams dealing with hunger, thirst, oxygen, physical movement, sleep and excretion, which are essential for survival, then sex for procreation. These are all *self*-oriented. The roots of such basic instinctive consciousness lay in the top regions of the spinal cord, which, from a bud-like shape at the time of conception, grows into a bulbous flowery shape during the nine months of pregnancy. These constitute the inner primitive brain, which is enveloped by the cerebral cortex.

The next higher level of consciousness amongst the lower order group has a predominantly selfish streak in a worldly sense. The *self* involved here is guided by the *pleasure-pain principle* (according to which, every living cell everywhere in the body and the brain, has the basic need of 'deriving pleasure and avoiding pain') which every living creature essentially follows for its survival and stability.

As you have noted in chapter four, the *self* (or, the ego) and its guiding 'pleasure-pain principle' are also related to the *creaturely psychological needs* which are typical of the inner or lower portion of your brain. These needs are: desire to win by making others lose; need for 4As (namely, attention, acceptance, affiliation and appreciation) and, dislike for 'attack' (which means direct criticism).

Therefore, although at the cortical level, the two sides of the brain are getting divided into two distinctly different (or, shall we say, opposite) streams of consciousness, both the streams get contaminated with the urge to protect the *self*. The positive (such as love, affection, fellow-feeling, friendship, co-operation, and so on) as well as negative (anger, jealousy, hatred, unhappiness, remorse, depression, shyness, fear, etc.) emotions are all related to the *self*. So, the right half of the brain has the roots of self-consciousness.

In day-to-day life, the feeling of *self* creates its own logic, and that logic is influenced, is biased. So, the left is governed by the right. When we read, see, or hear something, we immediately relate to the *self* inside us. When we speak, write, or draw something, it certainly carries a reflection of the inner *self*. When we plan or programme something, take a decision, or solve a problem, there is always the inner selfish *self* that is the major influencing factor. In the consciousness hierarchy, the second level thus has the *self*-related worldly consciousness—divided into two mainstreams, logical and emotional.

At the third step from the bottom, we will place the 'pure logical' and the 'pure emotional' consciousness. At these levels, you have conquered and transcended your *self* (or *ego*).

The former is active in someone who is doing something with total detachment, with no desire for the fruits of his labour. Is it possible in the materialistic form of existence as most of us happen to be in? Yes, of course, it is, when we are reading, doing, listening to, or experiencing something purely for selfless learning, not for selfish pleasure or any gain, like passing an examination or getting a job or a promotion.

Pure emotional consciousness is active when your mind is widely open. You are not guided by any specific likes and dislikes. Everything, everyone—whether good or bad, is the same for you. There is no discrimination in your mind; you are absolutely fair, truly balanced in showering your love, the 'feel good' feeling to everyone. You 'give pleasure and avoid giving pain' to every individual. You are altruistic; you are loving, affectionate, helpful, and cooperative, in the truest sense of the terms.

The peak is where there is pure cosmic consciousness, a condition which Pandit Gopi Krishna beautifully portrays when he says: 'The real object of the system of *Kundalini Yoga* is to develop a type of consciousness which crosses over the boundaries confining the sense-bound mind, carrying the embodied consciousness to super-sensory regions' [21].

If we now consider the *self* to be the inner or lower primitive part of the human brain, containing the basic instincts essential for survival, security and stability, since the worldly logical and worldly emotional consciousness are also contaminated by self-orientation, biologically we can explain it by saying that there are very strong neural connections between certain parts of the cerebral cortex and the primitive inner brain; as well as there are regular electro-chemical communication between them.

There are certain parts of the cerebral cortex which are not connected, all the time, with the primitive inner brain. So, when those parts become active and they get delinked from the inner brain, true logical or true emotional consciousness starts prevailing. To attain that higher level of consciousness, one must have regular practice of selfless concentration, or meditation.

The peak of super-sensory consciousness is attainable through more rigorous physical and mental practices, which have been elaborated in the *Hindu shastras* and also in the doctrines of other developed religions like the Christianity, Islam, Sikhism, Zoroastrianism, Buddhism, Jainism, Confucianism.

REFERENCES

[1] 'Get up, sitting for long can kill you', *The Times of India, Kolkata*, 22 January 2010, p. 16.

[2] 'Running can help jog memory', *The Times of India, Kolkata,* 20 January 2010, p. 16.

[3] Carter, Rita, *Mapping the Mind,* Phoenix, London, 1998, pp. 34–35.

[4] Greenfield, Susan, *The Human Brain: A Guided Tour*, Phoenix, London, 6th Impression, 2000, p. 176.

[5] Chaudhuri, Prasun and Mudur, G.S., 'Ever Since Double Helix', *The Telegraph Know-How*, Kolkata, 25 January 1999, pp. 1–2.

[6] Das, Asish, 'Don't ignore headaches', *The Telegraph KnowHow*, Kolkata, 21 January 2002, p. 3.

[7] Heppenheimer, T.A., 'Penetrating the Mind', *Span*, Vol. XXX, No. 5, May 1989, pp. 16–19.

[8] Bogen, J.E. and P.J. Vogel, 'Cerebral commissurotomy in man. Preliminary case report'. *Bulletin of the Los Angeles Neurological Society*, Vol. 27, 1962, p. 169.

[9] Sperry, R.W., 'The great cerebral commissure', *Scientific American*, Vol. 210, No. 1, 1964, pp. 42–52.

[10] Gazzaniga, M.S., 'The split brain in man'. *Scientific American*, Vol. 217, No. 2, 1967, pp. 24–9.

[11] Sperry, R.W., 'Hemispheric deconnection and unity in conscious awareness', *American Psychologist*, Vol. 23, 1968, pp. 723–32.

[12] Sperry, R.W., 'Lateral specialisation in the surgically separated hemispheres', In: *The Neurosciences Third Study Program*, (eds. F.O. Schmitt and F.G. Worden) Cambridge, Mass, MIT Press, 1974.

[13] Gazzaniga, M.S., 'Consistency in brain organization', In: Evolution and lateralisation of the brain'(eds. S.J. Dimond and D. Blizard), *Annals of the New York Academy of Sciences*, Vol. 299, 1977, pp. 415–23.

[14] Sperry, R.W., 'Consciousness, freewill and personal identity', In: *Brain, Behaviour and Evolution*, (eds. David A. Oakley and H.C. Plotkin), Methuen: London, 1979, pp. 219–228.

[15] Fuster, J.M., *The prefrontal cortex,* 2nd edition, Roger, New York, 1989.

[16] Luria, A.R., *The working brain*, The Penguin Press, Allen Lane, London, 1973.

[17] Brewer, W.F., 'Visual memory, verbal encoding, and hemispheric lateralization' *Cortex*, Vol. 5, 1994, pp. 145–151.

[18] Walsh, Kevin, *Neuropsychology: A Clinical Approach,* B.I. Churchill Livingstone, New Delhi, 3rd edition 1994.

[19] Levy, J. 'Psychobiological implication of bilateral asymmetry' In: *Hemisphere Function in the Human Brain* (eds. Dimond S.J. and Beaumond, J.G.), Elek Science, London, 1974.

[20] Blakeslee, Sandra, 'Forever in two minds' (reproduced from the New York Times), *The Telegraph KnowHow,* Kolkata, 25 January 1999, p. 2.

[21] Gopi Krishna, Pandit, *Kundalini: Path to Higher Consciousness*, Orient Paperbacks, New Delhi, 1976.

KEY TAKE-HOMES

- Routine, familiar activities (such as, cycling, driving, knitting, operating a machine and the like) are performed *unconsciously* as the brain and the body are in the auto-pilot mode. In any situation, for performing something non-routine, you can do it *semi-consciously* or *consciously*. The former method will lead to wastage of time, effort, energy and money for you and also for the organisation or family unit that you represent. So whatever you do, you must try to do it *consciously* for maximising the '*Return on Investment (ROI)*' of the human assets invested in performance.
- So far, we have used the terms *'conscious'* and *'consciousness'* too generally. *Consciousness* has different levels. The lower structures of our brain—the primitive *creaturely* portion which is the seat of the lowest level of *consciousness,* is *unconscious* because of millions of years of conditioning, whereas the higher structures—the relatively new *neo-cortex* has the potential for functioning *semi-consciously* and *consciously*.
- Just above the *creaturely consciousness*, for right-handed persons, the left half of the brain is logical, intelligent and rational, whereas the right half contains emotions which are self-conscious. Thus an inferior level of *consciousness* would be when the left is controlled and governed by the right. This is the second level of consciousness. It may happen *unconsciously, semi-consciously* or *subconsciously*.
- The third level of *consciousness* is the pure logical and pure emotional (it is better to call these propensities 'feelings' rather than 'emotions')—detached from the 'self' or 'ego'. This should be our goal in the practice of *conscious management*. It is not difficult as it just calls for patient and restrained self-management.
- The fourth level, pure *cosmic consciousness* is the beginning of your journey into the higher levels of *consciousness*.
- These higher levels of *consciousness* are attainable through practice; and, the higher your goal is, the more rigorous and painstaking would be the physical and mental practices.

CHAPTER 6

Two Organisational Scenarios

THE ORGANISATIONAL SCENARIO TODAY: WHAT YOU SEE

- Many people are stretched to their limit, working too hard whereas there are others who consider such over-stretched people as 'stupid' as they themselves are 'shirkers'; they are there just for their reasonably good income and other employee benefits.
- Few people feel really 'valued'. Instead many of them feel threatened as they are ruthlessly managed. It is not that they are not empowered but empowerment with regular reporting and review is most stressful for many.
- Pleasing the boss is given a high priority instead of delighting the customers and suppliers—both external and internal.
- Frequent restructuring of the organisation, change of duties, responsibilities and job locations make people insecure. Some express their *stress*, while most others suppress. The smart ones quit while those who cannot leave their present job due to some reason or the other continue to perform, but their performance varies between 'good' (51 to 60%) and 'very very good' (71 to 80%) in comparison with the benchmark of an extraordinary standard. Silly excuses are provided to justify why performance never reaches the *peak level* (95% and beyond) and all past records are not broken by showing 'great' and 'super-great' grades of performance.

- Organisation's vision, mission, policies, objectives and goals are displayed and distributed throughout the establishment. But, how many *leader-managers* have their own and help other inter-dependent organisational members to develop their respective dreams, visions, mission, policies, objectives, goals and targets related to organisational performance, progress and growth?
- Teams turn out to be individuals put together in groups but each member fighting for his own stand either in an aggressive way by arguing and trying to dominate or in a suppressive way by withdrawing himself and becoming non-participative.
- Some employees have more than one person to report to; both may be formal; or, one may be formal and the other informal (because of his bullying nature or greying hair). This creates confusion and stress which affect hassle-free performance.
- 'Change-seekers' and 'change-makers' are very few. And, most unfortunately, those very few persons' ideas, suggestions and proposals are not even heard by the 'change-resisters'.
- Most people are *controlled* by their respective bosses. The seniors' habit of *controlling* their small kids in their family roles get replicated at their workplaces resulting in unhappiness as individuals are coerced to accept tasks and targets they feel diffident to accomplish and meet. They are scared that they will be pulled up for their mistakes, lapses and failures where their bosses are also to be blamed to a great extent.
- Statements like 'People are our greatest asset' or showing human resource in the upper rungs of the list of 'core values' are considered to be merely lip-service as, in practice, these are not followed.

Reflections on the Family Scene

Mr Manager, are you one of those rare balanced persons who can separate, in their minds, their work roles from the family roles as if the moment they are out of their work roles, the pleasures and pains of their work roles get out of their minds? I don't suppose you are. For a 'me too' person who does not qualify to be so balanced, the stimuli that are received in the work roles—whether pleasant or painful, and the responses that are made—whether reactive or proactive, are carried home inside the body and mind and those certainly have an impact on the playing of the family roles.

Therefore, how do the happenings in the organisational scenario have reflections on the family scene today?

- Most families resist any changes. Even if they accept any change, that would take place unhappily. Such families are commonplace and we call them 'me too' families. Change-seeking and change-making propensities are hardly encouraged. The 'odd man out' change-seeker or change-maker, if he happens to be in a 'me too' family, looks for opportunities to break away.
- A typical 'me too' family today has some 'overstretched' members and some 'shirkers' just like it happens in a 'me too' work organisation. The latter lot is enjoying the fruits of the former lot's labour.
- There is too much pressure on the parent members of a 'me too' family to keep up with their neighbours, colleagues, friends, relatives and their families. Being unable to practice *conscious management*, they transfer their pressures to the family's children members by setting high performance standards for them in academic and other extra-curricular activities.
- The senior members—grandparents and parents try to *manage* the youngsters as their focus is on performance as highlighted just now. There are very few *leaders* in the right sense.

THE ORGANISATIONAL SCENARIO TOMORROW AND THE DAY AFTER: WHAT YOU WANT TO SEE

Dear Mr Manager, an essential part of your *conscious management* portfolio is: what you want see as your organisational scenario tomorrow and the day after, you'll have to try and create. You have to contribute, heart and soul, in bringing about the changes that you'd like to see around you. A *conscious manager* is a change-maker in spirit. He acts as a positive *change-agent* and works out according to a plan.

However, first of all, you'll have to *visualise* what you want to see. You may like to include the following in your list of pictures or visual scenarios:

- People are working with balanced workloads, neither 'over' or 'under' what they can manage with a little pressure and they are all very well technology-task-talent-matched and thus *intrinsically motivated* and not focused mostly towards *extrinsic rewards and benefits*.
- Different people's different 'strengths' (knowledge, attitude, skills, intelligences and talents) are appreciated which makes them feel great and valuable. They are all empowered but in different degrees and with periodic control (not too tight but loose and mild by way of progress data and feedback sharing) by their bosses.

- Everybody makes it a point to delight the concerned external and internal customers and suppliers. There are genuine endeavours, on the 'customer' front, to convert 'prospects' into 'customers', 'customers' into 'clients (regular customers)', 'clients' into 'advocates' and 'advocates' into 'evangelists'; and on the 'supplier' front, to convert every 'party/offer-maker' into a 'supplier', 'suppliers' into 'vendors', 'vendors' into 'co-makers' and 'co-makers' into 'business partners/associates'.
- Performance attained for any employee or a team is never less than the *peak level* (95 per cent and beyond) and there is always an endeavour to break the previous records. And, so that people can perform at a stress-free level, they are generally consulted prior to any restructuring, change in the job content, context, or transfer.
- Every manager sets his own and helps his each team member to set the personal and team's vision, mission, performance policies, objectives, goals and targets.
- Teams are well-knit, well-managed, and well-participated. Agendas are set, activities are identified, tasks are distributed, checks and tests are built in, progress reports shared periodically.
- Spans of control and chains of command are well-defined to remove ambiguities.
- *Change-seekers* and *change-makers* are identified, appreciated, motivated to think out productive changes, even very small ones, and encouraged to discuss and share. Good suggestions are accepted and implemented jointly so that the credit for any productive and positive change is shared with and between all who had contributed, to eliminate the smallest possibility of any heartburn.
- People are not 'controlled' in the literal sense of the term which smacks tightness and rigid, uncompromising attitude on the part of the boss; instead, they are 'managed' with the help of shared policies, plans and programmes; organised, directed and their performances reviewed regularly to maintain a fast pace of progress and growth.
- People are truly considered as *capital assets* and all steps are taken to identify their *capital base* (namely, knowledge, attitude, habits, skills, intelligences and talents), ascertain their present 'worth' or 'value', train them up formally and informally for *value-addition, new value-creation*, and *optimal asset utilisation*. This system is in-grained in the organisational *Performance Management Process (PMP)* [1].

Profile of a Consciously Managed Family of Tomorrow and the Day After

Mr Manager, along with your vision for an ideal organisation of tomorrow and the day after, I'm sure you would like to visualise a *consciously managed* family where:

- Babies are lavished with motherly affection and thus they are less likely to become anxious and stressed adults [2].
- The senior members *consciously* try to 'lead' the juniors rather than trying to 'control' and 'micromanage' them.
- Performance standards are not imposed—rather those are mutually agreed upon or even, in some cases, set individually due to trustful empowerment. And, every member strives to attain peak performance being motivated generally intrinsically.
- Members share the family workload *happily* as they feel 'valued' because their inherent personal assets (knowledge, skills, intelligences and talents) are being recognised and opportunities are created to have them gainfully utilised in the interest of personal and family's collective growth.
- The family ambience is positive. There are few members who are so tensed that they do not want to move beyond their 'comfort zones'. Each member is ready to take risks—some small, some medium, and some big, by being a change-seeker or a change-maker.
- The family often chats about societal issues and current events (instead of mere casual chats) like the Gulf Oil spill, or the Commonwealth Games, which creates simple mathematical models of events in the minds of the young family members. They become motivated and it is not only that their number sense is improved it also has a positive impact on their academic performance [3].

WHAT IS WRONG WITH YOU

Mr Manager, you would have been told in workshops and training programmes, you would have read in books and articles, you would have also seen in specially made management films and videos how one should behave and manage effectively and what are the good management practices, but still why do you and most other people act and manage in ways which lead to wastage of resources, loss of opportunities and profits and make people that you deal with reactive and unsynchronised, sometimes even non-cooperative and unmanageable? Have you ever asked yourself this question?

In most cases, the answer would be only one and a very simple and straight 'No'.

You actually act like a robot. You manage the way you've been managed right from your childhood—by the *'command-control-coerce-coax'* rule.

Your parents and elders, including your teachers and tutors, had always tried to *'control'* you under the presumption that you were just a kid and could not *manage* yourself. They never encouraged you to do things independently, nor did they ever make you feel that they were also dependent on you for your feelings of affection, respect, faith and trust.

When you had tried to behave independently, they *'coerced'* you to do things the way they wanted you to do. And, when you revolted or went into your shell, they *'coaxed'* you to get back into your normal 'kid-self'. You took the *'coaxing'* as their shower of love and cooled down to take their *'command'*.

Coercing Style   Coaxing Style

Fig. 6.1: Command-Control-Coercing Style and Coaxing Style

Such childhood experiences have gone deep into your brain in its inner and lower structures and got stored permanently in terms of some *acquired programmes-reflex (AP-R)*. So, whenever you are required to relate yourself to and manage others, the same software is being used again and again as the operating system of your brain. You are not using the innovation power of your cortex—the outer and upper floor of your brain and your higher levels of consciousness, which helps you to be situational and contextual in your behaviour. Your brain is behaving as if it is resistant to any change in your management behaviour and leadership style.

'KID NATURE' STUDY

How Kids ('Care-receivers') React to their Parents' and Elders' ('Care-givers/providers') 4-C ('Command-Control-Coerce-Coax') Handling Style

Kids who are quiet, submissive and obedient by nature (Obedient Kid-self or 'OKS'): They respond favourably and accept the care-givers' 4-C style *obediently* as they know that there is no choice. They are convinced that this is the only way that care-givers deal with the care-receivers. As a result, they grow up with this obedient attitude towards their authority figures and, when they enter the work arena, inadvertently they expect their seniors to deal with them in the 4-C fashion. In fact, if the reality does not match with their expectations, they get confused and, interestingly, surprised and may not be able to *perform* at their best. So, in their *work role* too, they would need to be 'manager-managed' (as they are weak in 'self-managed' work performance) in the same 4-C style. The Conscious Manager must be aware of this and mobilise performance from them using the most appropriate handling style to produce 'First Time Right (FTR)' and 'Zero Defect (ZD)' activities.

Kids who are smart (Smart Kid-self or 'SKS'): They are very sharp and intelligent to be fully aware about their kid-identity. They know that if they do not succumb to their care-givers' dictates, they will be deprived of their due care provisions and it will be difficult for them to sustain themselves. When they grow up, their intelligence makes them behave very smartly. They adjust themselves according to the circumstances and become situational. In other words, if the situation demands them to be obedient with overpowering, autocratic authorities, they behave obediently. On the other hand, if the boss and other seniors behave like friends and ask for ideas and suggestions, they open up and try to meet their requirements. And, in an extreme case, if the senior behaves helplessly and would like the junior to give him tips on how to solve a problem, the clever junior will reverse his role and turn into a care-giver.

Independent Kids (Independent Kid-self or 'IKS'): Some kids are very independent-minded and they always want to have things their way. If they are forced into anything by their care-givers, they rebel and become aggressive or keep a distance from the authority. The best way to handle them is just to withdraw the 4-C programme to manage them. Especially the last 'C' (that is, 'coaxing') should be used discriminately. Such subordinates should be ignored and left on their own to deprive them of the 'attention' which they are extremely hungry for. Having been left out, when they reach their limits of tolerance, they will themselves get back to the authority with a lot of humility with strong hunger for the seniors' attention and to be affiliated into the team. This is the time when they should be handled toughly and made to make some concrete performance-oriented commitments.

Emotional Kids (Emotional Kid-self or 'EKS'): Some kids are very emotional and they become your pets if you start with the last 'C' (that is, 'coaxing') in a positive manner. Start with a 'pat'—that is, some appreciation of his abilities, skills, and talents which will boost him up. Then, go on to the first 2-Cs (that is, 'command' and 'control'). Such kids grow with the same emotionality in their nature, and behave exactly in the same way when they take up their 'work roles'. In some cases, if 'coaxing' is done properly, the juniors may even be prepared to accept the seniors' 'coercion' without any objection.

Logical Kids (Logical Kid-self or 'LKS'): Some kids are very logical. If, as a care-giver, you explain to them why they should do what you're commanding them to do, they'll do without any hassle once they are convinced. You'll have to satisfy them with specific answers to their questions. They will have the same attitude when they grow up to undertake any work responsibility and should be dealt with accordingly.

Playful Kids (Playful Kid-self or 'PKS'): Some kids are very playful, game and fun-loving. They love and adore like-minded care-givers. When they grow up to perform in 'work roles', they can be handled well with humour, jokes, periodic hooplas, celebrations, games, and activity-oriented exercises.

Every grown-up individual carries in his mind his characteristic *kid-self (KS)*. It does not get erased from his mind despite the kid grows into an adolescent and then into an adult. On the contrary, every time the grown-up individual interfaces with an authority figure—his controlling manager (who represents the 'parent/elder') his typical *kid-self (KS)* appears from the hiding and comes to the surface to interact with the controlling person.

> If you observe inter-personal behaviour closely and analyse coolly, you'll find this happening in most cases, barring a few rare exceptions. The incidence of response from the 'kid-self' may grow day by day as in today's small, nuclear families with both parents being extremely busy, children are deprived as regards the emotional needs of their 'kid-selves' while they are growing up because of lack of enough quality time and attention provided by their care-givers. Thus their *KS*, with its unfulfilled desires, would tend to come to the mind's surface even when they are grown-up, during their adult-to-adult family, social and work role-related transactions.

WHAT YOU OUGHT TO DO

The right stand for your brain—an intelligent strategy, Mr Manager, would be to study each person that you're dealing with separately from the others (as no two persons are identical in their nature) and determine who should perform better if left to himself (that is, more of being 'self-managed' and less of 'manager-managed') and who needs to be more 'manager-managed' than 'self-managed'. You may be able to see very clearly, if you are *conscious,* that there are still a few left out who would work best with a balanced approach on your part; that is, being 'self-managed' and 'manager-managed' almost fifty–fifty. There needs to be a reviewing done inside your brain to adopt this kind of *flexible* approach and, that is possible, only when you're alert and conscious.

The *conscious manager* studies the 'kid-nature' or 'kid-self (KS)' in each individual that reports to or interacts with him [see the 'Kid Nature' Study' box above for details of how to study the 'kid-nature' or 'kid-self (KS)'] and deals with him accordingly to produce the desired outcome. He also studies the 'kid-personality' of the team; in other words, which dominant 'kid-nature(s)' or 'kid-selves (KSs)' is/are present in his team to guide the team's working in a manner so that it leads to 'First Time Right (FTR)' and 'Zero Defects (ZD)' performance.

REFERENCES

[1] Ganguli, Siddhartha, *Performance Management: 'First Time Right'*, Platinum Publishers, Kolkata, 2008.
[2] 'Mom's love inoculates kids from growing up stressed', *The Times of India, Kolkata,* 28 July 2010, p. 16.

[3] 'Family chats beneficial for kids: Study', *Hindustan Times, Kolkata*, 28 July 2010, p. 14.

KEY TAKE-HOMES

- In the practice of *conscious management*, you have to visualise two scenarios: one of the real-life present—what is happening at the moment, today, here and now; and the other of your desired future—what you want it to be like—both for your organisation and your family.
- You will realise the gap between the two but you'll not be able to bring about much change to bridge the gap and move towards your vision because of the pull of the inherent automatic software inside your *creaturely brain* and the dominant control of certain *acquired programmes-reflex (AP-R)* stored in the human portion of your brain, picked up from the styles and strategies that your parents adopted in dealing with you when you're a little kid and the way you responded to it. Your brain is resistant to change and it is saving energy by retrieving an old preserved behaviour from the brain's store room and not adopting any better behaviour and ways of handling others.
- The *conscious manager's* job is to study each individual's *kid-nature* or *kid-self (KS)* whosoever reports to or interacts with him and deal with him accordingly to produce the 'First Time Right (FTR)' or 'Zero Defect (ZD)' performance. He should study the 'personality' (dominant or core nature present) of each team and handle team performance adopting the same dealing strategy.

CHAPTER 7

Your Work Role under a Microscope

WAYS OF GENERATING MONEY

There are three honest ways of generating money for livelihood through three different kinds of 'work roles'. The easiest and most common of them is to get employed and earn as an *employee* who is under contract with his organisation to *take* something in return of what he *gives*. For his *giving*, 'performance standards' are set. The second way is to earn through *self-employment* by being a trader, an artisan, a craftsman, or a practicing professional like a doctor, a lawyer, an accountant, an insurance adviser, an architect, or a management consultant. The third and last one is by being an *entrepreneur*—an owner of a business or an industrial firm.

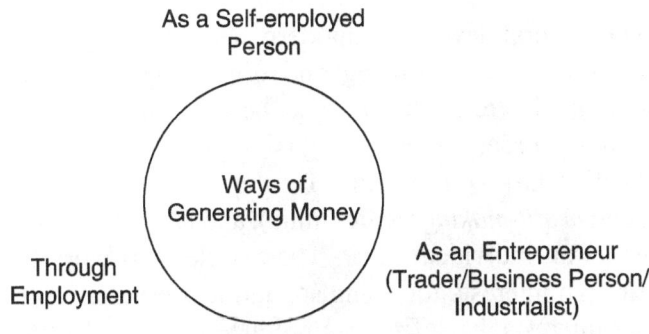

Fig. 7.1: Ways of Generating Money

In the first choice, obviously the employee's *self-interest* is primary as he has taken up the employment for generating enough money for his own and his dependents' upkeep. If one employment does not satisfy an employee, he will look for another more suitable employment and move to a greener pasture. In the case of the *employee* existence for an individual, the enterprise or the risk element is missing which is the main differentiating factor between an employee and a self-employed person or an employer. In the case of an employee, the risk has been and is being taken by his employer.

INSIDE THE HEART OF A *FIRM*

Self-employed people and business persons can set up *firms*, each with its own sociological profile: proprietorship, partnership, family firms, joint stock companies, and so on. But, there is a feature that all forms of firms have in common and, that is, the promoters of the *firm* who had set it up initially had taken a *risk*. All organisations are thus identical at some basic level. However, there exist differences between organisations that have profit-making as their goal and those that do not. Organisations, therefore, also have their typical *personality profiles* in terms of the *basic interests* that they try to pursue directly and indirectly in whatever actions they take or avoid.

To quote the Cornell University sociology professor Richard Swedberg:

> "There are general advantages of looking at firms in *interest* terms: it allows the strength or the power of the actors to be better taken into account; it helps to explain why one type of action rather than another is chosen; and it helps to understand how a number of actions can add up to a powerful dynamic.
>
> On a general level, the modern share-holding firm represents a special way of mobilising and organising a number of different economic interests. It can also be said to constitute a legitimate economic order, which assigns to a number of individuals the collective task of producing for the market. This order is centered around *profit-making* (italics mine), and it is legally as well as socially seen as an individual actor. The people who work for a firm have their own interests for doing so, and it is essentially by appealing to those interests that a firm can produce what it sells. In pursuing their own economic interests as well as those of the firm, the actors inside the firm also tend to develop group interests, which may or may not

be of help in producing profit. The modern firm takes many different forms and must not be automatically identified with the giant joint-stock corporation controlled by a huge number of owners [1]".

A *FIRM'S* INNER DYNAMICS: A HISTORICAL PERSPECTIVE

Way back in 1776, the founder-father of *Economics*, Adam Smith had pointed out that people are not as careful with 'other people's money' as with their own; and that this makes the interests of the owners of a joint stock company diverge from that of its managers.

> "The directors of such companies, however, being the managers rather of other people's money than of their own, it cannot well be expected that they should watch over it with the same anxious vigilance with which the partners in a private co-partnery frequently watch over their own.... Negligence and profusion, therefore, must always prevail, more or less, in the management of the affairs of such a company [2]".

As to the internal organisation of the firm, another stalwart of classical economic theory Alfred Marshall had pointed out, amongst other things, that a joint stock company that is headed by a (salaried) manager has a tendency to shy away from 'innovation'. According to him:

> "The owner of a business, when contemplating any change, is led by his own interest to weigh the whole gain that it would probably bring to the business, against the whole loss. But the private interest of the salaried manager or official often draws him in another direction: the path of least resistance, of greatest comfort and least risk to himself is generally that of not striving very energetically for improvement; and of finding plausible excuses for not trying an improvement suggested by others, until its success is established beyond question [3]".

Nevertheless, Marshall also discusses the place of *loyalty* in a corporation and how it makes the employees take pleasure in its success and in its good reputation, a bit like people who love their country. 'This loyalty', he adds, 'is being furthered by a multitude of movements, designed to give the employees a direct interest in the prosperity of the business for which they work' [4].

THE MODERN VIEWS

The range of organisational actors that modern thinkers like March alone and March and Cyert jointly discuss go beyond the ones mentioned by old-timers Smith and Marshall, and includes suppliers, customers, governmental agencies, trade associations, trade unions, different types of employees and so on [5, 6].

The similarities between March and Cyert's ideas and so-called *stakeholder theory* that has gained ground in modern management thinking, are obvious [7, 8].

According to Cyert and March, neoclassical theories of the *firm* such as by Smith and Marshall recognised the principle that economic actors are self-interested, but *conflicts of interest* internal to the *firm* were ignored or assumed to be resolved through a prior contract by which employees agreed to pursue the *interest* of the entrepreneur [9].

Some suggestive additions to the theory of *conflicts of interests* inside the *firm* can be found in Nobel-laureate Herbert Simon's writings on the role of organisations in the economy. In a few of these writings, Simon discusses the *loyalty* of employees and notes that it represents a pervasive and important phenomenon in its own right which, we feel, only *conscious managers* can understand, appreciate and tackle squarely [10, 11].

Simon adds to Marshall's analysis of *loyalty* by emphasising its quality as an *economic emotion*. *Loyalty*, to Simon, is more than just a way for the employees to identify with the interests of the *firm*; it also represents a powerful source of aggression as *loyalty* generates certain expectations in the employee's mind and he becomes aggressive if those expectations are not met or even partially met. According to Simon, where there are *conflicts of interest* between the two main groups, that is, the employers and their authorised representatives—the empowered managers (who can be called 'we') and the employees (who can be described as 'they'), both the groups are not only very protective about their rights and privileges but are also prepared, should the situation demanded, to be aggressive to claim and fulfil their own respective *interests* [12].

YOUR 'WORK ROLE': YOU'RE AS MUCH AN EMPLOYEE

You're as much an employee to the organisation as the other members in your team and also as all others around you who are employed in it. Your team members are not in the employer-employee relationship with you. Their employer is the organisation as much as it is yours. You're all on an equal footing in that sense—sailing in the same boat.

You may not have this simple realisation. Common sense may not dawn upon you as sometimes inadvertently you feel that you can do whatever you want to do with those reporting to you. Actually, you can't. You may not even have the power to sack any one of them for *non-performance* or promote another for *super-performance* or give a double or triple raise. You have to follow the *Performance Management Process (PMP)* of which *Performance Appraisal (PA)* is an integral and important part. And, the most effective way to 'detoxify' (that is, remove your personal bias or prejudice, if you have any) the *appraisal* is to incorporate three things: a *self-appraisal*, an *appraisal* by the *boss*, and an *appraisal* also by the *boss's boss*; which is called the 'child-parent-grandparent' method of performance appraisal. Although a little too elaborate or cumbersome, the best bet and the most bias-proof appraisal system is the *360-degree feedback* where the appraisee is appraised by everyone with whom he has some interaction or transaction while performing in the 'work role' including, if possible, by external suppliers and external customers and other stakeholders, to the extent applicable [13].

The work environment of an employee becomes *pro-performance* when the organisation provides a very good compensation package, excellent infrastructure and employee welfare facilities (like good arrangements for refreshments, physical and mental recreation, spacious office or shop-floor, breaks for stretching and relaxation, car or coach pick-up and dropping facility, housing, health care, children's edu-care and so on). However, if the manager, who supervises the performance of the employees reporting to him, follows a standard 4-C management style which does not suit all employees equally well, then the same plush work environment may turn *anti-performance* for them. In the words of the British organisational behavioural analyst Di Kamp: '…… when people are put under pressure to perform, you may squeeze a better performance out of them for a short while, but in a longer-term perspective the results deteriorate as people rebel overtly or unconsciously against such pressure' [14].

WALKING THE TALK: YOU BECOME A ROLE MODEL

So Mr Manager, your emphasis should first be on *self-change* and *self-development* rather than rushing to lay your hands on others to change and develop them. Only then you'll be walking the talk and others will take you seriously and, may be, also follow you if you develop yourself into a *role model*. You may try this out even if it works fully with only a few and partially with some others.

The *Obedient Kid-self (OKS)* is likely to copy you almost totally while the *Smart Kid-self (SKS)* and the *Logical Kid-self (LKS)* may pick up certain features which they feel would add value to their personality. The *Emotional Kid-self (EKS)* and the *Playful Kid-self (PKS)*, if handled gently and softly, would follow your direction and path. The only person that you may face problem with and who will be reluctant to follow you is the *Independent Kid-self (IKS)* but you should not give up. It is a challenge for you to identify strategies which will turn them around.

AN ORGANISATIONAL REALITY: THE PRINCIPLE OF 'INTER-DEPENDENCE'

At this juncture, it is necessary for you to be exposed to one more organisational reality: the *principle of inter-dependence*.

Dependence to Independence: Single to Split Personality

At birth, you were *dependent* on your care-givers—especially your mother. As you grew into childhood and then into girlhood or boyhood, the state of dependence on your parents continued although the degree got reduced as your personality started taking a concrete shape. Your dependent nature represented a *single personality*.

The teens made you turbulent as rapid biological changes brought, in their stride, rapid psychological changes too. Throughout your adolescence, you wanted to be most *independent* at home and *dependent* outside on your peers—representing, in a way, some kind of a *split personality*.

Entry into youth turned you *inter-dependent* as you partnered with your chosen person and eventually set up a home with the same one or someone else. But as you embarked on your career, in your 'work role', you became *dependent* again—on your boss and other seniors as they were more advanced than you in knowledge and work experience. That period in your life represented your 'career-childhood'.

Once you acquired sufficient knowledge and practical experience to carry out your duties and responsibilities mostly on your own, you started feeling *independent* and behaving independently again: not taking your boss's commands obediently at times particularly if he happened to be a newcomer compared to your tenure in the organisation or you belonged to the parent or holding company and he was a recruitee of the new joint venture; arguing with him when you found he was not right in what he said; and, commanding and inflicting your ego on your subordinates. This stage in your career represented your 'career-adolescence'.

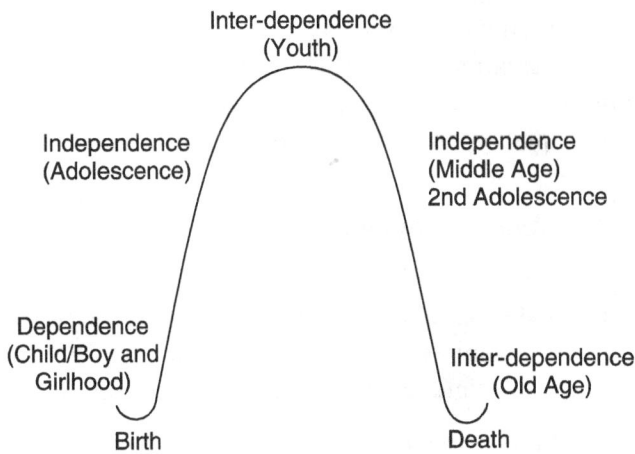

Fig. 7.2: Dependence-Independence-Interdependence-Independence-Dependence Cycle

The Reality: Inter-dependence

However, such an egoistic and independent attitude is based on the wrong perceptions which may be prevailing in your subconscious mind, driven by your biology. Such wrong perceptions include: 'I can do many things independently myself'; 'I know much better than many'; 'I have every right to be reactive with those who do not agree with me and are on an altogether different wavelength'; 'I can certainly criticise my colleagues, peers and juniors who are doing things wrongly' and so on. The reality is that we are all *inter-dependent* whether it is in the family, social, or work roles.

The Details of Inter-dependence

In the work role, you are dependent on your boss and other seniors for their instructions, direction, guidelines and appraisal of your performance. They too, in turn, are dependent on you for completion of some parts of their job responsibility. You are also dependent on your direct subordinates and other juniors for their assistance in getting things done to complete parts and portions of the whole assignment which you have been entrusted to perform. They are also dependent on you for your instructions and so on.

You are dependent on people engaged in other departments and units of your organisation for supply of goods, services and information as your performance depends upon processing of material inputs in machines with the assistance of men using certain systems, methods and procedures with some specific information and know-how. If there was any shortfall in any of these, your output will not meet the performance standards set for you in terms of time, quality, quantity, cost, profitability, safety, durability, etc.

The Internal Supplier-Customer Concept

This is the reason why we divide the organisation's functional units and people into 'internal suppliers' and 'internal customers'. You also have the same department or unit and the same person plays the dual role of 'internal supplier' and 'internal customer' in different contexts.

The realisation of this *principle of inter-dependence* must make you aware that, as far as any internal supplier of yours is concerned, you must make it very clear to him your specific requirements (which are objective/quantifiable/calculable) and also your emotional expectations and value system (which are subjective and non-quantifiable).

On your part, as an internal supplier to any of your internal customers, you must find out before you start performing, his requirements and expectations. Your realisation and implementation of this principle will lead to hassle-free performance and peaceful relationship with people.

In the 'family role' too, the principle of inter-dependence and the internal supplier-customer concept equally apply. No family member should consider himself or herself as an island. The husband is dependent on the wife in certain respects and *vice versa*. Same is true for the parent-child relationships. All the family members are internal suppliers and customers to each other in different ways. The attitude and behaviour of an adolescent boy Raju Srivastava, student at the senior secondary level, towards his mother took a 180 degree turn when he realised how much he was dependent on his mother—for what all tangible and intangible things. He ended his third session in our Winning Child clinic with tears in both his eyes. His father, Anil Srivastava, a senior manager of a reputed company, reported to us subsequently that Raju had now become very sober in his behaviour and most loving and respectful towards his mother

Anjali—a really welcome change which had converted the unhappy mother into a very happy person.

REFERENCES

[1] Swedberg, Richard, *Principles of Economic Sociology,* Princeton University Press, Princeton, 2003, pp. 74–75.
[2] Smith, Adam, *An Inquiry into the Nature and Causes of the Wealth of Nations,* 2 Vols. Oxford University Press (original 1776), new edition, Oxford, 1976, p. 741.
[3] Marshall, Alfred, *Industry and Trade*, Macmillan, London, 1919, p. 324.
[4] Marshall, Alfred, *loc. cit.* p. 327.
[5] March, James, 'The Business Firm as a Political Coalition', *Journal of Politics,* 1962, Vol. 24, pp. 662–78.
[6] Cyert, Richard and James March, *A Behavioral Theory of the Firm,* 2nd edition, Blackwell, Oxford, 1992 (published in 1963 by Prentice-Hall, Englewood Cliffs, N.J.).
[7] Donaldson, Thomas and Lee Preston, 'The Stakeholder Theory of the Corporation: Concepts, Evidence and Implications', *Academy of Management Review,* 1995, Vol. 29, No. 1, pp. 65–91.
[8] Jensen, Michael, 'Value Maximization, Stakeholder Theory, and the Corporate Objective Function', *Journal of Applied Corporate Finance*, Vol. 14 (Fall), 2001, pp. 8–21.
[9] Cyert, Richard and James March, *A Behavioral Theory of the Firm, loc. cit.*, p. 215.
[10] Simon, Herbert, 'The Role of Organizations in an Economy'. In: *An Empirically Based Microeconomics*, Cambridge University Press, Cambridge, 1997, pp. 33–60.
[11] Simon, Herbert, 'Organizations and Markets', *Journal of Economic Perspectives,* Vol. 5 (Spring), 1991, pp. 25–44.
[12] Simon, Herbert, 'The Role of Organizations.......', *loc. cit.* p. 54.
[13] Ganguli, Siddhartha, *Performance Management: 'First Time Right'*, Platinum Publishers, Kolkata, 2008.
[14] Kamp, Di, *The 21st Century Manager: future-focused skills for the next millennium,* Kogan Page, London, 1999.

KEY TAKE-HOMES

- There are different channels for generating money in the modern economic social system and different people choose different channels according to their likes and dislikes, strengths and weaknesses, opportunities and threats. Nevertheless, most people go for employment in work organisations which also possess different 'personality profiles' in the shadow of their promoters or top authorities. Work organisations cater to the various needs of people who have come to work as employees and, in turn, get their services to produce whatever products or services they are dealing with.
- According to the old school of thought, the interests of the owners and promoters of any firm would naturally differ from those of its employees including those who are at the helm of management. The risk-averse employees, although they may display loyalty, become standardised and mechanical due to the generally repetitive nature of their work and do not serve as potential source of any perceptible change and innovation.
- The modern *stakeholder theory*, however, includes suppliers, customers, governmental agencies, trade associations, trade unions, different types of employees as 'key' organisational actors apart from the shareholders and investors. Amongst all these stakeholders, the *loyalty* element is highest in the employees, which can turn them aggressive if their interests are not fairly fulfilled. To be a *conscious manager*, you have to recognise this and bear it in mind while dealing with the employees and their formal and informal *Performance Management Processes* (PMP).
- In the *conscious management* of work organisations and families, you have to recognise another organisational reality: the *principle of interdependence* and provide due honour and importance to the performer of any work role.

CHAPTER 8

Your Personality Development

YOUR PRIME TARGET: YOUR ATTITUDE

Mr. Manager, you need to concentrate on your personality development to become a *role model* for others to follow. And, to qualify as a *conscious manager,* you'll have to build your personality *consciously* like a 'dwelling house'.

You should remember that this 'dwelling house' must have a solid foundation. If your personality is comparable to a house structure, its foundation should be your *attitude*. And your *attitude* resides in the subconscious levels of your iceberg mind.

'SUBCONSCIOUS' DEVELOPMENT: FIRST STEP TOWARDS THE *'CONSCIOUS MANAGER'* GOAL

Dear Mr. Manager, there is one very important message for you.

As the very first step for you to take to reach the ultimate goal of being a *conscious manager,* you have to clean up the 'self'-oriented portion of your *subconscious* mind, remove all the junk 'self'-oriented values and beliefs that you might have picked up from your environment (by seeing, hearing, reading and copying others and also by trying out yourself) since you were a kid; and install there a new solid and sound value-based attitudinal framework supported on four legs, each represented by the capital letter 'L'.

'Self' will certainly feature in that framework; but, not alone—along with some other equally vital factors. If you do not consider those other factors on an equal footing and give them equal importance, your *attitude* will not be balanced. In short, you ought to develop a *4L attitude*.

Let us discuss the details for you to follow.

The First 'L': Love for Your Profession

As we had already discussed, your 'Work Role' has two sides. To describe it most simplistically, we have to say, it has a 'technical' or 'professional' side 'T' where you're using your technical/professional knowledge and experience to perform and mobilise others' performance. (Refer to Fig. 3.1 in Chapter 3)

It may be related to: fine arts or draughtsmanship; mechanical or electrical engineering; or, safety and health; or, administrative discipline and labour laws; or, selling techniques; or, quality assurance. In order to attain peak performance in your relevant technical or professional domain, you have to follow certain norms, certain standard systems and procedures which, if you forget, you can always refer to drawings, specifications, manuals, and other relevant documents. This side of your 'work role' can be described as 'functional management'.

The other side of your 'work role' is the 'trans-technical' or 'trans-professional' part 'TT' which involves your dealing with people, all around you, and influence them positively to reach the 'peak performance' goals and targets. It can be described as 'general management' as each situation is different, each individual that you deal with is different, each group that you face is different; even the same individual or group is different at different times. It poses strategic and tactical challenges to you.

As you move higher and higher along the organisational ladder, the 'general management' part of your 'work role' assumes a bigger dimension than the 'functional management' part. A manager in the top portion of the pyramid does not perform in any specific 'functional management' area; his primary concern is with the 'general management' part.

However, both the 'functional' and the 'general' management parts are included in your professional practice. Now, the combined effect of both

Your Personality Development **97**

these—how does it appeal to you? Or, would you rather have your work to deal with 'functional management' mostly; or the reverse (that is, 'general management'). Please evaluate your present attitude and give yourself a score out of a total score of '100'.

The Second 'L': Love for Your Job

The work that you do, that is your job, would normally have three components: 'Self-Engagement (SE)', 'People and Social Engagement (PSE)' and 'Physical Engagement (PE)'.

SE involves application of your upper brain (the cerebral apparatus); PSE involves application of your speaking, listening and all other verbal and non-verbal skills (the communicative apparatus). PE involves the application of your bones, muscles, tendons, ligaments and joints (the muscular-skeletal apparatus). Which of the activities is predominantly present in your job? Do you love it? Or, is your job a balanced combination of all the three and does it give you satisfaction? Evaluate your own present satisfaction level from this point of view and give yourself a proportionate score out of 100.

The Third 'L': Love for Your Brand

Your 'brand' is your 'organisation'. There are some international brands which have become household names particularly in the FMCG or consumer durable product and service categories (such as Tata, Unilever, Phillips, Sony, Pfizer, GlaxoSmithKline, Colgate, National Panasonic, Vodafone, Airtel, Reliance, Samsung, LG, Toyota, Ford, Mercedes, Lenovo, HP, Compaq, IBM and others whose products are well-known).

Similarly, in an industry, one company or a few companies may be the *brand leader(s)*. Such as, in the cement industry, there are ACC, Ultratech, Lafarge, and Ambuja who are nation-wide brand leaders. In the FMCG industry, Hindustan Unilever, Proctor & Gamble, Dabur, Emami and a few others are national brand leaders. Similarly, there may be 'regional' or 'local' brand leaders. A young man or a lady may have dreams to join such a brand leader.

Do you feel you have developed a love for your brand? Evaluate what are the 'satisfiers' and 'irritants' you find in your organisation and, accordingly, give yourself a score to your satisfaction level out of 100.

The Fourth and Last 'L': Love for Self

Do you love yourself? Do you have high self-esteem/self-confidence? Do you have the feeling of 'I can' in any situation and with anyone you deal with? If you have, then you certainly love yourself.

If your 'self-image' is strong, you can give yourself a score of '100'. Otherwise, make a list of your 'achievements' (situations/events where you have received formal or informal appreciation from others in any field such as academic curricula, extra-curricular activities, in landing up/being selected for a good job, doing well in your work career etc.) and analyse the strengths/talents/knowledge/skills/attitude etc. which have contributed to each such achievement event and make a list of the highest common factors. These are your *core competencies*.

Now try to think where you're applying these *competencies*. If you would apply any one/a few/all of them, you will achieve success.

Please evaluate your self-love score out of '100'.

This 4L *subconscious* of yours should be in constant touch with your *conscious*, so that every 'conscious thought', every 'conscious feeling', and every 'conscious action' of yours should be largely influenced by your 4L *attitude*.

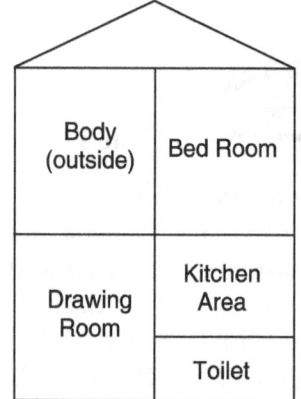

Fig. 8.1: The 'Dwelling House' Model of Your Personality

YOU: THE DWELLING HOUSE

Visualise yourself as a beautiful 'dwelling house'.

The External Façade: Your Body

Every dwelling house has got an outside—the external facade, which is visible from outside and everyone passing by the road on which the house is located, can see it. Your outside is your *body*; the *skin* covering your body is the *wall* of your house. The *doors* and *windows* are your *eyes, ears, nose* and *mouth* which you can open and close just like you can do with the *doors* and *windows* of your house. You stand with your *arms* crossed across your *chest* and it becomes a *balcony*; you extend your *arms* fully along with your *fingers* extended horizontally in front of your *chest*, and they look like a *long cantilever* verandah or a canopy on top of your front entrance door.

When a passer-by passes by your dwelling house if he finds it to be a well-maintained property with sleek, nice-to-look-at wall surfaces with all doors, windows, balconies and other projections well-kept, he gets satisfaction and makes a positive impression about the owner or occupant of the house. On the contrary, if he finds it to be a palatial structure but very badly maintained with plaster peeling off and cracks on the wall surface with some window glass panes broken, a negative impression pervades his mind and he feels how such an aristocratic, well-to-do family can neglect the maintenance of their property. He concludes that it must be their lack of *consciousness* which has been responsible for this neglect.

Just like a well-maintained dwelling-house reflects the *maintenance awareness* of the landlords or occupants, similarly an individual (an employee, a self-employed professional, or an employer) who is not healthy and fit, not neatly and cleanly groomed and dressed up, represents absence of a *conscious attitude* that 'I should look good and present my overall personality which is reflected through my constitution, gait (style of walking), gestures and postures, which all together constitute my 'static' and 'dynamic' *body language* in a descent fashion because all these make the first impression which becomes the lasting impression'.

The Inside of the House: Your Mind

Every house has got an inside—the rooms; likewise, you have your inside too, represented by your mind. Just like you have a few rooms inside your house, your mind also has a few rooms which you use at different times without being conscious about their existence and functional utility. To be a *conscious manager*, you'll have to be fully aware about all these features.

The Drawing Room

This area of your dwelling house is where you welcome guests and entertain them to maintain positive human relations. It represents the 'courtesy zone' of your house. Similarly, when you are greeting a person (by saying 'Hello!', 'Hi!', 'How are you?', 'Good morning', 'Namaste', 'Good bye', 'See you again') and exchanging pleasantries, you're behaving from the drawing room of your mind. Do you generally fight or become argumentative with your guests and invitees in the drawing room area of your house where you entertain them? The answer I expect is: 'No'. Similarly, when your objective is to maintain good relations with people, you ought to be conscious so that you don't behave badly with people under any circumstances. You'll have to maintain the drawing room of your mind with every person you meet, be it your internal suppliers (on whose work, service, instruction, or report your activities are dependent) or internal customers (who all are dependent on you for their activities) or your external suppliers (on whose supplies from outside your work activities are dependent) or external customers (the outsiders who are dependent on your supplies from inside the organisation). By using your mind's drawing room, it is possible for you, on the one hand, to turn a 'party' or 'trader/offerer' into a 'supplier', a 'supplier' into a 'vendor', a 'vendor' into a 'co-maker' and a 'co-maker' into a 'business partner' and, on the other hand, to convert a 'prospect' into a 'customer', a 'customer' into a 'client (regular customer)', a 'client' into an 'advocate' and an 'advocate' into an 'evangelist'.

The Bed Room

This is the private area of your dwelling house, representing the 'intimacy zone'. Just like you do not allow any outsider to enter into your bed room as that would be considered as an encroachment, similarly you do not like anybody who is not close to you asking you very personal questions as that would be considered as an 'intrusion'. The bed room of your mind contains your very private thoughts and emotions which you store in the subconscious part of your mind as those relate to your past pleasant and painful memories and your future dreams, hopes, ambitions and aspirations. Such personal data you would not like others to know except for those who are very close to you. That group which is proximal to your mind may not even include your spouse, children, brothers, sisters and other kith and kin. Nevertheless, in your work role, you ought to have (and I suppose you already have) one or two or even a limited few persons with whom you would like to share your very personal feelings: your joys and sorrows, your self-perceived achievements and failures, your confidential impressions about people inside and outside your organisation. While you would allow a few such people to enter into the bed room of your mind, you must not enter into the bed room of others' minds unless they allow you. If you are not welcome, it would be considered as 'intrusion'. Therefore, you will have to decide on the 'inclusion' (whom would you allow to enter into your mind's bed room) and 'exclusion' (whom you would not allow into your mind's bed room).

The Kitchen

A well-run household kitchen is an excellent example of what effective management means. The kitchen is run by a kitchen manager who represents many roles rolled into one. She first finds out who are going to be her 'customers' (the people who will consume the food). Her family members are her 'internal customers' whereas any set of invited guests are her 'external customers'. Then, she does the production planning (that is, planning the menu: what all items are to be cooked and of what quantity and quality—she customises the products according to the likes and dislikes of the customers). Once the production plan is ready, she prepares the materials requirement plan: what all materials (raw materials like rice, wheat, dal, vegetables, non-vegetarian items and consumables like salt, pepper, spices and so on) would be required. Then she would check up the inventory position: what all stocks she has in her store including in her fridge. Once she is able to find out what all are available and what else have to be procured, she prepares a procurement list and sends somebody off to the market. Once the materials are procured, she does the inspection and if she is satisfied with the quantity and quality, she will accept the materials; otherwise, she will reject and ask for good replacement quickly. Then she will start the manufacturing process by lighting the oven and following the set procedures. From time to time, she will do the quality checking. Once the food is ready, she will serve the food to the customers and remain in waiting to see if any help is required. She will promptly attend to any request from anyone. One may wonder why she takes so much care in the execution of her duties and responsibilities. There is a definite answer and, that is, her only motto is 'customer satisfaction'. If you go back to the remote past and think about your grandmothers and mothers playing the kitchen manager's role, you would find that quite often they would have a sacrificing attitude and go out of the way to offer their own shares to the customers. We don't have to go far away to distant places; we can learn the art of customer satisfaction from our mothers and grandmothers.

The Toilet

All that we consume as the products of our household kitchen does not get digested; on the contrary, some of it turns into waste products and we use the toilet area of our dwelling house, to eliminate those waste products. Similarly, our mind also generates waste products by way of negative emotions: unhappiness, depression, irritability, anger, anxiety, fear and the like. Whoever has created us has kept a little area to be used as toilet just like an architect allocates a small area of any dwelling house for toilet purposes. Unfortunately, now-a-days, we find people who have a disproportionately large mental toilet area.

There are tips ready for your mental toilet control. The first one is to install a *study room* inside your mind which means you have to do your knowledge management by keeping all your relevant knowledge up-to-date. You have to keep yourself up-to-date in technical professional subject or domain knowledge; knowledge about your organisation and its changing environment; knowledge about practical psychology: that is the likes, dislikes, strengths, weaknesses and most interesting points or unique features of people with whom you interact; and, knowledge about yourself—your likes, dislikes, strengths, weaknesses, and life's goals. If you do not have a study room inside your mind, you get frustrated when you find others having well-developed study rooms in their minds and you feel you'll lose in competition.

You'll have to install a *prayer room* in your mind which would mean you'll have to think beyond self as we do when we visit a temple, a church, a mosque or a gurdwara. Thinking beyond self means you would have to think about others. We get upset if we don't get any attention, acceptance, acknowledgement, affiliation, or appreciation as we are very selfish. The moment we just turn our attention to others and feel for them, our selfish emotions disappear. We feel happy if we make others happy by satisfying their emotional needs and expectations.

You would also have to do a *store room* audit where your mental *store room* means your memory—the memory of your achievements and failures to analyse your 'strengths' and 'weaknesses' as for your achievements, your 'strengths' and for your failures, your 'weaknesses' are generally responsible. You must take steps to use and sharpen your strengths and utilise them more and more consciously to multiply your achievements and remedy your weaknesses to minimise your failures.

The last tip for toilet control would be to make sure for you to have a *terrace* or a *garden* or a *balcony* to be used to grow small plants. This part of your mind would be the source of new ideas and innovations. You will be free from frustrations if you're a regular idea person.

Evaluate Yourself

You have to check out now whether you have all the above features in your personality and, if you do not have, where you lack and to what extent. This may be described as *gap analysis*. The next step for you would be to prepare time-bound action plans for filling in the gaps and then take actions for personality improvement and self-development.

KEY TAKE-HOMES

- A *conscious manager* has to build himself and develop his personality like a 'dwelling house'—outside of the house being the 'body' and the inside rooms representing the 'mind' which is in the 'brain'.
- The 'dwelling house' must be placed on stable footing. So, the *conscious manager*'s attitude should be founded on four solid pillars: love for the profession, love for the job (the work that you do), love for the brand (that is, the organisation), and love for 'self' (that is, self-esteem).

CHAPTER 9

Conscious Right Brain Management

THE 'DWELLING HOUSE' MODEL *VIS-À-VIS* YOUR PERSONALITY

How does the 'dwelling house' model relate to your personality? Just like the external facade of the house can be seen from outside, similarly your *body* and all its features can be seen from outside. However, just as much to know about the inside of the house you have to have an idea of its interior—the rooms, to know about the *mind*, you have to know about the *brain*.

YOUR BRAIN: A FRESH VISIT

You had a glance at the human brain in chapter 5 where we said that a very simple model of the human brain would be analogous to a two-storied structure. The inner or lower floor is the primitive portion, containing the *limbic system* and other survival-oriented structures which we have inherited from our ancestors like the chimpanzees and other apes. This structure is responsible for all our basic instinctive needs and desires.

Incidentally, for human beings the brain's inner or lower floor is also responsible for learning anything without understanding, for developing any skill merely through practice and also for any inherent skills like singing, dancing, ball throwing or shooting, and for any routine work including routine data entry into the computer or carrying out any task following a set of routine procedures where there is no scope for introducing or bringing about any change.

The outer and upper structure, known as the *cerebral cortex*, is specially developed in humans and there is functional asymmetry between the two halves—the left cerebral cortex (the left brain/LB) and the right cerebral cortex (the right brain/RB). As you are already aware, the layout of nerves coming out of your brain is such that there is cross-lateral control: the LB controls the right side of the body and the RB controls the left. Therefore, in brain study, consideration of the individual's handedness is extremely important as a left-handed person's brain functions are just oppositely designed in relation to those of a right-handed person.

For a Right-Handed Person (RHP), the most prominent LB functions are: intelligence (logical-analytical-rational thinking); power of calculation or arithmetical skill; appreciation of science and the ability to develop and change products, systems and procedures; the power of expression through verbal language—grammar, composition, vocabulary or stock of words, usage of words in reading, writing, speaking; and, factual memory—memory for facts and figures (names, addresses, hard data like anniversary dates). The LB powers, being quantifiable and linear (true or false, high or low), are being taken over by the computers.

For the same RHP, the RB has a few prominent functions, which are: feelings; imaginative and creative thinking; motivation; leadership quality; and impressionistic memory (which include the ability to store and retrieve information such as images, sounds, and emotional impressions—pleasant or unpleasant). There is a great deal of variability in the RB powers and they are holistic. Therefore, these can be described but not quantified or measured. Thus they are still beyond the reach of computers.

A DEEPER INSIGHT INTO YOUR BRAIN'S FUNCTIONS

The upper and the lower portions of your brain can work simultaneously. Examples are galore, such as: you may be carrying out a routine task like typing or knitting which has been developed by you through practice as a '*skill*' and talking to another person at the same time; or, walking and talking on the cell phone; or doing some household work and singing; or driving and listening to music. In all these instances, the former is a function of your inner or lower brain whereas the latter is the function of the upper and outer portion.

Nevertheless, as regards the upper brain, the left and the right halves cannot work together at any moment. You cannot do some serious work (LB) requiring concentration and listen to music or watch a movie (RB) at the same time. For the RB work, you have to take your attention off from the LB work and vice versa. However, such inter-hemispheric change-over can take place at a split second and the faster it happens, the better and higher is the quality of the brain. Such power provides you with the ability for smooth, stress-free multi-tasking: switching from one task to another as a manager's job menu may demand. A *conscious manager* makes such shifts possible *consciously*.

There is yet another very important point. While the LB powers are objective, quantifiable and determinable, your RB powers are subjective and moves between two opposite poles—positive and negative. There could be positive feelings (love, affection, care, fellow-feeling, respect, faith, trust, loyalty and the like) and negative feelings (unhappiness, depression, irritability, anger, anxiety, fear); positive imagination (good taste) and negative imagination (bad taste); positive motivation (socially acceptable) and negative motivation (socially unacceptable); positive leadership (constructive) and negative leadership (destructive); positive impressionistic memory (remembering pleasant things) and negative impressionistic memory (remembering unpleasant things).

RIGHT BRAIN MANAGEMENT: THE RIGHT STEP FOR *CONSCIOUS MANAGEMENT*

The fuel for our body and brain is blood. Blood is a fluid which has its physical and chemical properties including the common ones like pressure and temperature. As long as the RB remains positive, the pressure and temperature of blood remain positive and it can flow freely and quickly to the LB and make it active. The moment the RB turned negative, the properties of blood will change quickly to become negative and it will not flow freely to the LB until the RB turns positive again. That is the reason why when you are angry, sad or nervous, your logic does not work and your decision-making gets affected.

Thus to be a *conscious manager*, you have to do *RB management* consciously. You will not only have to ensure that your RB remains positive and LB remains active but you'll also behave in a way that others with whom you're interacting, their brains also do not turn negative and they act sensibly and logically. For this, you'll have to *consciously* adopt a 'proactive (think before you act)' behaviour.

Imagine, your interaction with any person is about to turn towards a tussle or controversy or getting a little sentimental (which would mean a 'mental accident' leading to spoiling a good relationship, imagine yourself being placed at a busy road crossing. Hold yourself and stop as if the red light is on. Inside you, your stress hormone *adrenalin* is about to come out from your adrenalin glands; you can hold its level by breathing deeply, consciously following a rhythm: deeply in: 1, 2, 3, 4, ... hold: 1... deeply out: 1, 2, 3, 4, 5, 6, ... up to 8. Do it a few times to prevent your RB from turning negative. This will stop you from becoming 'reactive (behaving impulsively in a negative manner—either becoming aggressive or becoming defensive)'. Such stance will allow the traffic (emotions) from the opposite direction to pass and you'll see the 'amber' sign. Now, you put yourself in the green light action mode—you behave logically. You've just averted a 'mental accident'—a conflict.

Right Brain Management is thus the right step for *conscious management*.

EMOTING FIRST, THINKING SECOND

Everyone emotes ('emoting' means showing emotion in a very obvious way) first, thinks second. In most of us, the emotional reaction is primary, the rational response is secondary. Unfortunately, this stark reality is overlooked by the management community. Managers do conduct performance appraisals of their team members and others associated with them; and, they claim that the system which they follow for this purpose is an objective one; but very few, almost none of them realise that the process they adopt has an emotional base.

Even, in the context of handling customers, this truth is ignored. Measurement systems in the field of marketing tend to rely on what customers think (and consequently say)—what their response was to a promotional campaign, or a product, as opposed to how do their emotions govern their judgement and what do they infer as their impression about those.

Dan Hill comments regarding how marketing and sales get affected due to lack of proper perception of this reality: 'Currently, branding risks failing for two reasons, both of which can be addressed by taking into account what brain science tells us about the importance of creating an emotional connection with consumers' [1].

CHANGE OVER TO THE 'PEOPLE FIRST, PROCESS SECOND' ATTITUDE

Marketing and sales professionals are too much 'product-focused' and least 'prospect (potential customer)-focused'. In the same note, management professionals are mostly 'job or work-process-focused' and least 'people or performer-focused'. They fail to motivate their people to perform at their peak level as they neglect their emotions which vary from person to person. They always want them to lay stress on work performance and reach their goals by attaining the performance standards set by the organisation for a particular period. They have to reorient their attitude by changing over from the 'process first people second' to the 'people first, process second' mind set which, if you remember, represents the attitude of true 'leadership'. Thus *conscious management* has got, integrated into it, both the functions of 'leading' and 'managing'. And, we can say that it is 'managing by leading'.

A SCIENTIFIC FINDING

The recommendation for this attitudinal reorientation is based on the findings of past 25 years of brain research using most modern MRI (Magnetic Resonance Imaging) techniques, the practical applications of which were so far limited to the corridors of neurobiology, medicine, surgery and health care. The main finding is that people are primarily guided by their emotions, irrespective of their backgrounds and the work roles that they have.

How the 'work' or 'task' performer *feels* about his or her work or task is much more important than the *logical priority* (in the urgency-importance two-dimensional scale) of the activity. Such reactions based on emotions and feelings are 80% faster than responses based on logical and analytical thinking. *Therefore, 'relationships' are more crucial than 'rationality'* because the primary emotional impressions 'colour' (or, shall we say, 'contaminate') our secondary rational inferences.

OUR THREE-IN-ONE BRAIN

The human brain is a three-in-one mechanism. The ground floor consists of a real lower or street-level consciousness (the ancient fish and reptilian brain portion which is an extension of the *spinal cord* culminating in the bulbous *brain stem*) and a 'mezzanine' (the original mammalian brain which houses the *limbic system*—the seat of your 'emotions'). This 'mezzanine' is most active in chimpanzees with which we share almost 99% of *DNA*s ('deoxyribonucleic acid') with only around 1% dissimilarity [2, 3].

The first floor, the *cerebral cortex*, as we have already known, contains two entirely different minds located in two different apartments, which are typically human—unlike the emotion-ridden mind of the chimpanzee—in right-handed people, the left half—the 'thinking mind' and the right half—the 'feeling mind'.

THE HUMAN BRAIN'S NATURAL UNCONSCIOUS WORKING PROCESS

Any *stimulus* in the environment external to us—be it a physical, a chemical, or an emotional one, is first received by the concerned receptor organs (eyes for sight, ears for sound, nose for smell, tongue for taste, skin for touch, and mind for others' behaviour expressed through communication). From the receptor, it is quickly transmitted by concerned specialised nerves to the brain's ground and mezzanine floors.

Thereafter, it is picked up by the 'feeling mind'—the right half of your brain's first floor, as that is usually (when we behave spontaneously and thus *unconsciously*) the first choice for taking a spot impulsive and instantaneous decision. If the emotional decision is not taken *unconsciously* there and then, the stimulus gets 'coloured' (and thus 'contaminated' as it loses its purity) by some emotion rooted in the right brain, it is passed on to the left brain—the 'thinking mind' which takes a decision which, in all probability, is *biased* according to the relationship that the individual enjoys with the *transmitter*—the person involved in the transaction who had transmitted the 'stimulus'.

Emotional data being subjective, non-measurable, soft information which is non-specific unlike objective hard data—unless it is offered in a large quantity, at least ten times larger in volume which would make it reasonably understandable and perceptible, the receiver would tend to develop a *bias* which may either be 'positive' or 'negative'.

CONSCIOUS BRAIN MANAGEMENT (CBM)

In this process, the energy available to your brain (normally 20% of the total energy requirement of the body-brain combination), undergoes a colossal wastage which is contrary to the principle of *human resource economy* that must be followed for *managerial effectiveness* and *peak performance*. To prevent this from happening, the *transmitter* or *sender* must adopt a very special influencing strategy to develop a cordial emotional relationship with the *receiver* or *addressee*. The role of your left half of the upper brain—the 'thinking mind' is to make it happen. And, this is what we would describe as *Conscious Brain Management (CBM)*.

NATURE STUDY FOR CORDIAL RELATIONSHIP-BUILDING

To be *aware* about a person in your external environment is a function of the ground floor of your brain—the real ground floor. To *like* or *dislike* the person is a function of the mezzanine floor which has got close connectivity with the right half of the first floor—the 'feeling mind'.

So, the feeling as to whether the person would be 'liked' or 'disliked' is routed *via* the first floor right apartment to the first floor left apartment. Therefore, even if the person conforms to a flawless specification in his or her family background, qualifications—both academic and professional, and personal grooming, dress code and so on, the true *personality* of the person will reflect from how he stands, sits, walks, speaks, listens, writes, and behaves. All these will determine whether the person will be acceptable or unacceptable to the transmitter or the transacting person.

So only if the *transmitter* or *sender* complies with the communication and behavioural requirements and expectations (which are feelings-based) of the *receiver* or *addressee*, he/she will become acceptable.

In practical life, you and I lay emphasis on the 'what' (the background, qualifications and experience) of people rather than 'who' they are—their *nature* (their perceptions, likes, dislikes, beliefs, value systems, strengths and weaknesses). This is wrong; it should be the other way round. The people—two in a pair or more in a team situation, involved in any transaction, get motivated and work well together if their wavelengths match. If there is such wavelength matching or mental harmony that you enjoy with someone, then he or she will accept most of whatever you say, do or propose to do. [4]

The secret thus is you would have to touch the other person's 'I' or 'me' and not impose your 'I' or 'me' on him/her.

REFERENCES

[1] Hill, Dan, 'Reach for the Emote Control', *Brand Equity: The Economic Times, Kolkata,* 3 December 2008, pp. 1–2.
[2] Greenfield, Susan, *The Human Brain: A Guided Tour*, Phoenix, London, 6th Impression, 2000, p. 21.
[3] Rose, Steven, *The 21st Century Brain*, Vintage Books, London, p. 92.
[4] Ganguli, Siddhartha, *Business Communication: The S-M-A-R-T Roadmap for Your Career Growth*, Platinum Publishers, Kolkata, 2009.

KEY TAKE-HOMES

- The human brain is like a two-storied structure: the lower floor, the *creaturely brain* is primitive, inherited from our animal ancestors; and, the upper floor is the *cerebral brain*, which has all the human mental powers.
- For a right-handed person, the Left Brain (LB) is the 'thinking and planning mind' and the Right Brain (RB) is the 'feeling and human relations' mind. This functional allocation is in the *cerebral brain.*
- Since the RB has closer network connections with the lower creaturely brain, deprivation of any creaturely physical, physiological or psychological needs leads to negative feelings and the RB turns negative, displaying 'fight-or-flight' symptoms. *Conscious management* thus involves effective RB management. Two effective strategies are: slow and steady deep breathing (physical); and, proactive instead of reactive behaviour (mental).
- *Conscious Brain Management (CBM)* involves cordial relationship-building and relationship management with other people. For implementation of CBM with difficult people, one has to do their nature study.

CHAPTER 10

Developing Self-Consciousness

Here, you learn to look at yourself in an altogether different way and develop a new brand of self-consciousness.

YOUR BIOLOGICAL HARDWARE

Your *body* and *brain* are nothing but biological hardware. The same analogy applies to the body and brain of any other living organism. The moment the creature is dead, its biological hardware becomes a chemical junk waiting to get decomposed. The living biological hardware possesses unimaginable capabilities for stimulus 'input' reception, processing, and 'output' production in each *cell*. And there are millions of operating programmes—the software, keeping the hardware active and busy in action, with varieties of minute specialisation.

YOUR BRAIN'S SOFTWARE

Inside your brain, there are approximately 10,000 million brain cells *or neurons*. Each *neuron* is an input-processing-output device like a computer. The hardware of each *neuron* being its organic structure, there are two types of software by which these computers run.

The first type is represented by the *inherent, innate* or *Inherited Programmes (IP)* which are inborn and thus absolutely natural to you, while the second type consists of the *Acquired Programmes (AP)* which you have been picking

Developing Self-Consciousness **113**

up from the environment through the various sensory modalities like seeing and hearing, then doing, reading and trying out; in other words, by learning or experiencing.

The *IP* represent your basic instincts (that is, the instinctive propensities) or those stimulus-response processes which are survival-oriented, namely, the creaturely physical and physiological needs (that is, hunger, thirst, need for oxygen, sleep, excretion, physical recreation, sex and the like) and the creaturely psychological needs (that is, the desire to win by beating others, the need for attention, acceptance/acknowledgement, affiliation, appreciation and the dislike for attack or direct criticism) as well as your natural traits or endowments—your inherited *strengths* (skills, intelligences, talents) and *weaknesses* (physical as well as mental—body as well as brain-related). These *IP*s include, firstly, certain common 'strengths', inherited by you from your mother's and father's and their family genes, which you cannot claim as exclusively your own as they may be possessed by other kins of yours in different degrees in your environment.

These are the 'strengths' that have been talked about by Buckingham and Clifton [1, 2]. According to them, any 'strength' is a positive trait that one possesses; by developing on which one can attain a near-perfect performance again and again just like any phenomenon can be established as 'scientific' if the same results can be obtained through repeating the same experimental process. Let us call them *Inherited Programmes: Ordinary (IPO)*.

The 'Inherited Programmes' also include your talents, intelligences and skills which are your inherited 'strengths', really very special to you and not found in any other person in your environment. These are so special that others are totally dependent on you for the services that you render to them using those 'strengths'. This is the category that has been described as your *'Unique Buying Propositions'* or *UBP*s as these provide you with uniqueness and a cutting edge compared to others in your operating environment [3–5].

Let us call them *Inherited Programmes: UBP (IP-UBP)*.

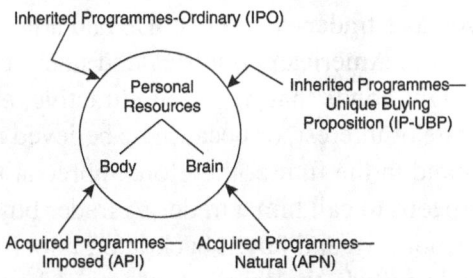

Fig. 10.1: Inherited and Acquired Programmes

A few examples of *'Inherited Programme: Unique Buying Proposition (IP-UBP)'*

Example 1

There are some people, whom you and I know, who are simply excellent in work execution or performance. Let us call them *performers*. They are most active; they execute; they implement. Any role other than a *performer*'s would certainly not see the best in them. Performance should be regarded as their *UBP*.

There are some others we have met, who possess a very well-balanced and attractive *personality* so much so that it makes them an ideal fit in the *leadership* role. They possess the power to lead and get the best possible results by, through and from people. They themselves may not be strong performers but they can harness high performance from *performers*. For them, their *personality* is the *UBP*.

There are still a few others we see whose priority is to explore and develop own inherent yet hidden *potentials* and/or to help others to nurture and hone their natural *potentials* through tutoring, coaching and mentoring. These people are spontaneously oriented towards human resource development—be it for self or others. For these people, their urge to nurture *potentials* would constitute the *UBP*. They may be described as the *potential-shapers*.

In real life, we also find two-in-ones (combination of *personality* and *potential-shaper*; or *performer* and *personality*; or *performer* and *potential-shaper*) as well as three-in-ones (combination of all the three *UBP* propensities). These are *Inherited Programme: Multiple Buying Propositions* or *IPMBP* in short.

Example 2 [6]

Carlos thrived as a trader-economist. He had a large network of friends in the various Latin-American countries and knew exactly what took place there. He bought bonds that he found attractive, either because they paid him a good rate of interest, or because he believed that they would become more in demand in the future, therefore appreciating in price. It would be perhaps erroneous to call him a trader. A trader buys and sells (he may sell what he does not own and buy it back later, hopefully making a profit in a decline; this is called 'shorting'). Carlos just bought—and he bought in

Developing Self-Consciousness

size. He believed that he was paid a good risk premium to hold these bonds because there was economic value in lending to these countries. Shorting, in his opinion, made no economic sense.

Within the bank Carlos was the emerging-markets reference. He could produce the latest economic figures at the drop of a hat. He had frequent lunches with the chairman. In his opinion, trading was economics, little else. It had worked so well for him. He got promotion after promotion, until he became the head trader of the emerging-market desk at the institution. Starting in 1995, Carlos did exponentially well in his new function, getting an expansion of his capital on a steady basis (i.e. the bank allocated a larger portion of its funds to his operation)—so fast that he was incapable of using up the new risk limits.

An excellent example of IP-UBP indeed!

Example 3

(This example is based on one of our own latest experiences)

In a senior management HRD workshop, we came across a middle-aged engineer Mr P, designated as 'senior manager'. In the same batch, there were six assistant general managers, three deputy general managers, two general managers, and one senior general manager—all senior to him in the plant management hierarchy. P was being called out from time to time by the chairman's secretary. Our workshop had incidentally coincided with the chairman's visit to the plant, located roughly 400 km away from the corporate office at Kolkata. The chairman was visiting the location for a few days to review the progress of community development projects which formed a part of the Group's corporate social responsibility or 'CSR'. And, once P went out, he was missing for one to two hours each time. He came back each time and asked for apology. He was an exceptional case as no other participant, even those who were much senior to him like the senior general manager would be called out, even for once.

On asking him he explained to us that he was the only one available in the plant here who not only had avid interest in community development activities, but was also involved very deeply in the ongoing projects and also in the future planning. He had been entrusted with the prime responsibility of initiating and seeing through all the community welfare projects at this location. His interest and deep knowledge of community development projects was the UBP that brought him close to the company's top management—particularly to the chairman, again and again.

The *AP* constitutes the *acquired programmes* which you have picked up from your environment (during your childhood, boy/girlhood, adolescence, and youth) and are still picking up, and will continue to pick up from one's family, social and work environments. These include: *Automatically Acquired Programmes* which are those knowledge, values, beliefs, skills and habits acquired by you according to your body-brain's natural propensities. For instance, those who have a natural flair for dancing can pick up a special, new or novel form of dancing quickly and spontaneously while others may be struggling or are unable. Similarly, some people who possess a linguistic flair can pick up any language other than their mother tongue very fast—speaking and understanding at least; and, some people reading and writing too. Let us call them *Acquired Programmes: Natural (APN)*.

There are *AP*s *'Acquired due to Imposition'* which include those knowledge, values, beliefs, skills and habits that have been imposed upon you by your external environment. In fact, you have acquired them much against your wishes (members of the human species are no strangers to such compulsion as it was also prevalent during their pre-historic cave-dwelling days to meet the requirements of survival). In these areas, your performance would be rather erratic (and not uniformly high) despite all conditions for a high level of performance being satisfied and all other input requirements being adequately met. Let us call them *Acquired Programmes: Imposed (API)*.

One very contemporary example of *AP* is being presented below:

Technological advances and saturation-level promotion for every type of computer-based product explode around us daily. The focus is clearly on the younger generations—Digital Natives—who form the most avid consumer group, worldwide, for technology-based products. From cell phones to iPods, computers to gaming systems, the sales of digital products to young people dwarf the acceptance rates of other market segments. However, how does this fascination with and adoption of technology relate to brain development? Is brainpower generationally defined?

Every generation is influenced by the events, major personalities, and trends of its time. For these newest generations, its technology and social networking. Harvard's John Palfrey and Urs Gasser, describe the generation this way: 'These kids are different. They study, work, write, and interact with each other in ways that are very different from the ways you did growing up... And they're connected to one another by a common culture. Major aspects of their lives—social interactions, friendships, civic activities—are mediated by digital technologies. And they've never known any other way of life' [7].

Can you now sit back and identify your *IPOs*, *IPUBPs*, *APNs* and *APIs* like Samir Bakshi, Life and General Insurance Consultant, as he did in our 'Planned Success' consultation session?

Samir Bakshi's Case Study

Samir Bakshi had been dropping into our 'Planned Success' clinic, several times, of late to help him to make a career choice: whether he should continue as a self-employed professional marketing life and general insurance schemes; or he should appear in competitive tests for a govt. clerkship job; or, he should take up an ordinary non-executive job in a private firm. The first alternative had the scope for a high level of income in three to five years' time if he would struggle now for the next few years. The government job, although the income would be enough to ensure his subsistence would provide him with job security; (however, for this he had to clear the written and oral tests and he was almost going to reach the upper age limit in another two years' time). Opportunity for the third choice was readily available as he was having a few clerical job offers from some private firms due to his father's influence; (Samir's father had been and still was in a high level govt. job—from which he was going to retire in a year's time and unless Samir availed of the opportunity at present, he would lose it when his dad retired).

Samir Bakshi's following set of neuro-cerebral software identification is based on self-analysis and analysis of feedback from others:

IPOs: +ve: Friendliness, sociability.

–ve: Emotional sensitivity; low tolerance limits; hesitation to develop relationship with people; lack of natural ability to influence/convince people; a strong urge for job security; suffers from low energy and low confidence level problems.

IP-UBP: Fantastic knowledge about Kishore Kumar and his songs; Samir happens to be a moving encyclopaedia on Kishore Kumar's songs. (This IP-UBP of Samir apparently is of no value in the insurance marketing profession that he has taken up unless he uses it strategically in developing relationship with people—which he can if he applied his practical intelligence; he can also listen to Kishore's melodies for reducing his stress and increasing his energy level which happens to be a regular need for him as he gets hurt easily, gets sentimental and depressed whenever he fails to influence a prospect and to convert an existing customer into a client who takes his services on a regular basis.)

APN: Power of expression in Bengali (mother tongue and second language), English (first language as he went to an English medium school), and Hindi (third language); playing cricket (past hobby during student days)

API: Selling, business promotion and developmental skill.

Can you now take the decision for Samir Bakshi?

Ronit Roy's Case Study

(Do you remember in chapter one we had talked about the 11-year-old boy Ronit Roy and his parents Mr and Mrs R. Ronit had stopped studying at home due to the frustration caused by his parents regarding his interests in snakes, reptiles and herpetology. If not, please go back to chapter 1 and read Ronit's case study once again)

On analysis of Ronit's IP-AP, we observe that he possesses:

IPO +ve: Sobriety, seriousness and sincerity, simple habits, obedience.

IP-UBP: Extraordinary painting talent; unique life's aim: to be a herpetologist.

IPO –ve: Still immature (possibly due to his tender age) as he is not logical in thinking; it has not clicked in his mind that in order to become a herpetologist in the long run, he has to complete his studies at the secondary, senior secondary, graduate and post-graduate levels and then go for his doctorate in herpetology, specialising in serpents.

APN: Power of expression in Bengali (mother tongue and second language), English (first language as he went to an English medium school), and Hindi (third language); playing the violin.

API: Elementary knowledge of Russian language as his father Mr Roy is an accomplished Russian language expert.

Just like we have analysed the salient IP-AP traits of Ronit here, try to discover your child's 'strengths', 'deficiencies', ambitions and aspirations and try to counsel him accordingly. If he is properly guided, he will develop *self-love* which is one of the foundation pillars for an individual's personality and will be able to choose a proper channel for his unhindered progress and growth in life.

REFERENCES

[1] Buckingham, M. and D.O. Clifton, *Now Discover Your Strengths*, Pocket Books, Simon and Schuster, London, 2005.
[2] *Clifton StrengthFinder Resource Guide*, The Gallup Organization, Princeton, N.J., 2005.
[3] Ganguli, Siddhartha, 'Human Resource Economics: New Insights Into Man's Personal Resources', *Globsyn Management Journal,* Vol. 1, No. 1, 2007, pp. 19–27.
[4] Ganguli, Siddhartha, *Performance Management: First Time Right*, Platinum Publishers, Kolkata, 2008.
[5] Ganguli, Siddhartha, *Live Happily, Work Happily,* Allied Publishers, New Delhi, 2009.
[6] Taleb, Nassim Nicholas, *Fooled By Randomness: The Hidden Role of Chance in Life and in the Markets*, Penguin Books, New York, pp. 81–82.
[7] Herther, Nancy K., 'Digital Natives and Immigrants: What Brain Research Tells Us', *ONLINE,* Nov/Dec 2009, Vol. 33, No. 6, pp. 14–21.
[8] Palfrey, John and Gasser, Urs, *Born Digital: Understanding the First Generation of Digital Natives,* Basic Books, New York, 2008.

KEY TAKE-HOMES

- Inside your brain, there are around 10,000 million brain cells (neurons) representing your brain's hardware. The operating software are of two types: for day-to-day survival—inherent, innate, inherited programmes (IP) and for further higher functions, programmes developed due to family and social conditioning from your childhood—acquired programmes (AP).
- There are inherited programmes—ordinary (IPO) and also inherited programmes which are unique to you (IPUBP). The acquired programmes are also of two types: AP-normal (APN) and AP-imposed (API).
- In *conscious management*, it would be wise and worthwhile to use this technique for studying one's own propensities and others' too for more effective self-management and man management.

CHAPTER 11

Conscious Change within Yourself

BRINGING ABOUT A CONSCIOUS CHANGE WITHIN YOURSELF FOR BETTER PERFORMANCE

Your *APN* and *API* would include *knowledge, skills, talents, habits, values, beliefs, cultural attributes* that you might have received as inputs from your environment by seeing, listening, reading, and through teaching, counselling, coaching, mentoring and any other kind of value diffusion strategies. These have shaped your *attitude* during your formative years. Today, they reflect in your *behaviour* as your behaviour is a reflection of your *attitude*.

You must be able to *consciously* evaluate which of your behavioural ingredients are good and which are bad for you, which are appropriate and which are inappropriate for you to use to perform effectively in the context of your *work role* in the organisation—both in its 'Technical (T)' and 'Trans-technical (TT)' parts. This evaluation must be done on the basis of an analysis of the *pay-offs* as you will see from the discussion below.

However, stop for a moment and ponder over what other thinkers have to say in this regard: 'We all have beliefs and we all make assumptions about the right way of doing things. This is certainly true when it comes to managerial leadership. Although our beliefs and assumptions can make us effective, they can sometimes make us ineffective' [1, 2].

One example of our *belief system* is that we'll age and die one day. This is just a *belief*. It is not the *whole truth*. The *whole truth* is that if you take good care of your body and brain by following the appropriate scientific principles, you can reverse the ageing process.

THE PRINCIPLE OF PAY-OFFS

We are essentially selfish creatures and we make *changes* when we can see some *pay-offs* for ourselves. This we may call the *Principle of Pay-offs*. However, what we think these *pay-offs* will vary according to our own values and the particular context we work in.

Examples of some common *pay-off*s of *conscious management (managing and leading happily)* are:
- The change will make my life easier. I would be able to *hand over* responsibility to my team member(s) and shall have more time for myself (other likely outcomes in this group would be: I'll feel good; I shall have mental peace; I'll have less hassles; I'll get to smile/laugh more; I'll have a more comfortable life; I'll have reduced pressure and stress).
- I'll get to learn more.
- I'll have some role to play in motivating and developing people who do not consider themselves as important and feel they have almost reached a dead end and thus have nothing to look forward to.
- I'll have a sense of achievement leading to satisfaction and fulfilment.
- I'll be seen by higher-ups as achieving results; so, I'll be recognised more and sooner—that will open up opportunities for me to get more rewards, earn more and to get promotion, prestige and status.
- I'll have more power.
- There will be much better teamwork and less intra-team conflicts to deal with.
- There will be happy suppliers, happy customers and happy stakeholders.
- I'll be liked and people will do things for me.
- There will be quality service and products; my organisation will grow and that will open up greater and bigger opportunities.
- I'll have a peaceful family life which will lead to more effective time management for myself and all the other family members. The children will develop and grow faster.
- I'll now look forward to coming back to a real happy family nest.

FOCUS ON EMOTIONAL CHANGE

If you have to change, the most important change has to be in your emotions. Emotions relate to your *creaturely psychological needs* which emanate from the *limbic system* which is, as you know by now, a very vital part of the inner and lower part of your brain. These *needs*, present in all our ancestors including our closest cousins chimpanzees and bonobos, are equally strong in most of us when we are not *conscious*.

You have to recognise that it is extremely important for you to satisfy these emotional needs in others by transcending your own emotional needs consciously with the help of your *feelings* which dwell on the right side of your outer and upper brain.

This recognition should prompt you to set the following strategic goals:

- *Goal 1*: Being situational and using customised transactional style (pay-off: peak performance).
- *Goal 2*: Being 'proactive' rather than 'reactive' (pay-off: peak co-operation).
- *Goal 3*: Being a *role model* for your team members with the expectation that they will follow you to a large extent as suitable to their natural propensities (pay-off: near-model to model behaviour from the team members).

Priority Analysis

Goal	Urgency	Importance	Priority and Application Phase
1	High	High	I (1st Phase)
2	High	High	-Do-
3	Moderate	High	II (2nd Phase)

HOW WOULD YOU DEVELOP A POSITIVE FEELING TOWARDS ONE, TWO OR A GROUP OF INDIVIDUALS

It is easier to say that you transcend your own *creaturely* emotional needs with the help of your *feelings* which dwell on the right side of your upper and outer brain, than it is done. If you have ill feelings towards one, two or a group of individuals, there are the following alternative ways of detoxifying your mind.

- One way is to have an altruistic view like we belong to the same species.
- Another way is to think about how the other one or two persons or a group of persons had served you in your bad times when you needed some help.

- A third way is not to allow the negative feelings (such as feelings of deprivation, conflict etc.) to invade your mind-space; instead fill your mind with the noble attribute of forgiveness.
- A fourth way is to look at each individual as being different from another. Each individual is really a product of her or his genetic propensities which are freaks of Nature, over which the person has no conscious control like one has on the voluntary sensory or motor activities. You thus have to look at each person as an individual entity—with the combination of the natural good and bad characteristics.
- A fifth way is to ascertain as to in what respects or in what ways you are dependent on the person or persons concerned; and, this dependence must be acknowledged.
- A sixth way is to determine whether for any of your achievements, the person or persons concerned must be given credit.
- Another way is to recognise that you all are members of the same family and children of the same mother—your organisation. Sibling rivalry would be there but it gets resolved quickly amicably. You may not be sharing the same genes but you certainly share the same vision, mission and objectives.

YOUR BRAIN'S CONSCIOUSNESS AND WHAT CHANGE IS CALLED FOR

Inside your brain, cell-to-cell (inter-neuronal) communication is a continuous activity even while you relax, take rest or sleep. (If you're keen to know details of the behaviour of your neurons, refer to Appendix II; otherwise skip it).

This inter-neuronal communication is an outcome of the neuron's *consciousness* of which, of course, the neuron itself is not aware. Here *'consciousness'* signifies the presence of life and does not mean 'awareness'. Thus live neurons possess *consciousness* and dead neurons are devoid of it.

Our objective is to make you *conscious* about the *consciousness* of the neurons and what important a role inter-neuronal communication plays in the activities of your daily living and working and how it contributes to your success or failure; your superiority, mediocrity or inferiority in comparison to others in your circle.

The neuronal communication processes inside the human brain has no analogy and is, therefore, unique. Different chemicals (neurotransmitters) get released from different input sources converging on a single cell and active at any moment. In addition to the degree of activity of these inputs, different amounts of chemical transmitters get released. Finally, each transmitter docks itself into its own receptor that has its own characteristic way of influencing the voltage of the target cell.

Thus at every stage there is room for an enormous flexibility and versatility in the brain, using different combinations of transmitter chemicals. But, unfortunately, you do not take advantage of your brain's profound flexibility and versatility as you choose to follow the *path of least work* which helps you to keep your 'proactive' thinking and planning to the minimum. And, this *path of least work* means using all readily available software: that is, your brain's *Inherent Programmes (IP)* and *Acquired Programmes (AP)* which you have acquired from your family and social environment during the process of being brought up from infancy to youth and which may not be the right ones to apply in certain situations. The *path of least brainwork* is a corollary of the *law of conservation of biological energy* which is essentially to be followed for maintaining *homeostasis* (of Greek origin, 'homeo' and 'stasis' meaning 'like or similar' and 'condition' respectively) or a 'steady state' of equilibrium [3].

Most interestingly, therefore, no external intelligence programmes your brain: it operates spontaneously according to its own wishes—just because it 'feels like it'. It is thus guided by feelings which are closely networked with your emotions located in the *limbic system* of your brain's inner and lower structures.

This spontaneous strategy might not help you to perform and mobilise performance from others effectively in your 'work role'. Thus there is a need for you to programme your brain *consciously* and not fall a prey to your brain's in-built software.

Most of your actions, including behavioural actions, are *unconscious*—taking place automatically, spontaneously. In order that an action is *conscious*, it must be created mindfully.

Consciousness of mind gives rise to thoughts or impulses of creative intelligence. They come out in an organised manner, as the mind has organised them. This organisation leads to a conscious action. Endocrinologist turned wellness expert. Deepak Chopra says that the power to organise thoughts may be called *knowledge*.

To quote Chopra's words:

> First, we have consciousness, in which reside all the impulses of creative intelligence. These are expressed as thoughts in our minds. When expressed in an organised manner—via organising power, or knowledge—they lead to action and result in material creation. This process taking place in us is paralleled throughout nature on a universal scale [4].

WHAT IS 'PERCEPTION'

'Perception' is a learned phenomenon. Perception in each individual is different from the other. The reason is simple. As far as our *Inherent Programmes (IPs)* are concerned, although similarity between individuals exists to a large extent, dissimilarities also do exist due to difference in natural propensities and brain selectivity to learn different things from the same environment to which all present in the environment are exposed. The second reason is the difference in *Acquired Programmes (APs)* as different people have been brought up in different environments and exposed to different stimuli.

According to Deepak Chopra:

> The power of awareness would make no difference in our lives if Nature had outfitted us all with the same response to experience. Clearly this didn't happen; no two people share the same perception of anything [5].

Interpretation of anything or any situation arises from an individual's internal self-interaction in a silent mode, which may be described as *self-talk, mind-chatter* or *internal dialogue.* Thoughts, judgements and feelings are ceaselessly swirling through our mind: 'I like this, I don't like that; I'm afraid of A, I'm not sure of B' etc. Internal dialogue is not random mental noise; it is generated from a deep level by your beliefs and assumptions.

HOW PERCEPTIONS DIFFER

You suddenly see a snake passing by. It stops for a while in front of you. You jump back in fear. You become aware of your muscle reactions, which are an automatic outcome of the trigger by chemical signals from your nervous system (in other words, your *IP*). Your increased heartbeat and panting breath are other visible signs that the hormone *adrenalin* has responded to the situation, as would be quite natural. It has been secreted by the *adrenal cortex,* housed in your brain, in response to *ACTH,* a specific movement-related brain chemical sent from your *pituitary gland* also located inside your brain.

You reacted according to the programme that is installed in your brain. (This incidentally would be the general biological response of the human being while confronted with what he perceives as a dangerous situation). A snake collector and charmer, for whom exhibiting snakes in public is the means of livelihood, would look at the situation with a lot of interest. A Hindu religious-minded villager might have his mind filled with respect and devotion, so much so that he may bow down and lower his head in awe.

PERCEPTION OF CONSCIOUSNESS

The *consciousness* that we want you to develop can be described as an alert, agile and active state under a little *stress* which is essential for dynamic activities in the body and brain.

And to deserve the title of a practitioner of *conscious management*, can you study different persons' different *perceptions* to the same situation, or of the same problem? If you can, then you would develop *Multiple Perceptual Intelligence (MPI)* and your physical as well as mental happiness, comfort, compatibility and tolerance limits will increase and the corresponding zones will be much bigger and wider, compared to another individual who is limited in his perception and points of view (See Fig. 11.1). *MPI*, on the one hand, can be your asset; on the other hand, it can become a liability for you if your tend to use it too much in every case. You may become a viction of *paralysis by analysis*. Therefore, you should apply your practical intelligence discriminately as to where and when to use it and to what extent.

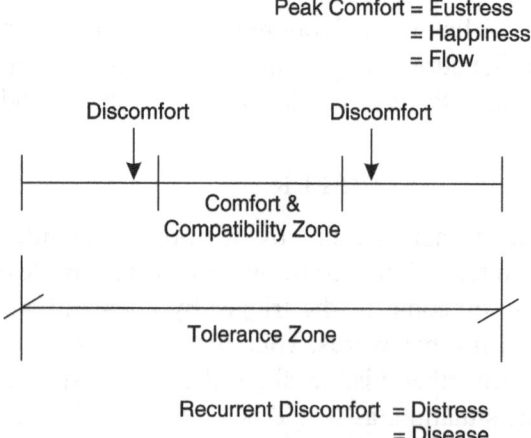

Fig. 11.1: Happiness, Comfort, Compatibility and Tolerance Zones

PURE AWARENESS

When we wake up in the morning there is usually a second of *pure awareness* before the old *perceptual conditioning* becomes active to give us protection and provide shelter from what we perceive as danger or make us active to derive pleasure. At that moment of the awakening of pure awareness, you are just yourself, neither happy nor sad, neither elated nor depressed, neither proud nor modest, neither old nor young. Such an awakening is unconscious.

Can you bring such pure awareness *consciously*? Yes, you can. Consider the following tips.

- You'll operate from a *pure awareness* level if you look at every failure as an 'opportunity' to learn, not as a 'threat' as when you consider any failure as a 'threat' your thoughts are contaminated with your 'self'—your ego.
- You'll operate from *pure awareness* if you look at what you feel as negative circumstances as an 'opportunity' for you to develop resilience, shock-absorbing capacity as your feeling of negativity is contaminated by your 'self'—ego.
- You'll operate from *pure awareness* when you face something you dislike, you consider this as good luck as unless you confront what you dislike, and how would you know and appreciate what you like. Your dislike is considered a dislike as it is affected by your ego. A glass or bottle half full is not half-empty, it is half-full. That is *positive thinking*. And positive thinking comes when you're in *pure awareness*.

Pure awareness prompts you to use and utilise the present, do not ponder over what you did or had in the past; nor should you think about your future except for chalking out a flexible plan on what you want to be, where you want to go. This understanding is of utmost importance.

THE *COMPENSATION PRINCIPLE*: BE CONSCIOUS ABOUT YOUR AND OTHERS' HIDDEN STRENGTHS

In a blind person, it is generally known, other sensory powers like sound, smell, taste and touch are much more developed than in normal persons who are not visually handicapped. Many orthopaedically disabled people are seen to develop tremendous determination and willpower—they do not consider their physical disability as a deterrent or barrier towards their success.

Some mentally challenged people—both male and female, are known to be physically extra strong so much so that physically they can achieve many things which their normal counterparts cannot. In the disabled people, the deficiency present is *compensated* by some special trait which is especially predominant in them creating a 'uniqueness' in them, serving as a discriminating factor compared to those who are normal.

In other words, there is a *compensation principle* working in all of us. Just in the same way as it happens in the case of disabled people, in each normal person also, some critical deficiency (which may be termed as a 'constraint') is compensated by some hidden strength waiting to be discovered.

As a little kid, Albert Einstein had to really struggle to remember words and written material. He would often be told by his teacher that his future would be bleak. What the teacher didn't know was that 'Einstein's deficits shared the same brain with his extraordinary vision as a physicist—one that profoundly changed the ways we understand our world' [6].

One deficit in you may be the indicator of a solid strength hidden in your personality—you have to discover it with the help of your own insight and the insight of others both close and distant to you. Those who are close to you may not be so sensitive about your *powers* as much as they would notice and point out your *weaknesses*; whereas your *strengths* may strike those distant from you.

Orfalea, who suffered from *dyslexia*[1], but turned into a top businessman, states in his autobiography:

> I've often thought that the obstacles I faced in school helped to shape me as an entrepreneur. It wasn't until business school, when I was able to concentrate on business and economics that I really came into my own. That experience taught me that everyone has their strengths and challenges. It highlighted the importance of teamwork and showed me that the combination of many different strengths produced a better outcome than one person working alone [7].

In another context, he puts it beautifully:

> How many innovators, I wonder, are lost to us simply because their talents and skills cannot be perceived or measured? And why are we

---

[1]Yale dyslexia expert Sally Shaywitz defines *dyslexia* as 'a reading difficulty that is unexpected for a person's age, intelligence, level of education or profession'.

so hung up on measuring everyone, anyway? The very bedevilment we are so eager to cure in a person may hold the key to his genius [8].

HOW TO MANAGE YOURSELF CONSCIOUSLY

For activities that are performed with attention or conscious effort, there needs to be a constant referral to the *cortex*—the outer and upper structures of your brain. It is your *cortex* that is known to play a key role in conscious attention.

Once a movement can become automated, either by internalised triggers in the *basal ganglia* or from sensory inputs fed through the *cerebellum* (both of which are located in the inner and lower structures of your brain, the *cortex* is free for other functions, such as explicit memory, the remembering of facts and events [9]. Therefore, for conscious self-management, you must focus your mind only on one task or matter at a time; otherwise you will not be successful.

REFERENCES

[1] House, R.J. and Podsakoff, P.M., 'Effectiveness: Leadership Past Perspectives and Future Directions for Research' In: Jerald Greenberg (ed.) *Organizational Behavior: The State of the Science*, Lawrence Erlbaum, Hillsdale, N.J., 1994.

[2] Quinn, Robert E., Sue R. Faerman, Michael P. Thompson, Michael R. McGrath, *Becoming A Master Manager: A Competency Framework*, John Wiley & Sons Inc., Hoboken, N.J., 2003, Third edition, p. 1.

[3] Ganguli, Siddhartha, *Human Engineering for Better Management*, Kwality Book Company, Calcutta, 1977, p. 33.

[4] Chopra, Deepak, *Creating Health: Beyond Prevention, Toward Perfection*, Grafton Books, London, 1988, p. 90.

[5] Chopra, Deepak, *Ageless Body, Timeless Mind*, Random House, London, 1993, p. 2.

[6] Orfalea, Paul and Ann March, *Copy This!*, Workman Publishing, New York, 2005, p. vii.

[7] Orfalea, Paul and Ann Marsh, *Copy This!*, *loc. cit.*, p. viii.

[8] Orfalea, Paul and Ann Marsh, *Copy This!*, *loc. cit.*, p. xix.

[9] Greenfield, Susan, *The Human Brain: A Guided Tour*, Phoenix, London, 6th Impression, 2000, p. 176.

KEY TAKE-HOMES

- You may need to bring about a *conscious* change within yourself by segregating your personal qualities which would be of relevance and value for your effective performance, from those which would not be. Once you have identified and segregated those qualities, you must concentrate on their proper maintenance, sharpening and value-addition.
- Frequently work out the *pay-offs* of *conscious management (managing and leading happily)*. It is not unlikely that every time you do this exercise, you may be able to add on one or two items to the list of your pay-offs.
- Transcend your own emotional needs to satisfy others' emotionally with the help of your feelings which are higher than emotions.
- Create all your actions including behavioural actions *consciously* (that is, mindfully). Try to bring pure awareness also *consciously*.
- Be *conscious* of your own and others' hidden strengths and focus yourself only on one task at a time.

Chapter 12

Conscious Brain Skills Management: Conscious Intuition

"Close your eyes and pretend you are a baby looking at the world for the first time. The world is not what you see. There are no trees, no clouds, no houses, or faces of animals or humans. Your existence is a blur of pointless shadows and pieces of coloured light. As time goes on you would begin building patterns from the information that you receive from your senses and with the assistance of your Guardian Angels. Eventually you will understand all the patterns you would see for the rest of your life. Whether you see white clouds floating across a cobalt blue sky and felt peace or monstrous shadows reflected on your bedroom wall at night and felt fear, you are giving birth to your imagination. From this imagination, you interpret reality, become creative, create inventions and discover your connection with the Universe and your Guardian Angels."

—M.E. Slappery

BRAIN SKILLS MANAGEMENT: WHAT IT IS AND WHY IMPORTANT

During your momentary existence in the *pure awareness* state of your brain, as discussed in the last chapter, you may get access to some of the brain powers hidden in your brain cells (*neurons*) and the products and services of the electro-chemical processes which constitute their activities.

Let us describe all these different brain powers collectively, by the general term *brain skills*, for brevity's sake and take you for a round through the glossary of brain skill terms so that you get specifically familiar with each of them. This glossary will also include terms representing the outcome of the practical application of your brainpowers. However, some of the brain skills defined in the glossary are inborn and, for those who do not show such inborn propensities, these cannot be developed so easily without long painstaking practices like specialised meditative techniques.

By *conscious* brain skills management, we mean invoking some specific brain power at will at times of need to deal with a difficult situation or to solve a problem.

GLOSSARY OF BRAIN SKILL TERMS

Brain Skill

A *skill* is a power which can be developed and retained with regular and repetitive practice and habit formulation, if the individual has some flair for it—such as sketching, drawing, painting, reciting, singing and dancing—which are not original but produced by copying or mimicking. A few common 'brain skills' suitable for managing and leading at the workplace and at home, which can be developed through practice by applying certain proven methods or techniques include: strategic or situational thinking, planning; decision-making; problem-solving; and, innovation.

Intelligence

It is a brain power which prompts the individual to explore, investigate, and find out the cause-and-effect relationship by asking questions like, why/what is the purpose/what are the objectives; what benefits can be obtained and when; who all are involved; for whom; where; what; and how. Intelligence is generally indirectly associated with its economic value/worth or economic return on investment. We normally talk about *academic intelligence* or *General Intelligence* (GI) which can be measured through IQ tests with an average base of 100. Below 100 begins the degree of dullness and above 100 begins the degree of sharpness. But there are *multiple intelligences*.

A few examples are: *visual-spatial intelligence* (how a space can be utilised gainfully); *arithmetical intelligence* (calculation power); *scientific intelligence* (looking at everything and explaining things scientifically); *linguistic intelligence* (the capacity to pick up languages fast); *emotional intelligence* (the ability to control and use own emotions by watching and studying the emotions of the other person or persons leading to a positive outcome); and *business intelligence* (a natural capacity to scan the external environment to identify the business 'opportunities' and 'threats' bearing in mind own organisation's 'strengths' and 'weaknesses') [1].

Intuition

It represents the gut feelings—some feelings which come to you suddenly absolutely uncalled for and most spontaneously, independent of any matrix of thoughts or organised origin. It also includes the ability to recognise and communicate intuitively with spiritually strong beings/with one's own inner self. Intuition is useful for bridging difficult gaps in a problem. In addition, intuition always bespeaks the future.

Instinct

It prompts a mother to protect or save her child; *intuition* tells her what to do immediately for its recovery once harm occurs.

Insight

It is the 'Aha!' 'Eureka!' or the 'light bulb' moment of reaction on realisation of some truth which was being sought. *Hunches* are immature or incomplete insights—mainly resulting from a limited understanding of the big picture 'movie'.

Sixth Sense

It denotes the very special and rare faculty of psychic or spiritual perception which is distinct from, and higher than, the five physical senses.

Inspiration

It is the ability to receive information from some extraordinary source (some believe the spiritual world)—information about the processes and laws of Nature.

Perception

In contrast to *consciousness*, perception is concerned with objects external to the mind, with things having actual existence. To have good perception is not only to be aware of sensations pertinent to an issue, but to enrich the meaning of that sensation by meshing it with related past experiences.

Idea

It is a patterned quantity of mental energy—incomplete in its form. Ideas contain embryonic mental images—called *percepts* which make one aware of something. In the earliest stages of a developing idea, it has vague, hazy and partially formed images. Yet such ideas are so fleeting that mind's failure to grab them immediately may be a missed opportunity for you. It may never come back, nor may it be possible for you to retrieve as it might not yet have been stored in your short-term memory. This is why creative people who produce great works always have pen and paper or a laptop or a cell phone handy to make instant notes. Concrete ideas are tangible, quantifiable and measurable whereas abstract ideas are intangible, non-measurable and non-quantifiable.

Concept

It is any formulated thought without a mental picture. In other words, it is abstract in form.

Images

Some images are reflections or likenesses of material factors outside one's mind while some other ones are psychologically and/or philosophically symbolic. The composite of a few images constitutes *imagery* and the art of thinking in images is called *symbolism.*

Imagination

It is the act or power of forming a mental image of something not present to the senses or never before wholly perceived in reality. The images are usually visual pictures although they do occur with other forms of perception and may involve one or more of the senses.

Vision

It is a picture of something that the mind sees clearly and concretely—and to the point as to suggest concrete reality.

Fancy

It is anything conceived purely in the imagination whether it combines the elements of reality or is pure 'invention'. Most cases of fancy are of a light nature. Besides, fancies are whimsical and elusive and ornamental in quality.

Fantasy

It is an imaginary product often in literary and artistic form, most of which has no correspondence with objective reality but is an unrestrained product of the mind.

Dream

It applies to the ideas and especially to images present to the mind in sleep.

Daydream

It is wishful thinking in an attempt to escape the experience of one's self.

Creativity

It is not the creation of something out of nothing. Rather, it is the process by which two different things are linked together by a similar idea or thought. A few of the criteria for creative thinking are: (i) novel (impressively unusual, striking and unprecedented)—different from just thinking outside the box; (ii) the seeing of the common in the uncommon ('How is a dog like a flower?'—'They are both living things') or seeing the uncommon in the common or linking the common with the uncommon; (iii) a workable product, whether intangible or tangible, which solves some known or unknown problem.

Talent

It is a brainpower which cannot be measured or quantified as an intelligence of any type can be. Manifestation of each talent has a touch of originality or novelty in it. There could be: creative talents; musical talents; culinary talent; artistic talent (drawing, sketching, painting, sculpture, model-making, craftwork, furniture design, interior design, fashion design etc.); choreographic talent (dancing and visual-spatial movement), linguistic talent (poetry writing, story writing, drama writing, copy writing etc).

Task

It is a work activity or a set of work activities to be performed by an individual, or two individuals together, or by a team or by individuals or sections or departments placed in internal supplier-internal customer relationships.

Domain

It is a particular discipline such as a stream of engineering (mechanical, electrical or chemical) or a 'core business' line or staff function (like sales or production or marketing or HR or finance and accounting).

Field

It is a specialised area, a collection of *domains*. Evaluation or judgements of actions (or *tasks*) performed in a *domain* are put forth by individuals knowledgeable in that *domain* by members of the *field*. It is simply not possible to tell whether a *task* has been executed satisfactorily by people who are not from the *field* to which the *task* belongs; although it is not that in the absence of such judgment, a *task* or work activity accomplished would be considered as inadequate. The term *field* has been suggested by the Harvard psychologist Csikszentmihalyi [2]

Giftedness

An individual is considered 'gifted' if he has a natural aptitude for some *task* and advances quickly compared to others in that *task area* or *domain*.

Prodigiousness

It is an extreme form of *giftedness* in a *domain*.

Expertise/Expert

An individual qualifies to be an expert after he has worked for a long time within a *domain* to develop certain *skills*. *Expertise* thus can be described as mastery of some *skill* which can lead to high performance in that *domain*. However, there is no implication of originality, dedication, or passion in such a performance; *expertise* is better conceived as a kind of technical excellence.

Memory and Learning

Sensory inputs received by sensory receptor organs from the external environment in the form of external stimuli reach the brain through nerves. These, received in the form of altered signals, by way of chemical changes in the connections between nerve endings (known as 'synapses), are processed by the brain cells or 'neurons'. The brain is thus able to convert new sensory information into 'memories'—and this is the basis of all learning. Lasting memories are formed by structural rearrangements that occur in the contacts between nerve endings. Our cerebral cortex, where these memories are stored, has nearly 400 trillion such contacts. The contacts may become larger or smaller, fewer or more in number, or may change positions to carry a novel memory. The new memories get stored as a change in the brain circuitry.

Mastery

Some creativity can be manifest prior to deciding if someone has attained *mastery* over a subject or in a domain.

Genius

This highest honour should be reserved for those persons who have not only proved to possess *expertise* and *creativity* but the products or services of their thoughts have assumed universal or even some quasi-universal significance and have transcended their era to attain long-term significance or virtual immortality for as long as we can visualise. Examples are: Isaac Newton, Charles Darwin, Shakespeare, Rabindranath Tagore, Goethe, Rembrandt, Van Gogh, Picasso, Beethoven and Mozart.

A recent research study led by scientist Szabolcs Kri of Semmelweiss University in Hungary has revealed that there is only a fine line between genius and madness as both share a particular gene. Creative people have a gene called *neuregulin 1*, in common, which is also linked to psychosis and depression—in fact, it plays a role in brain development but a variant of it is linked to mental illnesses like schizophrenia and bipolar disorder. Molecular factors that are loosely associated with severe mental disorders but are present in many healthy people may have an advantage enabling us to think more creatively [3].

Your Body and Physical Stamina

Your workload at the workplace and at home today demands that you should have a sound health and a good amount of physical stamina. According to the Australian anthropologist Peter McAllister, the modern men—you and I, are no better than wimps. According to McAllister our cave-dwelling ancestors were much stronger than us, the modern humans, in muscle power. The reason was simply they worked physically much harder than us. We are so inactive these days. He says, many pre-historic Australian aboriginals could have outrun world 100- and 200-metre record holder Usain Bolt in modern conditions. McAllister points out that a Neanderthal woman had 10 percent more muscle bulk than the modern European man [4].

In order to get the best out of your body in its present state today, you can be guided by the following tips:

- Our bodies work the best when we do not worry about them.
- We are likely to face serious problem when we give too much comfort to our bodies. The body works best when it is efficiently used with clear knowledge about its capabilities and limitations. By being lazy one deprives oneself by default (underload). Overuse of the body also leads to problems (overload)—such as health problems, fatigue, diminished efficiency, and may even face accidents. Therefore, look after yourself and take good care.
- One should make oneself fully aware of the realities of the human body. There are natural changes like getting old, slowing down of its internal systems. One should accept these changes in good grace, and make the necessary adjustments in life.

Your Brain and Intellectual Stamina

Compared to our prehistoric ancestors who used to survive 70 to 80% on body power, we are much stronger in brain power due to millions of years of evolutionary progress by virtue of tool design and development and performance in teams by adjusting with different types of attitude and behaviour displayed by different involved people. Looking microscopically into our brain, the *posterior cingulate cortex* part developed to provide us with the power of strategic decision-making—making a choice amongst new alternatives. The frontal and the parietal lobes also developed to give us the skill of performing numerical tasks. This skill became associated particularly with the *intra-parietal cortex* which is a region of the *parietal lobe* [5].

THE 'EYE OF THE BEHOLDER' PRINCIPLE

In *conscious* brain skills management, the '*eye of the beholder*' principle has to be followed as the prime one. In other words, the *conscious* brain skills manager must not manage his skills to satisfy himself but to provide delight and happiness to the customer/user. *Conscious* brain skills applications must be user-friendly.

DEVELOPING THE RIGHT AMBIENCE

Can brain skills be accessed under pressure/stress from within one's own self or from the external environment (by an individual like the 'boss' or a parent or as a part of the individual's performance standards set by the organisation or the family)?

The answer is a simple and straight 'No'. The reason is: under pressure or stress, negative brain chemicals (such as *adrenalin* and *cortisol*) and negative brain electricity (*beta-negative:* 25 to 32 cycles/second) are generated which help the brain to cope with the stressful situation rather than making the cerebral environment congenial for utilisation of *brain skills*.

For access to brain skills, one needs to have a reasonably balanced level of positive brain chemicals (namely, *endorphin, dopamine, serotonin, oxytocin* and *melatonin*) and flow of positive electricity (beta-positive: 14 to 24 cycles/second).

For developing the right ambience for *conscious* brain skills management, one option for you would be to practice 'Achievements Audit (AA)' by retrieving from memory, starting with one, the vivid sensory-motor experiences of major achievements where you had been solely responsible (and not as one member of a 'pair' or a 'team' or a group') - namely 'individual' and not 'collective' achievements and living with that memory for a few minutes.

The other options for developing the right ambience would include: deep breathing exercise involving the entire breathing department from lower abdomen to the throat level, colour meditation (meditating on an imaginary natural scenic picture like the sunrise, sunset, or green hillside, bright sunny, light blue sky or deep blue sea waves); and music therapy (listening to slow instrumental musical melodies).

BRAIN SKILLS *VIS-À-VIS* YOUR BRAIN'S STRUCTURE

Skills are usually related to the inner or lower *creaturely* position of our brain. For a Right-Handed Person (RHP), *intelligences* are related to the left side of the outer and the upper brain-the left *cerebral cortex* (LB) and *talents* to the opposite side of the cortex—namely the right side (RB).

INTUITION

Intuition is a right brain skill. Many supervisors, executives, managers, self-employed professionals, entrepreneurs and parents get guided by intuitive flashes at crucial times. I don't know whether you have ever experienced a spontaneous *intuitive power*, where your gut feeling has turned out to be true. Have you? If you have, that's great.

Magical Intuition

Some people, in fact, perceive *intuition* as such a magical power. They claim that there is a deep level of wisdom residing in each of us, and our job is to make contact with it, to use it as a psychic ability that can guide us over the hurdles of life. Some others look at *intuition* as a special gift or talent typified by some very special sensitivity.

These advocates of *magical intuition* suggest that whenever we are confronted with a complex decision-making situation, we ought to get in touch with these unconscious forces, representing an ESP (extra-sensory perception) power, deep down inside our brain.

Muscular Intuition

I am quite sure that even if you might not have come across your *magical intuition* power, there are certainly some functional areas of your job where you have developed a *special proficiency* by practice. Klein [6] prefers to describe it as *muscular intuition* where a skill can be acquired as *strength* that can be enhanced and expanded through practice. The more you practice, the more repetitions there are, the stronger you get.

Conscious Intuition

While *muscular intuition* can be developed as a *skill*, *magical intuition* is a *talent*. In between the two, there is a level where *intuition* can be based on your *intelligence* (that is, application of your logical-analytical-rational thinking power located in your brain's left *pre-frontal cortex* or *PFC*). This may be called *conscious intuition* as you are coming to the decision by applying your brainpower 'consciously'.

The key to using *intuition* effectively is conscious 'experience'- more specifically, meaningful experience—that allows us to recognise patterns and build mental models. Thus, the way to improve your intuitive skills is to strengthen your experience base. The most meaningful type of experience, naturally, is real-life experience. You can't beat the real world when it comes to meaningful experience. It tends to teach the truest lessons and make the biggest impressions.

There are a couple of problems with relying on the real world for all our experience though. One is that many of us simply do not get the opportunities to accumulate enough real-life experience in a particular field to develop expertise, leading to the formation of a base for intuition. Another is that many of us cannot afford to wait until we're doing something for real to learn from our mistakes. That's the paradox. When you take up a job, you're expected to be proficient at that job. Naturally you wouldn't be given the responsibility otherwise. But how can you develop the expertise to be proficient at a job before you've actually been on the job for some time? Mental conditioning works best when it is experiential— that is, learning by doing.

Comparison: Development Time of Three Intuitions

1. *Magical Intuition:* a talent, hence inborn; it is the individual's inherent quality and, therefore, the question of development time does not arise.
2. *Conscious Intuition:* a matter of application of mind; hence, development time is moderate; you need only stronger and more specific mental models.
3. *Muscular Intuition:* development time is long; you really need a richer experience base.

MAKING A CASE FOR CONSCIOUS INTUITION

Our eyes contain a *fovea* and a *periphery*. The *fovea* lets us see fine details. In contrast, *peripheral vision* is useful for providing the overall perspective that lets us keep ourselves well oriented in space.

We need both the fovea and the periphery to carry on our lives. Of the two, the peripheral vision system is more important. Diseases that destroy peripheral vision, such as *retinosa pigmentosa*, leave the victims helpless, left only with their foveal vision, which is like seeing the world through a straw. The fovea only shows a small amount of the world at a time—if you hold out your arm and focus on your thumbnail, that is, about the area covered by your fovea.

If we lose our foveal vision to diseases such as macular degeneration, we have suffered a loss, to be sure; we can no longer read or perform fine-grained visual tasks. But we can still navigate and get around.

Our intuitions (gut feelings/hunches) function like our peripheral vision to keep us oriented and aware of our surroundings. Our analytical abilities (that is *conscious intuition*), on the other hand, function like the foveal vision to enable us to think precisely. We may believe that everything we think and decide comes from our analytical thinking—the conscious and deliberate arguments we construct in our heads, but that's because we're not aware of how our intuitions direct our conscious thought processes.

Sometimes we need to rely more on intuition and other times we need to draw on analysis or *conscious attention*. When the situation keeps changing, or when the time pressure is high or when the goals are fuzzy, you just can't use analysis. You have to depend upon your *magical* or *muscular intuitions*. And, when you have a lot of experience, you can just recognise what to do without having to weigh all the options.

In contrast, when your decision involves a lot of computational complexity, such as determining whether there is a cost advantage for purchasing a new colour copier instead of leasing one, you can acknowledge your intuitions, but you're sunk if you do not whip out the calculator.

If you have to resolve conflict between different people or groups, you can't go with one person's intuitions over those of the other people. To help everyone arrive at a fair compromise you may want to compare the options using a common set of criteria, so that everyone can keep track of what he or she is getting and giving up with each option. If you have to find the best option to solve a problem, and not just a workable one, you may want to analyse the strengths and weaknesses of each alternative. And, if you have made a decision but are pressed to justify your choice, the most convincing way is to line up your options and explain why your solution was the wisest choice.

Conscious intuition is to use the brainpower of logical-analytical-rational thinking to take a decision. To what extent that set of thinking could be used so that there is no 'paralysis by analysis' in the crossroad where one may get held up is the challenge for you.

Limitations of *Intuition*

The stock market is too complex to allow accurate intuitions. No one has the expertise to reliably outperform the market. Stockbrokers have learned the routines of their job. They can provide us with explanations for their recommendations. They can talk knowledgably about various indices. What they can't do is make reliable forecasts. We may feel intuitive preferences for certain stocks, but most of us who carefully watch the track record of these preferences soon realise that they are not trustworthy. Of course, the stock market is too complex to be predicted by analytical methods either, but that is a different story.

REFERENCES

[1] Ganguli, Siddhartha, *Success: Can be Planned and Earned*, Allied Publishers, New Delhi, 2010.
[2] Csikszentmihalyi, M., 'Society, culture and person: A system view of creativity' In: R.J. Sternberg (Ed.) *The nature of creativity*, Cambridge University Press, New York, 1988, pp. 325–39.
[3] 'Only A Fine Line Between Genius and Madness: Study', *The Statesman, Kolkata*, 1 October 2009, p. 4.
[4] 'Modern man a wimp, says book', *The Times of India, Kolkata*, 15 October 2009, p. 1.
[5] 'Scientists see numbers inside people's heads', *The Times of India, Kolkata*, 28 September 2009, p. 11.
[6] Klein, Gary, *Intuition at Work,* Currency/Doubleday, New York, 2003.

KEY TAKE-HOMES

- All your brain powers collectively can be described as 'brain skills'. Your brain skills ought to be used *consciously* to satisfy others and not just yourself. Your 'ego' has got to be dissociated.
- You have to generate the right ambience for getting access to and practically apply your brain skills.
- 'Intuition' and its various forms could be an attractive brain skill to be used *consciously*.

CHAPTER 13

Lateral Thinking and Other Approaches to Conscious Brain Skills Management

LATERAL THINKING

When our basic thinking follows a routine format, we have instinctive answers to questions and standard solutions to problems. This is a function of our creaturely brain.

Do we ever think or feel that there could be a better solution - better from the point of view of time-saving, quality or productivity improvement, cost-saving, income or profitability rise, safety, or information flow or the HR factor? Those who do, they are *lateral thinkers.*

Examples of routine thinking coming from your hidden agenda

Task: Write down the step-by-step procedure for making an egg omelette.

Assignment on lateral thinking

Task: Think out a time-saving and or cost-saving procedure for making egg omelette.

Assignment on lateral thinking

Task: Design a totally novel type of omelette.

Example of routine thinking

Task: Write down common, day-to-day applications of building bricks. (10 inches × 5 inches × 3 inches (25 cm × 12.5 cm × 7.5 cm)).

Assignment on lateral thinking

Task: Write down at least 2 to 3 totally uncommon and rare applications of common building bricks.

Task: (For use in a HRD/training workshop) Participants to generate at least 2 to 3 new practical ideas in their respective work areas—individually as well as in small groups or suggest action plans for practical problem-solving which can be implemented in 2 to 3 months later.

THE WORKING PERSONALITY PRINCIPLE (W.P.P.) FOR *CONSCIOUS* BRAIN SKILLS IDENTIFICATION AND MANAGEMENT

You are already aware that there are three types of *Working Personalities (W.P.)* corresponding to the three kinds of *work* in which we, the modern human beings, engage ourselves day-to-day [1, 2]. These three types of working personalities represent three different types of brain skills dominance.

The first type has been named by us as *Self-Engagement (SE)*. Those belonging to this group enjoy working alone on activities involving the brain—the 'cerebral apparatus'—the outer and upper portion of the brain which is most developed in us, the human beings, amongst all mammals. They are relatively stronger than the other two types of working personalities in cerebral skills, namely, thinking (logical-analytical—Left Brain or 'LB', imaginative—Right Brain or 'RB'), planning (linear—LB, visual-temporal—RB), decision-making (rational/lateral—LB, creative—RB), and innovation (LB-RB balancing), goal-setting (LB), and vision formation (RB).

The second type, we have named as *People and Social Engagement (PSE)*. The PSE type of people enjoys interacting with people—speaking and listening, one-to-one, one-to-a few or one-to-many. These people use their 'communicative apparatus' consisting of larynx, pharynx, vocal chord, mouth cavity, tongue, nasal passage, windpipe, respiratory mechanism, eyes and ears. They are relatively stronger in communicative brain skills (namely, clear, articulate and specific communication—LB/ artistic and colourful communication—RB).

The third and last type, we call *Physical Engagement (PE)*. The PE type enjoys physical activities and movement, indoor and outdoor, using their muscles, bones, joints, ligaments and tendons—the 'muscular skeletal apparatus'. They are relatively stronger than the other two types of working personalities in physical and sensory-motor brain skills (namely, problem-solving using the logical route—LB, problem-solving using the imaginative/creative route—RB).

All of us have these three components in our personality; but one of them may be more dominantly present and active in one individual than the other two. However, there are some people where two of these components are equally strong such as SE: 40, PSE: 40 and PE: 20 or PSE: 45, PE: 45 and SE: 10; or PSE: 35, PE: 35 and SE: 30. There are only a few people, who constitute a rare species, who have all these three personality components present in them in equal proportions.

Mr Manager, in the practice of *conscious management*, you will have to identify your WP to canalise your energy in the most effective manner. In managing and leading others in an organisation or in the family you will study the WPs of others and utilise them accordingly to produce the best results.

THE LEFT BRAIN-RIGHT BRAIN THEORY

You are already aware that the human brain can be compared to a two-storied structure where the ground floor is the 'creaturely' portion inherited from our primate and ape-like ancestors and the first floor which is most developed in human beings represents the 'human mind'.

The entire brain is made of two hemispheres joined up by the *corpus callosum* tissue bridge. The left side of the brain controls the right side of the body whereas the right brain controls the left side as the nerves originating from our brain is cross-laterally laid out.

The other interesting thing is that there are distinctions between people as far as *handedness* is concerned. There are right-handed persons (RHP) who are stronger and more active on the right side of the body. The left-handed persons (LHP) are oriented, since birth, in just the opposite way. Any change of handedness for any regular daily habit such as eating and writing would lead to 'nature-nurture conflict' and is most likely to affect the normal functioning of the upper brain particularly adversely.

For a RHP, the left upper brain is the thinking and planning mind as it is where the power of intelligence and logical-analytical-rational thinking is located; and, the right upper brain is the feeling and man managing mind as it is responsible for all feelings, imaginative thinking, creativity and motivation.

LATERAL THINKING—A LEFT BRAIN ACTIVITY

Lateral thinking, propounded by Edward de Bono in the late 1960s and popularised in the 1970s and 1980s, is a systematic approach to thinking out of the way (non-traditionally/non-conventionally). Bono has devised a number of formal techniques and tools for engaging the brain in lateral thinking.

Let us now try and add value to the knowledge that Bono has been sharing with us through his publications and courses. *Lateral thinking* is essentially a left-brain activity. Bono also confirms this in his own way, when he writes:

> "If an idea is not logical in hindsight then we would have no way of seeing the value of that idea and it would simply be a 'crazy' idea. If every valuable creative idea is indeed logical in hindsight, then it is only natural to suppose, and to claim, that such ideas could have been reached by logic in the first place and that creativity is unnecessary. This is the main reason why, culturally, we have never paid serious attention to creativity [3]".

Any imaginary idea—absolutely wild in nature, arising from the right half of our upper brain must be tested thoroughly with logic to make it acceptable to others and marketable, in that sense. Artistic creativity is not the brain skill that we mean by the term 'creativity' as is being discussed here. The creativity, which is our current concern and would benefit organisations, is 'practical creativity' (which is 'innovation' really).

BARRIERS TO LATERAL THINKING

The creativity, that Bono talks about, as the product of his *lateral thinking* activity is the ability to change concepts and perceptions. Thus, the main barrier to lateral thinking is an individual's inherent resistance to change and closed-mindedness.

The other significant barrier is posed by the belief that ideas just come like windfalls and mental flashes to some lucky people and, therefore, those cannot be generated by planning and using formal techniques.

Another barrier is the fear from which some people suffer that their ideas would not be accepted instead would be criticised and ridiculed by others although they have the ability to think and perceive differently.

People normally do not realise and also do not want to realise that generation of new ideas is just a matter of *conscious brain skills management*. Creative thinking (in Bono's language *lateral thinking*) is a special type of information handling. It should find its place alongside the other methods of handling information: mathematics, logical analysis, computer simulation, and so on.

LATERAL THINKING *VIS-À-VIS* THE WORKING PERSONALITY PRINCIPLE

While it is true that there are people who are highly creative by nature, as all individuals have all the three personality components (namely, SE, PSE and PE) present in them, it is possible for all to indulge in lateral thinking. Nevertheless, when it is a question of taking a decision in a non-routine way or finding a novel solution to a problem, it would come naturally and spontaneously to SE type of individuals. But, when the context is that of applying the lateral thinking method to communication or inter-personal transaction, it would come easily to the PSE individual. When the problem is one of thinking out new physical activities to produce the same results as standard physical activities or even better results (as in the case of 'motion study' for 'work simplification') it would suit the PE type better.

Generally, it is observed that an individual can be more creative on her or his own with the use of the proper brain skills rather than assigning the task of producing some creative ideas to a group through group 'brainstorming'—a process which had its origin in the advertising world. An open-minded person sitting down with the conscious intention of managing her or his brain skills (using a lateral thinking technique) systematically to generate an idea in a certain area should represent a normal state of affairs.

MOTIVATING SELF AND OTHERS THROUGH CONSCIOUS BRAIN SKILLS MANAGEMENT

When you take a decision, solve a problem or generate a new idea by managing your brain skills systematically using tools and techniques of lateral thinking or creativity, you feel motivated and the 'feel good' hormones fill your brain. Same thing happens when you encourage others to manage their brain skills well to produce good results. So, it is a good method for effective performance management. Brain skills management makes people interested in what they are doing; so they are more focused when they perform. It gives the possibility of some sort of achievement to everyone and makes life more fun and more interesting. It provides a framework for working with others as a team.

SOME BASIC TOOLS FOR CONSCIOUS BRAIN SKILLS MANAGEMENT

Focus: For effective brain skills management, *focus* is a very essential basic requirement. You have to avoid all distractions and concentrate on the problem, topic or project where you want your brain skills to be applied at a particular instance. For instance, when you're trying to find out ways and means of managing your time much better than at present, you must 'visualise' with full focus on where your time is being spent currently every day and also what you are looking for as your 'goal'.

Challenge: *Challenge* the existing idea by asking questions: Why is it done this way? Has it got to be done this way? Could there be any other ways of doing it? 'Challenge' is synonymous with 'provocation'—provoke yourself as much as possible to find out as many alternatives as you can. Evaluate each alternative by using the PP (Plus Points)—MP (Minus Points)—MIP (Most Interesting Points) technique for choosing the best.

A SPECIAL *LATERAL THINKING* TECHNIQUE: THE 'SIX THINKING HATS'

This *lateral thinking* technique, proposed by Edward de Bono represents six different thinking behaviours [4].

In this technique:
- The *white hat* represents data and information presented on a two-dimensional space having a white background, such as paper or a computer screen.
- The *red hat* has to do with emotions and feelings (including intuition and hunches).
- The *black hat* represents the 'control-oriented' style of behaviour—critical judgement, blunt and tactless assertiveness, and straight talk.
- The *yellow hat* is for optimism and the logical, positive view of things.
- The *green hat* is for new ideas and creative thinking.
- The *blue hat* is for setting the agenda for thinking, summaries, conclusions and decisions. It is generally used by the conscious leader of a team for organising and controlling the thinking process.

How to Use this Technique Gainfully

In a group discussion, each member of the group ought to find out first which of the six hats fits her or him best; and, as the discussion or the meeting starts, announce which hat she/he will be using most of the time. If there are more than one individual in a group in whose case one particular type of hat suits best, then there should be conscious pro-active cooperation rather than impulsive reactive competition amongst them which manifests usually through overt argumentation and spoils the purpose of the meeting.

An individual can also use the six *thinking hats*, one at a time for any exploratory study. The sequence of wearing the hats will, nevertheless, vary with the subject, the situation, and with the purpose of the study. Instead of using all the hats one after another, one can even use one or two of them selectively as the need may be in a particular case.

This technique can also be used for 'conscious' team-building and team performance management where the leader has the option or authority of choosing his team members.

EXERCISES FOR YOUR SELF-DEVELOPMENT

Exercise 1

(This exercise is meant for knowing your own *working personality*.)

Question: If you are asked to develop a totally new idea, what would you do? Choose any three in order of your own preference as 1, 2 and 3. Then associate each of your chosen options to a particular *working personality (WP)* type or a combination/mix of two types.

Answer

- You would do some thinking and try to work out a new idea logically.
- You would visit somebody whom you consider more knowledgeable than yourself and borrow her/his idea.
- You would wait for a windfall inspiration to dawn upon you.
- You would assign the task to a brainstorming group and encourage every group member to throw up new ideas and finally you'll facilitate to select some novel idea from amongst those suggested by the people present.

Lateral Thinking and Other Approaches to Conscious Brain Skills... **151**

- You would go to the library, search the racks, get some books and magazines, bring them to the reading table and hunt for some new idea.
- You will start calling up people on the phone and try to reach a few others through the Internet seeking their suggestions for new ideas.

Exercise 2

You are working in an organisation where your duty starts at 8.00 am. Strict discipline is valued in your organisation and thus there is no grace period.

You are single and have rented a room where you stay alone. Mid-day meal is no problem for you as you get it at a highly subsidised rate in your office canteen. For your dinner, you have an arrangement with a local hotel and they deliver the evening meal daily at your place in a tiffin carrier. The problem is with your early morning breakfast. Let us try and understand why it is a problem for you.

You are picked up and dropped every day by your office transport. From your place of residence the pick-up point is just 15 to 20 minutes' walk. You are supposed to be picked up at 7.00 am sharp. Your travelling time in the office transport is around 55 minutes. If everything goes well, you reach your workplace at 7.55 am. To meet this schedule you'll have to leave your residence at 6.40 am.

Now about your personal chores. You take 25 to 30 minutes in your toilet and 10 minutes for dressing up. You have to go to the toilet at 6.00 am at the latest.

Now about your morning meal. Your mother has given you strict instruction to have one or two eggs in the morning with toast. But, you do not get any time to prepare the egg and the toast although you have the raw materials readily available with you. You set the alarm to wake you up at 5.30 am but you cannot leave the bed before 6.00 am on any single day.

So, think out a few alternative ways of organising yourself so that you can have adequate time available to you for having your breakfast. Remember to include the preparation time as well as eating time.

Exercise 3

Fill in the right-hand column by your *lateral thinking* inputs (at least one idea for each row):

	Left-hand Column *(Routine/Standard Thinking)*	*Right-hand Column* *(Lateral Thinking)*
Time management improves	By enforcing time discipline	
Quality improves	By conforming to the Quality Standards	
Productivity improves	By increasing the speed of work	
Cost is saved	By controlling and reducing expenditure	
Profit is improved	By increasing the difference between revenue and expenditure over a particular period of time	
Safety is improved	By reducing accidents	
Information flow is improved	By making it a point to ensure proper message transmission and reception by cross-checking and/or seeking feedback	

Exercise 4

(The task in this exercise is always to form a known word either at the end or at the beginning of the letters already with you. Whatever you do, this basic requirement must be fulfilled. Only in exceptional cases, you can break this rule, disrupt the structural arrangement of the letters and introduce a new structure for the word.)

- The first letter that is given to you is A.
- This is followed by T; so you form AT.
- The next letter is R. Now if you put it after AT, ATR does not make any sense. So, you put R before AT and RAT makes sense.
- The next letter given to you is E. If you put it after R, RATE makes sense.

- Now you get a G and when you put it in front, GRATE makes sense.

Now, the next letter supplied to you is T. What should you do that the new word makes good sense?

Exercise 5

Choose any two problems that you are currently facing in your job and functional area which have got to be solved with practical creativity. You have 20 to 30 minutes to identify the two problems, do brainstorming, and come up with innovative solutions which ought to be acceptable to all the people involved and who may be directly or indirectly affected when you implement the solution. You will have to make an oral presentation and submit a brief write-up containing all the salient features, not exceeding 150 to 200 words.

Exercise 6

You use your telescopic thinking ability to anticipate two future problems which may affect your performance in 2 to 3 months' time. Now, manage your brain skills *proactively* to find out three alternative solutions to each of those two problems that you strongly feel you're going to face in the proximal future (Exercise 5 was one of *reactive* brain skills management where the problem is already there and you attack it reactively to find solutions. You could not anticipate those problems from beforehand).

From the above two exercises, namely, Exercise 5 and Exercise 6, we suppose you have become clear about the distinction between *reactive* and *proactive brain skills management*.

Exercise 7

A big festival is just a couple of weeks away. You and a few of your friends have decided to invest some money each to set up a stall for making and selling 'novelty omelette' at a location where there will be high demand and low competition.

You have to prepare a project report outlining all the following details: perspectives and prospects (demand and supply situation and the nature of competition based on some assumed demographic data); people (prospective customers—their age group, eating habits, taste etc.); place (feasible locations); product (totally novel designs in shape, size, colour, taste, smell—what special additives you propose to use and how you are going to serve it); price (including proposals for discount structure); placement (how will you distribute the product to your customers—from the stall/home-delivery/take-away service and so on); promotion (how are you going to promote the product and give it a good publicity); planning (the stall layout, distribution of duties and responsibilities, daily sales/ production targets, daily income-expenditure-profitability, total investment required and source of funds); performance (daily work schedule); post-performance review and plan readjustment (anticipation of threats and proposed precautionary measures for facing threats).

Use the *Six Thinking Hats* technique for coming up with a feasible proposal. Try to relate each stream of thinking to a specific thinking hat.

REFERENCES

[1] Ganguli, Siddhartha, *Performance Management: First Time Right*, Platinum Publishers, Kolkata, 2008.
[2] Ganguli, Siddhartha, *Live Happily, Work Happily*, Allied Publishers, New Delhi, 2009.
[3] Bono, Edward de, *Serious Creativity*, Indus (An Imprint of Harper Collins Publishers India), New Delhi, Impression 1993, p. ix.
[4] Bono, Edward de, *Serious Creativity*, loc. cit, pp. 77–85.

KEY TAKE-HOMES

- Could there be a better and a non-conventional way of doing something than how it is being done at present? If such a thought-process is nurtured by you then it is the dawn of *lateral thinking* in your mind. 'Lateral thinking' is just a little change laterally without deviating from the mainstream.
- In the practice of *conscious management,* you will have to identify your *Working Personality (WP)*—what type of work you enjoy most, to canalise your energy in the most effective manner. In *managing* and *leading* others in an organisation or in the family, you will study the *WP* of others and utilise them accordingly to get the maximum return on the investment of *human capital*.
- *Lateral thinking* is an activity of the intelligent-logical-rational Left Brain (LB) in right-handed people. It follows an 'assembly line' or 'chain link' type of thinking process and the thinker does not get convinced without justifiable hard data. However, the lateral thinking process, in practice, gets interfered with some barriers. So the lateral thinker has to be aware if any barrier is standing in the way and take the right steps to remove it.
- Any wild imaginary idea, which is the product of the Right Brain (RB) in a right-handed person can be tested with logic and reasoning to make it marketable and acceptable to others. Such practical creativity would be regarded as *innovation*.

CHAPTER 14

Conscious Communication for Relationship-Building

DIFFERENT STAGES OF OUR LIFE

Childhood, boyhood/girlhood, and adolescence are the specific stages of our life when we *learn* by seeing, hearing, listening, reading and doing in the campuses of schools, colleges, universities, and career-providing institutions. The first two are the stages of our life when we are largely 'dependent' on others.

Adolescence—the turbulent teens, represents the stage of life where one displays 'independent' behaviour and tries to prove that he is in no way less knowledgeable or less intelligent. Many of the youngsters belonging to this age group learn to have access to the vast world of information through the internet. They feel they have the information power. Right after adolescence, there is an increased tendency in the youngsters for information sharing. Many of them try to depend upon logical and rational thinking—a propensity which we learn to carry from the post-adolescence and pre-youth stage of life.

Post-adolescence (21+ to 25 years) is the gateway to the phase of 'inter-dependence' or strong 'herding' and 'flocking' instincts—typical of the youth (25+ to 35 years) when the individual embarks upon a career and sets up a family.

Post-youth (35+ to 45 years) and *young old age* (45+ to 60 years) may be called the 'second adolescence' when the individual wants to feel and

Conscious Communication for Relationship-Building **157**

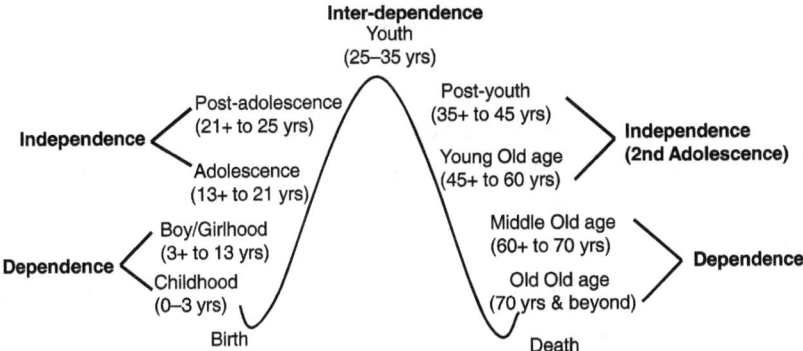

Fig. 14.1: Dependence-Independence-Interdependence-
Independence-Dependence Cycle
(Please note the 2nd adolescence here)

behave 'independently' by virtue of age and acquisition of experience (see Figure 14.1). A generation gap is automatically created between them and the younger generation people as the former group of people has the knowledge and experience power which are much more relevant at the workplace than information power which is the forte of those who are in their 20s and 30s.

Although the post-youth and the young old groups of people may feel that their thoughts and opinions have an objective base, in reality they have a more subjective viewpoint than others, being influenced by their own personal ideas. 'This trait is typically present among people in midlife and beyond who are generally less subject to the 'herd' behaviour that is so prevalent among youth' [1].

The phase of 'dependence' makes a re-appearance from the onset of the middle old age (60+ years).

All these different stages of life have been illustrated in Figure 14.1 with their normal relationship with 'dependence', 'independence' and 'inter-dependence'. However, an individual may behave differently from the norm and pose an exception to the rule. In *conscious management*, Mr Manager, these behavioural patterns—the normals and their exceptions, must be taken cognizance of in managing and leading individuals and groups at the workplace and in the family.

LEFT BRAIN-RIGHT BRAIN INVOLVEMENT

From the tender age of four or five, up to the age of 35, an individual's mental perspectives are commonly associated with the left side of the brain, being automatically canalised or guided that way by the educational and professional development systems as long as the young individual is performing in the 'student role' and thereafter by the methods, systems, procedures and processes of the work organisation when he is engaged in his 'work roles'. Then there is a gradual shift to the more intuitive and feelings-based perspectives which are characteristics of the right side of the brain [2].

Right brain is the seat of feelings. Therefore, if a young man or lady, who is a relatively newcomer in the organisation, wants to build up a cordial and congenial relationship with an old-timer who has crossed that age group and is a storehouse of practical knowledge and experience, the right gateway would be the right brain. And, for relationship-building, effective communication is the only tool. Therefore, one has to develop the power of *conscious communication*.

THEORY OF HUMAN RELATIONSHIPS

When you meet someone for the first time, it is just the stage of getting to know each other. Once you have come to know each other reasonably well, you have entered into the 'acquaintance phase' of human relationship. This means both of you have created a space for each other in the 'acquaintance zone' of your minds. Do you remember the 'dwelling house' model of human personality that we had introduced and discussed in chapter 8? 'Acquaintance zone' represents the 'drawing room' of your mind. It also stands for the 'comfort zone' where you feel comfortable and relaxed while interacting with your acquaintances.

However, the relationships pertaining to the 'comfort zone' or 'acquaintance zone' are loose relationships. It is certainly not the 'made for each other' situation. Real tight relationships pertain to the 'intimacy zone' when you become happy and feel really great in each others' company as you share some common interests—the same 'likes' and also the same 'dislikes' may be. Here comes the 'compatibility' factor. The more compatible you are with another person, the more comfortable you feel in her or his company and a 'happy' relationship develops when both compatibility and comfort are at their peaks.

True leaders set, as one of their primary goals, happy relationships with all, as much as feasible. All that we have discussed above are pictorially represented in Figures 14.2 and 14.3.

Effective relationships can be built only with the help of conscious communication.

There is yet another very interesting aspect. The most effective relationship-building happens with love. With more and more love, the comfort, happiness and tolerance limits increase as illustrated in Figure 14.2.

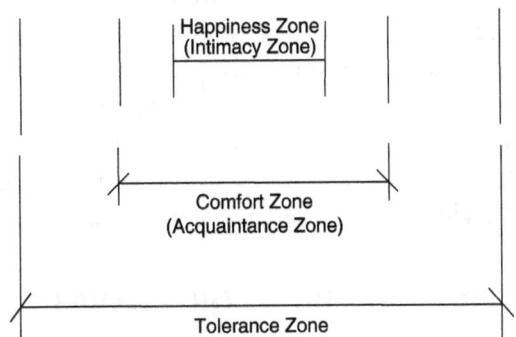

Fig. 14.2: Human Relationship *vis-à-vis* Happiness
(Love increases the 'comfort', 'happiness' and 'tolerance' zones and limits)

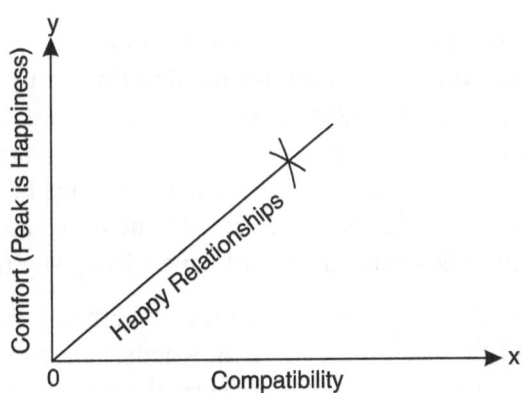

Fig. 14.3: Compatibility *vs.* Happiness in Human Relationships

WHAT IS COMMUNICATION

Communication is the expression of ideas, thoughts, feelings and opinions. It is also necessary for sharing of information. Most of our waking time, we spend in some form of 'communication'. Even when we are alone, thoughts pass through our minds and this form of communication is called 'self-talk' or 'mind-chatter'. During the 'dreaming' phase of our sleep also, we are communicating to ourselves, within our own mind.

MODES OF COMMUNICATION

Basically, one can say, that there are two modes of communication: *verbal* (what we express through a word-based language) and *non-verbal* (what we express through our postures, whole body movements, gestures, facial expressions, inter-personal distance and tone of the voice with its different modulations reflecting different attitudes, moods and emotions).

But, then, looking from another angle, we have different communication media. These are oral (spoken) written, auditory, (radio, telephone, cassette, CD, public address system), visual (sketches, paintings, diagrams, charts, tables, maps, route maps, posters, banners, billboards, cinema slides, 35mm slides, OHP transparencies, printed media, glow signs, signboards, traffic signals, computers, power point presentation), and audio-visual (TV, video, CD, cinema, computers).

COMMUNICATION: NATURAL OR LEARNT

While the 'non-verbal' part of the communication is natural or inherent to us, the 'verbal' or language-based part is learnt or acquired after birth, depending upon the social environment where we are brought up.

Human history is more than 2.5 to 3.0 million years old, whereas the ancient languages were introduced, for the first time, only a few thousand years (the general belief is 10,000 years, although we are not sure about it) ago. While it is true that the power of verbal communication has put man on the highest step of the evolutionary ladder, language being of relatively recent origin and linguistic ability being a skill acquired only after birth, in our language expression most of us still have a long way to go.

Speaking is a power, which comes from specific areas in the temporal lobe of the left side of the human brain. Then, whether one would be strong or relatively weak as far as speaking is concerned, depends to a certain extent on the construction and activities of the left brain's speech areas and, of course, on the learning part from childhood to adulthood.

WHAT DO WE MEAN BY *CONSCIOUS COMMUNICATION*

Let us go back to the 'dwelling house' model of human personality once again (see Figure 8.1). Just as much the kitchen of our family apartment or house functions as a food production unit, the kitchen of our mind serves us as the production centre of all our behaviour expressed through our communication—non-verbal as well as verbal—both in the oral and written forms.

Have you ever used a pressure cooker in your kitchen and, in case you've not, do you know how it functions? When a pressure cooker is used for cooking, neither can we see the inside penetrating our vision through the stainless steel body of the cooking vessel nor can we control the cooking process by reaching inside it in order to add some ingredient or water, if we suddenly decide as a result of an after-thought. Such actions are most conveniently and freely possible when we use some pots and pans for cooking in the conventional way by placing them on the oven. Pressure cooking is thus not within our control whereas traditional cooking is.

Let us draw an analogy now. The behaviour and communication which are emerging spontaneously and totally unconsciously from our *creaturely brain*, based on our creaturely psychological features, can be compared to pressure cooking, being outside our conscious control. Much though we may want to control it, sometimes it automatically comes out. *Conscious communication* is the one which is planned and implemented or delivered according to the needs of the situation or tailored to meet the requirements and expectations of the single receiver, more than one receiver, or a group of receivers. It is thus the pots-and-pans cooking situation.

Conscious communication is essential in order to get maximum cooperation from the people with whom you interact. Remember, you must follow the *principle of interdependence* (see Figure 14.1).

COMMON BARRIERS IN COMMUNICATION AND HOW TO OVERCOME THEM

One-way *vs.* Two-way (with Check-back/Feedback) Communication

Oral communication, which is our commonest activity, involves both speaking and listening. The speaker is the 'transmitter'.... he is transmitting a message and the person to whom he speaks is the 'receiver'—he must concentrate to receive the message. Very often, in our daily lives, we say something but never check back whether the message has been properly received and correctly understood. The receiver also does not respond by giving a feedback whether he has got the message correctly or not. Lack of check-back/feedback thus creates a barrier in the path of effective communication and the result may be an instruction, information, a reporting wrongly transmitted or wrongly received.

In telecommunication, it is always essential for the transmitter to check whether the receiver has got a message clearly by offering to repeat the message and requesting the receiver to point out any confusion or lack of clarity. In the same way, after receiving a message, the receiver on the other side should offer to repeat the message for the transmitter to cross-check.

Oral communication of a 'Message (M)' from the 'Transmitter (T)' to the 'Receiver (R)' is a 'one-way' *open circuit* process, which may lead to problems unless the loop or circuit is *closed* by a 'check-back'/ 'feedback' response. In day-to-day formal and informal, official and unofficial communication, it is essential to follow the '2-way communication principle', which is possible in the case of face-to-face, telephonic communication, fax, and voice-mail. Written communication, even e-mail has its limitations in this respect.

Golden Communication Formula

Many a times, we call up somebody or respond to a telephone call, very rudely because we do not make it a point to maintain *politeness*. This sort of callous attitude hurts the person on the other side....he considers it to be impolite. So, make it a point to follow a general 'golden communication formula' while playing the dual role of transmitter as well as receiver:

P: Start positively and politely to give pleasure.
L: Listen actively without interruption when the other person is talking.
E: Empathise with the other person (get into his shoes, cross into his world).
A: Attract attention of the receiver while speaking by being polite, humorous, vividly descriptive, specific, and interesting, as appropriate.

S: **Short**: Your whole message must be broken into '**short**' parts—not given at a stretch in one go, as our ears are not trained to listen and receive a message systematically; after giving a part, the transmitter must check back whether proper reception has taken place... only then the next portion should be transmitted; every word should be pronounced clearly and loudly enough to facilitate good reception.

- **Slow:** The speaking speed should be '**slow**' (approximately, 100 to 110 words per minute) so that proper reception can take place. Our ears neither have the capacity, nor are they trained, to receive fast messages.

- **Soft**: The tone of the voice, while transmitting or responding should be **'soft'**—it should not be commanding or terrorising, nor should it be too shrill and high-pitched reflecting aggressive mentality.
- Throughout speaking and responding, the quality of the voice should be kept **'strong'**, exuberating confidence.
- It is also important to maintain a **'steady'** voice without much ups-and-downs.
- The words to be used should be **'sweet' 'simple'** and **'specific'**. Harsh, rude, abusive, complicated, too technical jargonistic words and mannerisms should be avoided. It is equally important to avoid round-about or vague way of expressing things instead of being 'specific'.
- **Superlative positive:** In any language, when we want to express emphatically we use, either 'superlative positive' (such as, 'grand', fantastic', 'excellent', 'too good', 'remarkable', 'gorgeous', 'great' etc.) when we share our positive attitude, or, 'superlative negative' (such as 'too bad', 'horrible', 'horrifying', 'nasty', 'ridiculous' etc.) words, when we have a negative mind set. Develop the good habit of using only **superlative (positive)** words.

  (You have now got an easy-to-remember '10-S formula' for ascertaining to what extent your present style of communication is effective and where is the scope for your improvement).

E: End positively to give pleasure when you finish your conversation either as a 'transmitter' or as a 'receiver'; even if there had been a little heat generated in course of the conversation, the ending should be such that no hard feelings are left.

Personal Ego and Emotion Management

Mind you, when you are communicating officially, you are representing your organisation and your organisation's reputation is at stake if you bring your personal ego and emotions into your communication transactions.

Be Conscious about the Non-verbal Components

In face-to-face communication you should be extra careful to avoid negative body language signals (aggressive, jerky, signals like wielding the index finger as a 'baton', chopping, thumping, cutting and tapping as well as defensive freezing signals such as stiff postures, keeping hands and fingers hidden and away from the other person's sight). In telephone communication, since the body language of either party is not visible, you should concentrate on the tone of your voice, clarity of speaking, proper voice modulations, and choice of appropriate words and presenting them in the most effective manner. In this context, the '10-S formula' should prove to be useful.

Ensure Effective 'Transmission'

With many of us, it so happens that something goes wrong with our transmission. And, if transmission turns out to be defective, reception at the receiver's end also turns out to be ineffective.

Therefore, to overcome such a common barrier, we have to make use of a practical 'Transmitter' formula called 'TAG,'

- T: Translating your ideas, thoughts, feelings and information into a meaningful, purposeful message (every communication event has a purpose or objective and the message should be formulated and managed in such a way that the purpose is served, the objective is fulfilled).
- A: Attracting attention of the receiver (by establishing and cross-checking 'eye contact' as eye contact denotes attention; if eye contact is disengaged, to restore attention, you may take the help of the most helpful attention-providers like humour, case studies, anecdotes, vivid narration, diverting to a subject which the receiver likes).
- G: Getting a proper feedback message from the receiver, whether he has followed or not, whether he has agreed or not; if the feedback is not positive, then the transmitter has to see what has gone wrong where…if clarity is lacking then suitable clarification has to be provided—if supporting data is required, it should be organised.

Ensure Effective 'Reception'

Similarly, on many occasions, when we are playing the 'receptor' role the quality of reception becomes poor. To overcome the problems that such poor reception may lead to, a practical 'Receptor' or 'R' formula called 'EAR' ought to be followed.

In this formula,
- E: Establishing and maintaining free, natural eye contact.
- A: Attending to the message, with whole-hearted attention, without any interruption in between.

R: Responding to the message through an appropriate feedback. (if you have to disagree, disagree agreeably.... don't be bluntly straightforward in giving a negative feedback...instead, you have to be very diplomatic and tactful).

Organise Your 'Self-talk'

Any communication, before it is expressed orally or in written form, starts with a self-talk, meaning the thoughts and feelings passing through the mind. This 'self-talk' part has to be properly organised, otherwise the message expressed may be incomplete, unclear, garbled, confusing. If there is a fear of failure and fear of facing embarrassment (due to such failure), lack of confidence, or self-doubt, it will reflect in negative body language signals and improper tone of voice and disarranged words and sentences. Organisation of 'self-talk' requires just a little bit of self-discipline (one need not be vibrant with a high degree of self-confidence). The first question that you should ask yourself are: 'why' am I communicating; 'what' is the purpose or objective of my communication; 'what' do I want to achieve? Get a clear answer, to each. Next, ask yourself: 'with whom' am I communicating; what is the level of that person; what is my relationship with him; what are his 'likes' and 'dislikes'; what other special features are there in his psychology? You will choose your words, pitch your tone, select your body language and tonal signals, having all these information at the back of your mind.

Thirdly, you must know 'where' the communication is going to take place. In your own territory, you feel psychologically more confident... in the receiver's territory he feels stronger. Where both the transmitter and the receiver are equally strong, they must choose a neutral territory, where both will have the same confidence and mental strength level.

Fourthly, the timing of communication (that is 'when' the communication is taking place) is very important. Morning time, when our mind and body are fresh, is well-suited for complex, difficult communication; whereas, as the day advances, we become fatigued... so, afternoon and evenings should be kept for routine communication—routine instruction, routine reporting, sharing of routine information. Besides, you must ensure that the other person is free and ready for your message. If he is busy, he will not have any time to listen to you.

Based on specific answers to the four fundamental questions: why, with whom, where, and when, one has to decide on what to communicate and how. The basic objective in any communication (inter-personal or inter-group) event is to achieve a 'win-win' situation… meaning, both the transmitter and the receiver will be happy. 'I win—You lose' (power) or 'I lose—You win' (sacrificing) styles of communication should be avoided in 80% cases. Only in 20% cases, where one of these styles may be specially called for, one can adopt… otherwise not.

Be Conscious about Others' Creaturely Psychological Needs

We, human beings, despite our educational enlightenment and sophistication, have not been able to transcend a few creaturely psychological features, which have remained ingrained into our brain, as legacies of our animal past.

These features are (I suppose you remember them; still they are so important I feel no hesitation to repeat them here as it is very contextual):

- Everybody wants to 'win'; nobody wants to lose (so, as already highlighted, generally try to create a 'You win—I also win' communication situation).
- Everybody has a strong need for attention, affiliation, acceptance/ acknowledgement, and appreciation (Give a patient hearing when somebody talks with your sustained positive eye contact, show him respect, make him feel important, rather than making him stop abruptly showing your disinterest or disagreement; accept him by using your love and compassion despite his shortcomings; acknowledge his contribution in the outcome of any assignment where he was also involved with you and give him due credit instead of stealing credit from him; allow him to make suggestions and participate in decision-making, recognise him as a member of your affinity group, and appreciate his good points and any achievements).
- Nobody likes a direct attack (Do not criticise or disagree with somebody directly and abruptly; as already indicated, you can be assertive but with tact and diplomacy).

MUST WE LISTEN

Listen to Make Others Feel Important

Must we listen? By listening to others, are we not losing our importance? Pause for a moment and ponder. Rather than seeking importance yourself, it is important for you to make others feel important and listening attentively, without interruption, when others talk is an excellent way of giving honour. And, when you listen, remember to establish and maintain a link with the speaker through positive eye contact. Listening is an undervalued part of oral communication since each of us wants to feel important by making others listen to what we say. Perhaps it's an act which we have copied from our parents as young kids when they used to say very strongly in a commanding tone: 'Listen to us what we say!', 'Be quiet! Don't speak up!', and so on.

Listen Consciously

And, when you listen, listen *consciously*. *Conscious listening* would mean you analyse the context as well as the contents of the message: what is the speaker's purpose for communicating; why is she communicating in the specific way that she is; is it a command or an instruction, or sharing of information, or a feedback, or just a friendly remark.

Listen to Analyse the Message

You apply your brain's executive function to concentrate on the message being transmitted by the speaker to segregate the most important or interesting points and plus points from the minus points. Why—do you know? Get the answer below.

Respond by Using the 'Sandwich Technique'

While offering your feedback or comment, you must not be reactive (overtly negative by showing your irritation or frustration). Instead, be responsive and proactive by appreciating the most important or interesting points (and, if there are none such points, then some of the plus points). Thereafter, you put the minus points or the points with which you do not agree, indirectly in the form of a question: 'Don't you think….?', 'Don't you feel…?' etc. and top it up with some plus points. Such listening and post-listening activities constitute the key for effective inter-personal relationship building and relationship management. We call this proactive strategy the 'sandwich technique' and if you can use it properly, it is extremely effective, leading to a 'I win—you also win' situation.

Listen to Understand Each Other

Don't you think that the best way to understand a person is by listening? And, the reverse is also true. A true listener is much more understood than a non-stop, compulsive talker. Good listeners never suffer from loneliness which extroverted big talkers do and they have a positive energy that makes you want their company.

While listening, you must agree or acknowledge by a simple nod of the head, make a conscious effort not to let your mind wander or ask an occasional question or comment to recap what has been said and to ensure that you're on the same wavelength as the speaker.

KEY RESULT FACTORS TO BE FOLLOWED IN CONSCIOUS COMMUNICATION

('Key Result Factors' or 'KRFs' are the main factors which produce effective results.)

- *Time:* Time management in communication is most important. Neither the transmitter's, nor the receiver's time should be wasted. Message should be specific, crisp and clear.
- *Quality:* In communication, quality must be maintained so that the other person feels good throughout. Quality of communication depends upon the personal quality of the transmitter and the receiver both. The best quality of communication is maintained through direct interaction (face-to-face, on phone, or through exchange of e-mail) not using any via media or indirect method/mode. Best amongst them, of course, is the face-to-face mode as you can watch each other's body language. In phone conversation, you have to base your judgement on the voice characteristics only. The written mode including e-mail, although it has the plus point of creating a record or documentation, your judgement of the writer would require a lot of skill to reach near perfection.
- *Productivity/Speed:* While the speed of speaking should be maintained generally at 100 to 120 words per minute, the message must be 'productive'. In other words, the desired objective must be fulfilled and the goals reached. Plenty of fluffy and flowery communication, without any solid results, is useless.
- *Cost/Economy:* In communication, visible costs are the cost of equipment engagement time, long distance calls, and the invisible costs contain the cost of personal time of the transmitter and the receiver.

Every communication event must be cost-effective. There should be regular communication cost-audit. Standard economic guidelines should also be provided.
- *Income/Cash Inflow/Profitability:* Communication activities must be properly prioritised and planned. Those communication events that would lead to mobilisation of orders, collection of payments, reduction in costs, supply of equipment/tools/materials, reduction of downtime of plant and equipment, restoration of power/fuel supplies, machineries repairs and maintenance, etc. are top priority communication events. Low priority communication activities should be kept in abeyance and, whenever possible, dispensed with.
- *Safety:* Information/feedback regarding any accidents, health problems should be transmitted/relayed on an emergency basis.
- *Communication:* Communication equipment should be properly maintained—cleaned up and checked up technically, regularly, so that equipment downtime can be avoided. Each individual, in his own way, plays the important twin role of 'transmitter' and 'receiver' in any organisation. The contents and styles of communication of all employees in an organisation cannot be standardised much though one would have liked to do so. Therefore, every employee should indulge in habits and lifestyles leading to good health and fitness so that punctuality and regularity of attendance are maintained. In addition, one has to make sure to remain at his workstation (for urgent visit to other places, message should be passed on in advance indicating the whereabouts and contact details), so that no message is missed and, thereafter, received indirectly in a distorted form.
- *Information:* One has to keep track of what information can be asked for. If such information (facts and figures) is kept handy, no time is wasted and communication also becomes productive and result-oriented. No wrong or fake information should be given to anyone at all. If correct and adequate information are not available handy, one has to enquire how urgently the information is required. If it is not so urgent, then one can take the responsibility of collecting it from the right source and pass it on. In case the information required is most urgent and you do not have it at your disposal but know who can give correct information, it is your responsibility to direct the enquirer to the right person. Communication is an activity dealing essentially with information; so every member must be responsible enough to bear this most important point in mind.

- *Positive Thinking and Open-mindedness:* Every communication activity should be handled with a positive spirit. Even criticism should be regarded as learning opportunities and not as failures or lapses. Mind should be kept open to receive suggestions. In speaking to higher-ups and persons having strong, commanding personality and strangers, lack of confidence should not be allowed to stand as a barrier; success will automatically come if there is a little bit of advance preparation on the lines already discussed earlier.
- *Positive Attitude and Behaviour with All:* The organisational goal is the supreme, personal goal is secondary. Normally, when personal ego rises to the surface of the mind, one may tend to become negative in response to another person's behaviour. Such negative attitude manifests itself either through aggressive argumentation or defensive, suppressive communication. Communication is the behavioural vehicle through which a person's attitude gets reflected. If one can have the personal ego submerged by keeping it under the control of the organisational objectives and goals, then it may not become difficult to keep the attitude and behaviour positive with all.

HUMAN BEINGS: STANDARD *VS.* NON-STANDARD

There are two types of human beings: standard and non-standard. 'Standard' human beings are those who have a standard body—in height, weight and every other aspect. They walk into a ready-made garment store and try out some clothes and walk away with some standard fitting stuff. There are also others who are non-standard in shape and size. They are either too short or too tall—either too thin or too obese. Standard, ready-made garments do not suit their bodies. They must go to a tailor, who will take measurements of their body, cut the fabric and do the stitching as per those measurements and, should there be need allow the person to have one or more trials. People having non-standard bodies must go for tailor-made clothes.

People having standard bodies have standard minds. Their minds work logically and rationally and they get easily convinced provided you can furnish the necessary data to establish your claims. So, you need not work especially hard to influence them; standard talk with some amount of data would serve your purpose.

People having non-standard bodies have non-standard minds. They usually have some mental blocks or suffer from some complexes and idiosyncrasies. They do not get easily convinced even when you have the data to convince them. You have to study their nature and plan your talk or tailor-make your communication to suit their mental profiles. All these features are illustrated in Figure 14.4.

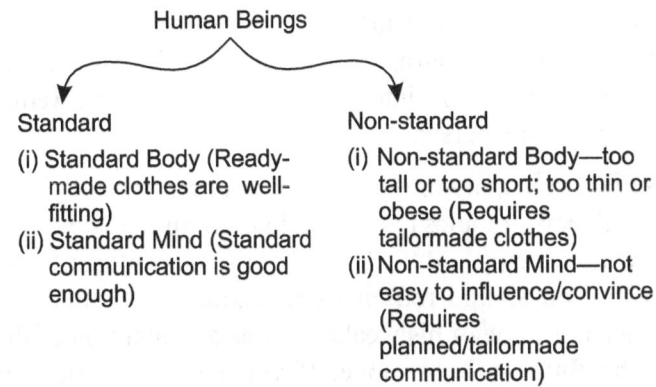

Fig. 14.4: Standard and Non-standard Human Beings

Human Nature Study

Our approach to human nature study is to collect information about an individual's: likes, dislikes, strengths (or plus points), weaknesses (or minus points), and any unique or interesting or special features (see Figure 14.5 below).

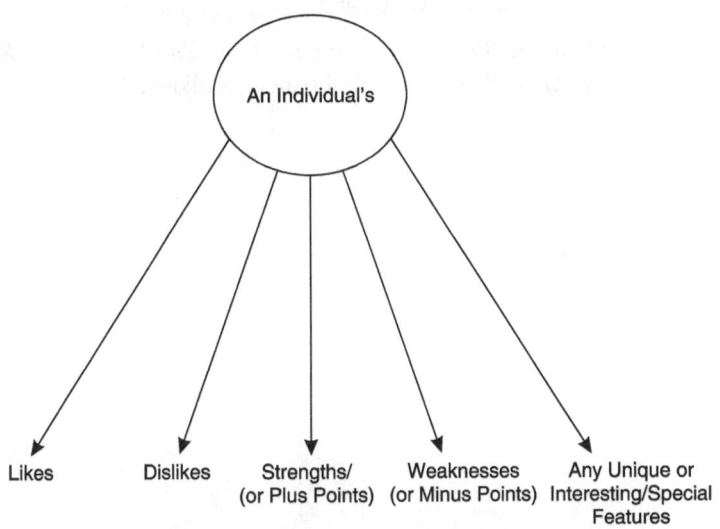

Fig. 14.5: An Individual's Nature Study

In order to do this nature study, you can use the 'LLF' formula where L: Looking around for 'displays' (artificial features like the watch, the pen, the glasses, the tie, the shawl, some photograph or painting, some decorative item, a jewellery, or a book or a magazine or an academic certificate or a prize or trophy) and 'details' (natural features like a beard or a moustache, or the hairline, or the salt-and-pepper combination of the hair and the sideburns). L: Listening with full concentration and eye contact without any interruption; and F: Feeling (empathy and genuine feeling for the person).

How do you apply the findings of your nature study? If you broach one of the subjects or topics the person likes or appreciate some of his 'strengths', he will be happy and 'feel good' hormones will start getting secreted in his brain. You should refrain from talking on a subject that he dislikes or criticising some of his weaknesses as any mention of these would put him in the fight-or-flight mode. If you have identified anything unique or interesting about him and if you highlight it in your communication, he will feel very good and will have a favourable disposition towards him [3].

REFERENCES

[1] Sisodia, Raj, David B. Wolfe and Jag Sheth, *Firms of Endearment: How World-Class Companies Profit from Passion and Purpose"*, Wharton School Publishing (Pearson Education), New Jersey, Fifth Printing, 2008.

[2] Pink, Daniel H., *A Whole New Mind: Moving from the Information Age to the Conceptual Age,* Riverhead Books division of Penguin, New York, 2005.

[3] Ganguli, Siddhartha, *Business Communication: The S-M-A-R-T Roadmap for Your Career Growth*, Platinum Publishers, Kolkata, 2009.

KEY TAKE-HOMES

- In *conscious management*, the different stages of life and their normal relationship with dependent, independent and inter-dependent patterns of behaviour must be noted along with exceptions to the norms. In *managing* and *leading* people, this is one very important aspect to be taken care of.
- *Conscious management* calls for the power of 'conscious communication' for relationship-building and effective relationship management. While you communicate, you have to remain conscious about the negative impact or noises created by any barrier and take the right step to remove it.
- For transmission of a message effectively in speaking or writing (including sending an e-mail or a text message using your cell phone) and also for good reception of any message through listening or reading, you have to follow certain proven techniques.
- In responding to a message to which you may not agree or do not accept, creating a 'You win—I also win' situation is a must.

CHAPTER 15

Conscious Time Management

All great men were 'toiling upwards in the night' while their companions slept!

—Extracts from Longfellow, American poet

The big secret in life is that there is no big secret. Whatever your goal, you can get there, if you're willing to work.

—Oprah Winfrey, American TV Personality

The two statements above imply that success can be achieved through hard work. Isn't it? Well, that would be the understanding of a common man. Let us add to these a third one from the master inventor of all times, Thomas Alva Edison, who had said: 'Success is only 1% inspiration; and 99% perspiration.'

But, is it really so? Do all hard workers reach the end of the success highway and climb the highest peak? Perhaps they do not. Let us examine where *conscious time management* features in bringing us success.

TIME IS OPPORTUNITY: A MATTER OF PERCEPTION

How many of us do realise that every day we are being endowed with a very special free gift, and that is, 86,400 units of opportunity? If we had been conscious of this fact, we would have stopped proceeding any further, down the lines, of this chapter. Nearly all of us are little aware of the reality that there are 24 hrs × 60 minutes × 60 seconds, totalling 86,400 units of time available to each of us each day. And, every unit of time is potent with some opportunity—big, medium or small, if we make it a point to utilise it positively and productively.

Possibly, proper perception of the unparalleled value of time escapes our conscious attention, as time is very much a man-made concept, developed by our ancestors only about eight to ten thousand years ago. It happened only with the dawn of civilisation, although our prehistoric forefathers had been reigning over the living world as the supreme species for 2.5 to 3.0 million years. In the prehistoric era, our predecessors used to follow, in their time management, only the 'day-and-night' and the 'seasonal' cycles. The planet earth used to take, as it still does today, exactly 1440 minutes to rotate on its axis once and precisely 365 and ¼ days to revolve around the sun. The human body used to have, as it still has today, sleep and wake patterns as also hunger and consumption patterns maintained by our 'biological clock' located inside the *hypothalamus* in the lower structures of our brain.

EFFECTIVE TIME MANAGEMENT

For us, in modern times, time management is most valuable as time lost means *missed* or *lost* opportunity and, in today's fast and highly competitive world, we simply cannot afford to miss any opportunity. Therefore, *effective time management* can be described as productive and positive utilisation of time so that every potent opportunity is tapped and we get the maximum return, in tangible and intangible terms, from the time invested by us in any activity.

TIME AUDIT

To ascertain whether you are an effective time manager at your workplace as well as at home, undertake a *time audit* by maintaining a 24-hour time-log for a certain period of time—may be a week, a fortnight, a month, or even three months. In your time-log, note down every significant activity in which you spend a reasonable amount of time, the minimum being 15 to 30 minutes. Keep the record right from the moment you wake up till the time when you go to sleep.

Now, when you are analysing your time spending pattern and segregating the productive and positive utilisation parts from the unproductive and negative utilisation parts, you are indulging yourself in some kind of an audit like a financial or cost auditor whose one main task is to identify the justifiable and the unjustifiable expenses.

You'll have to work on the unproductive and negative parts now separating out the *Time-Wasters (TW)* from the *Time-Killers (TK)* and *Time-Stealers (TS)*. *Time-Wasters* are activities (like, oversleeping, over-sitting at your workplace beyond the normal working hours, idle gossip, slow pace of work, indecision, procrastination etc.), which are very much within your control and you can take the remedial actions to reduce and gradually eradicate them altogether. Depending on the amount of *time-wasters* you have bred, set a target of 'Zero Time-Wasters' (ZTW) over a practically feasible time-frame but not exceeding 2 to 3 months. Regard these as 'Problem-Self (P-S)' and thrash them, one by one or the whole lot in one go with full gusto.

Time-Killers are those unproductive activities, which are not entirely within your control. These include; a feudalistic boss who wants to be surrounded by his subordinates, without any specific purpose, entirely for his self-satisfaction; a dull subordinate who demands a lot of your time and guidance unjustifiably; a telephone caller who goes on talking and does not get off the line even after completing what he has to say or receive specifically. Such *time-killers* can also be tackled by being a little assertive, tactfully and diplomatically, or with cooperation from the other person after you have explained to him your difficulty. When you need the cooperation of another person to sort it out, treat the case as a 'Problem-Pair (P-P)' and get cracking to solve it at the earliest opportunity.

Time-Stealers are activities over which you do not have any direct control. Examples are: lack of planning, in general, in the organisation or in the department; useless, unproductive meetings which go on for hours without serving any meaningful purpose and gainful results; general slow pace of working and sloppy, lethargic work culture. To reduce the incidence of time-stealers, one, two or a few persons cannot play a very useful role, as the problems are fairly widespread. People, at large, have got to be involved in bringing about an improvement and it takes time to bring about any perceptible positive change in such cases. These should be handled as 'Problem-Team (P-T)' but the team members should not exceed five in each team.

TIME BUDGETING: ADVANCE PLANNING

Once you have identified your *time-wasters*, *time-killers* and *time-stealers* and have taken the remedial steps, you will have to start the practice of 'time budgeting' (very much within your control), which is nothing but advance planning of your work activities. Prepare your next day's time budget on the previous day before you leave your workplace.

For such 'advance planning', you have to remember the following practices:

- *Prioritisation*: The 'urgent and important' activities are to be performed first (priority I). Remember the 'First Things First' (FTF) principle. Then, you take up the 'not urgent but important' ones (priority II). The 'urgent but not important' activities will come thereafter (priority III), and the 'not urgent and not important' activities should come last or be dispensed with (See Figure 16.1). This is nothing but the 'ABC Analysis' approach so familiar in the field of *Materials Management & Inventory Control*.
- *Delegation*: If you have a next lower level of people in your team below, some of the tasks, which do not need your personal involvement and can be performed capably by some of your subordinates, should be delegated to them.
- *Biorhythms*: Our physical and mental powers wax and wane corresponding to the day and night cycle. The 'complex', 'most difficult', and 'most disliked' activities are to be scheduled in the morning hours up to the noon. In the mid-day, afternoon, and evening times, simple and routine tasks are to be performed. Meetings and group activities, from which quick concrete results are sought, must be kept between 9.00 and 11.30 am.
- *Free Float*: Do not budget your time every minute to minute. Some free time (called 'free float') must be kept—anything between 30 and 90 minutes, depending on the nature of your work and your own past experience, so that any unscheduled events can be accommodated comfortably and you shall not be overcome by tensions.
- *Stretch Break*: Keep some time gap (5 to 7 minutes) as a break, after every work phase of 60 to 90 minutes, when you leave your workstation and stretch your body and limbs, with intermittent deep breathing practice for effective stress management.
- *General*: The general good habits related to effective time management, that we know of, include: punctuality, regularity, sincerity, fast work speed and hardworking attitude. Along with those, you will have to

inculcate a few more which are not talked about so much, such as, FTR ('First Time Right'), ZD ('Zero Defect'), JIT ('Just In Time'), Minimum 'Make-Ready' and 'Get Ready' Times (respectively at the duty commencement and completion times).

24 HOUR TIME SCHEDULING

A healthy lifestyle would mean that you do not become a *workaholic* (someone who is addicted to work and only works and does not play). Try to avoid taking work from your workplace to your place of residence. Leaving aside the 8 hrs of sleep and 10 hrs (8 working hours + 2 hrs extra for commutation), the balance 6 hours that you have at your disposal should be utilised as: 2 hrs. for personal chores, 1 hour for household and family duties, 2 hrs. quality time to be spent with spouse and children (including having meals, watching TV, listening to music, playing and chatting together), and 1 hour as entirely personal and private time to be spent in 3S (Silence, Solitude, Stillness). Also read the next chapter where tips on 'Work-life Balance' have been provided.

TIME SAVERS

It will be a wise move for you to keep in mind the use of some simple time saving devices and methods, such as: a diary or a desk diary; a daily or weekly planner; a 'To Do' list; checklist; a time schedule (advanced techniques include 'Gantt' chart & 'CPM/PERT' charts); a memory pad or a pocket note book; telephone and mobile; FAX and e-mail.

Meet people only by appointment. Keep track of the traffic situation before going out for an appointment by listening to the FM radio. Be clear about bypasses and alternative routes, which will take you to the same destination. Carry some reading/working material to utilise time well while waiting. Use tactful assertiveness to cut short a meaningless discussion or meeting. To collect, furnish, or report information or documents, practise 'Management by Walking About/Wandering Around' (MBWA). Do not keep any chairs in front of your working desk lest people sit down for an idle chat. For a special discussion, use the conference room or meeting corner. Remember to be very self-organised for effective management of space, paper, and accessories, which, if mismanaged, can cause serious problems.

HIDDEN AGENDA TO BE CHANGED

From our childhood, due to faulty (over-pampered or neglected) upbringing, we get wrongly conditioned and certain negative *hidden agenda* (biased attitude and bad habits) get impregnated inside our mind. These become responsible as barriers, adversely affecting our daily time management practices. These are: morning sickness, late rising; irregular eating, toilet and study habits; procrastination; poor self-organisation; poor (not clear and specific) communication; delay in decision-making and problem solving. There are many more. Such hidden agenda must be changed to incorporate the right kind of agenda inside our mind if we aspire to become effective time managers.

MODERN GADGETS: ACT AS BARRIERS TO PRODUCTIVE AND POSITIVE UTILISATION OF TIME

Bharat Dogra, writing against excessive consumerism and consumption, refers to a most revealing British case study published in *The Daily Telegraph*, which centres around a six-member British family having nine TV sets. All the family members were asked to switch off all the TV sets for three days. The 17-year-old daughter was too adamant to comply. However, a distinct improvement in behaviour was noticed in the three other children who could, in the absence of the idiot box, could seek out and enjoy each other's company although they were missing the entertainment they had been habituated to. Their mother Carol said: 'All sorts of things we had kept putting off doing got done. Bikes requiring minor maintenance got fixed up, books and book shelves were organised, rooms were cleaned up, and clothes got arranged in their cabinets. Planning their own entertainment did the children good.

In the ultra-modern offices and plants today, staff and executives alike are getting addicted to their desktop PCs. As a consequence, interactions between the leader and team members have considerably reduced. Their face-to-face meetings have gone down to such an extent that even the lady sitting next to a male staff in an office is sending an information to him by e-mail rather than communicating in person.

The regional director of a leading trade and industry association lamented that the young girl assistant sitting just outside his open door chamber would never meet him for any official communication; instead would communicate only via mail; and the top honcho has such a busy schedule of meetings and tours that most of such electronic inter-office communication would not be attended timely thus creating communication gaps leading to work-related problems.

This just shows that one ultimate risk of heavy high technology use diminishes empathy by limiting how much people engage with one another, even in the same room. This negative impact is causing a lot of concern today despite the fact that cell phones and laptops have allowed the users to escape their cubicles and work anywhere. They shrink distances and handle countless mundane tasks, freeing up time for more exciting pursuits

MULTITASKING: THE LATEST TIME-WASTER FOR YOU

In 2008, people consumed three times as much information each day as they did in 1960. And they are constantly shifting their attention. New research shows computer users at work change windows or check e-mail or other programmes 37 times an hour [1, 2].

Multitasking in the modern corporate world such as juggling e-mail, phone calls and other incoming information even from someone standing or sitting next to you who has come to give you a feedback regarding something can change how you think and behave. Your ability to focus is being undermined by bursts of information and, therefore, it poses a big threat as a *time-waster* for you. Heavy multitaskers have more trouble focusing and shutting out irrelevant information and they experience more stress.

Why is it a time-waster? Simply because the technology is under your control and you give it a command and it works. But the reverse is happening. With a clogged brain and a cluttered mind, you are being controlled by the technology; it has taken you over. Hence, it is a time-waster and neither a time-killer nor a time-stealer.

But, why modern technology tries to control you? Because the services provided by modern technology play to a primitive impulse to respond to immediate opportunities and threats as it used to happen to our cave-dwelling and jungle-treading ancestors. The stimulation provides excitement—a *dopamine* (which is the reward chemical in the brain) squint—that can be addictive. In its absence, people feel bored. The resulting distractions lead to significant time wastage and rising tension, cuts on cool creativity and deep thought, interrupting work and family life.

REFERENCES

[1] Richtel, Matt, 'Multi-tasking? Prepare to pay a high price.' *The Times of India, Kolkata,* 8 June 2010, p. 16.
[2] 'Tech-clogged Brain', *The Economic Times, Kolkata,* 8 June 2010, p. 9.

KEY TAKE-HOMES

- *Conscious time management*—positive and productive utilisation of time at your disposal is essential for *managing* and *leading* yourself and others towards success in any pursuit in the work as well as family roles.
- Periodic 'time audit' is useful for identification of *time-wasters (TW)*, *time-killers (TK)* and *time-stealers (TS)* and setting targets for minimising all the three. For *TW*, you need to set a *zero time-wasters (ZTW)* goal.
- It is essential for you to do advance planning of where your time should be spent by using the 'time budgeting' approach. Time required to accomplish various tasks and activities, according to their respective priorities, must be estimated and accordingly time allocated for each of them in your advance plan.
- In *conscious time management*, you have to keep a track of all the modern gadgets being introduced in today's fast-changing technological economy almost every day and also the new management and administrative practices and figure out which one of them would be your time-waster, time-killer or time-stealer and which one you can seriously consider as your time-saver friend in the work and family roles.

CHAPTER 16

Conscious Work-Life Balance

DAILY LIFE: A BIG REVOLVING STAGE

I often feel that our everyday life is just like a big revolving stage, divided into three segments—the family part, the social part and the work part. As long as we are in the family segment of the revolving stage, we are playing in different family roles as a spouse to our life partners, as a parent to our children, as a son or a daughter to our parents, or as a brother or sister to our siblings. The body language in each role is different from the other, so are the voice tonal quality and modulations and the choice of words and composition of messages. All the non-verbal and verbal contents of our communication change when we shift to some social roles, as a friend to our friends, as member of a social club, as a neighbour to a neighbour, as a customer in a local market or a shopping mall, or as a visitor to a religious shrine. At the workplace, we play different work roles—sometimes as supervisory persons and seniors to our juniors, at other times as juniors to our supervisors and seniors, and also as colleagues and peers to our colleagues and peers.

WORK-LIFE BALANCE: WHAT IS IT

The family roles and the social roles together constitute our 'life' and all the work roles combined, represent the 'work' part of our daily existence. Achieving a work-life balance would mean we do justice to both our 'life' (that is, family and social roles) and 'work' parts in terms of effective time management.

We do not bring any work home, unless there are exceptional circumstances (such as there is a very tight schedule to complete a work assignment and it is impossible to do it if we do not spend some time on it outside the normal working hours at the workplace itself or bring it home) nor do we steal any time from our working hours to attend to family or social role-related chores like visiting a relative or a friend at the hospital, attending the railway station or the airport to drop or receive someone close, or being present at a social function unless we are unable to make any alternative arrangements. Most of us are unable to prioritise our family/social role and work role-related tasks properly by assigning values in terms of 'urgency' and 'importance' and accomplish them on time as 'Just In Time' (JIT) and 'First Time Right' (FTR) persons and as such, we suffer from stress as some of the assignments do not get accomplished fully and it has its snowballing effect on other tasks and assignments. Most of us are time-mismanaged persons.

HAZARDS OF POOR WORK-LIFE BALANCE

We all know that the main hazard of poor work-life balance is *stress* which has its adverse impact on our body and mind in many ways. But, the fact that hazards of poor work-life balance in modern times on the part of the parents are taking a big toll on our children is not easily recognised by us as the ill-effects may not be immediately tangible.

The following examples, arranged from the newborn stage of life to the adolescence period, would serve as illustrations:

Example 1

How having a newborn baby would affect your performance in the work role adversely. A new study has found that parents lose out on a six months' sleep in the first two years after a baby's birth. On average, parents of newborn babies get just four uninterrupted hours of sleep at night—an hour less than the minimum they need to be able to function and avoid rows. Inadequate rest for the brain at night would leave you with a tired brain to work for you the whole day which is not desirable. And, it is also injustice to your work organisation or profession which is not getting full advantage of you in the form of *human capital* [1].

Example 2

Many of the modern mothers, particularly those who are working or are engaged in some profession or business do not want to breast-feed their kids. Breast-feeding, worldwide research has proven time and again, is essential for the newborn's all-round growth and development. Moreover, the child's coming in close physical contact with the soft body tissues of the mother produces the happiness chemical *oxytocin* inside the child's brain and helps in healthy brain development. Formula-feeding is not recommended by child health experts. In some cases, bottle-feeding when it is prolonged beyond 15 to 16 months, may lead to iron deficiency and a certain quantity of iron, as we all know, is essential for maintaining our blood's balanced composition [2].

Example 3

Children in the age group of 3 to 13, who are unfortunate not to have adequate company of their parents, particularly the mother, are found to lack social problem-solving skills which they are expected to learn from the way their parents solve social problems at their level. Such children are more at risk of becoming bullies or victims of bullying or both than those who enjoy the company of their parents even for 2 to 3 solid hours every day and who get exposed to their parents interacting with people of all kinds and dealing with them effectively at least for 2 to 3 hours every week. It is important that children see both the parents in parenting roles. When you don't see your kids every day, it can be tough to maintain a strong and tight connection [3].

Example 4

'Sixteen-year old Pritam Sarkar (name changed) could not sit for his Class XI final exam this year. He was in hospital. A nervous wreck. Pushed by his parents to 'be the best' in art and music lessons and under pressure to score well in school, he just couldn't take it any more and collapsed just before exams. He was something of a prodigy, starting singing at 3, and one of the best in school. No one knew what was wrong.

It wasn't a sudden reaction, psychologists found out. Pritam had a deep-rooted nervous disorder that festered since childhood, a result of being constantly pushed to perform.

Chances are, you may find a Pritam in your neighbourhood or even in your family. Schools admit 15% students are living on the edge. Psychologists say the burnout rate is more than 30%' [4].

A significant percentage of youngsters are growing up with a feeling of inadequacy which hasten *burnout*. And what kind of parents put such pressure on their kids: mostly those who are unable to maintain a work-life balance. Out of frustration, they drive their children to be big achievers.

Example 5

Parents' inability to spend adequate quality time with their children are prompting them to become addicted to TV watching, video or computer game playing and visiting social networking sites. Such sedentary habits are affecting the youngsters' health and well-being. These tend to distract them from sports, games and physical workouts, homework and studies contributing to a lethargic lifestyle and procrastination-oriented learning habit. Emotionally they also tend to suffer as they cannot have any direct face-to-face interaction or physical contact with the TV and game characters or even with the acquaintances being made through the social networking sites.

DAILY WORK-LIFE BALANCE STARTS WITH SLEEP IN THE PREVIOUS NIGHT

Let us break up the whole day into 24 hours. Out of this total time available to us, we must devote 8 hours for restful sleep so that the brain gets enough time for relaxation, for organisation of the newly acquired and reorganisation and updating of the old and existing information, arranging the innumerable files that it owns, and formation and consolidation of memory and learning.

Our sleep has two phases—the REM (Rapid Eye Movements) phase when the sleep is disturbed and as such the eyeballs underneath our eyelids rotate exhibiting restlessness when the brain has waves of the range 24 to 32 cycles per second. This is the phase, when we dream and whether it is a pleasant or an unpleasant dream, the wave pattern is the same. The other phase is the NREM (Non-Rapid Eye Movements) when we have sound, undisturbed sleep and the brain is calm and restful, having waves in the range of 4 to 7 cycles per second.

If in a total 8 hours of sleeping period, the ratio between NREM and REM is 6:2, then it is positive and acceptable. It prepares the brain for the next day with increased tolerance limits and higher shock-absorbing capacity. When we wake after such positive sleep, we have *alpha* waves (that is, 7 to 14 cycles per second) which may bring *pure awareness* or trigger creative-intuitive flashes and new and novel ideas, or practicable solutions to some prevailing problem. And, once we have left the bed with tossing around, after such a good night's sleep, we enter straight into *beta*-positive (that is, 14 to 25 cycles per second) which is a balanced state of mind—tranquil, stress-free and ready to take off to new heights during the day.

EARLY MORNING CHORES

After leaving the bed, a balanced life will mean going for the morning ablutions—brushing the teeth and clearing the bowels. It should be a daily habit. Once you have freshened up, have a cup of tea with milk and one and a half spoon of sugar with two to three biscuits (or, better, a handful of sprouted grams) and then in light clothes, in a cross-ventilated room, go for the morning stretching and bending workouts.

The exercise regimen should start with deep breathing in the standing posture, inhaling with expanding and exhaling with contracting the chest with both the horizontally extended arms and hands acting as the regulator. After 5–6 cycles of deep breathing, go for backward bending—breathing in while bending backwards and breathing out while coming up straight in the erect posture. Do it 12 to 15 times (after 2 to 3 months, increase it to 22 to 25 times). Now, go for deep breathing 4 to 5 times again. Next, you go for neck movements. First take up semi-circular neck rotation—clockwise (breathe in) and then anticlockwise (breathe out), 10 to 12 times each way, increasing it to 15 to 20 times after 2 to 3 months. Now, come on to forward (breathe out)-backward (breathe in) neck movements, considering the neck joint as a one-way hinge. Again, revert to the deep breathing 4 to 5 times, then start sideways bending following the rhythm: left (bend from the waist with your hands placed straight on top of your head)-centre-right (bend to the right now) and then again back to the centre. Now, finish off with deep breathing. Regular enjoyable physical activities like fitness exercises will generate brain's natural pain-killer chemical, *endorphin*, helping you to expand your tolerance thresholds.

These fitness workouts are to be followed by rhythmic walking or dancing rhythmically with rhythmic orchestrated music. Maintaining the rhythm is very important as it would produce *dopamine* eventually, which is our brain's natural balancer, helping in coordination—both physical and mental. Stationery slow jogging with music will also produce the same effect.

The entire phase of physical workouts and rhythmic movements should take 20 to 30 minutes. Now, you should hug, embrace, physically cuddle your family members or hold their hands so that the love and affection chemical *oxytocin* is produced.

Now, you finish your bath, breakfast and embark on your journey to the workplace.

THE WORKING HOURS

Planning for Your Work Performance

You have already planned for your today's work assignments' performance the previous afternoon or evening before you left your workplace for the day. And, in doing so you might have used, unconsciously, the *principle of prioritisation* as shown in Figure 16.1.

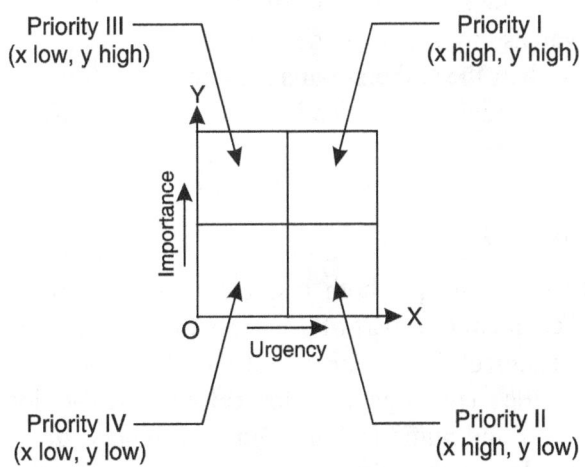

Fig. 16.1: The Principle of Prioritisation

Estimate performance time for Priority I assignments and schedule them for performance in the pre-lunch hours starting with the most complex of them the first thing in the morning. If the Priority I assignments can be completed in the morning before their respective completion times, and you have some free time available, then take up the Priority II assignments. Otherwise, you take up the Priority II assignments in the afternoon hours. Keep some free time for tackling unscheduled assignments, unpredictable visits, sudden meetings, business calls and mails. Do not pack every quarter or half an hour with prior work plans. The 'free float' (free time to be kept in hand) time should be kept according to your previous (1 or 2 months') experience. Some of today's Priority II and Priority III assignments, if not performed and left out for today, may become Priority I and Priority II tasks for you tomorrow. This type of analysis you have to do regularly consciously.

Making Your Performance 'Effective': 'Zero Defect (ZD)' and 'First Time Right (FTR)'

While performing any work assignment, get the right answers to the following questions: *why* do I have to perform; *what* is the purpose of the assignment; *who* would provide me with the resource inputs; and for *whom* would I have to perform/ *who* would be at the end of my work process to receive my output; *where* do I perform and *when*—from *what time* to *what time*; *what* specifically I'll have to do to perform; *what* should be the action steps and *which* one should come first and *which* one second and *which* one next and so on; *how* should I perform. To get a clear picture like this is essential for you as the 'self-managed' portion of your performance has to be much more than the 'others-managed' portion. You should be a self-starter. Train your juniors and kids in the family this way to become self-starters too.

Trans-Technical (TT) Roles

The interaction with people both inside and outside the organisation is beyond the 'Technical (T)' part of your job and that is the reason why we call it 'Trans-technical (TT)'. For your TT performance, you ought to use your hard skills (intelligence, logical-analytical-rational thinking, calculation power and numerical acumen, vocabulary, grammar and such other quantifiable attributes) and soft skills (non-verbal and verbal communication, human relations, intuition, imaginative and creative thinking) in a balanced way to get things done by other people willingly and happily—by keeping them motivated.

People will take your hard behaviour without getting sentimental and emotionally hijacked, occasionally—if the situation so demands when progress is slow and time happens to be the essence of the assignment, or work quality is poor necessitating rework, provided you maintain a very good relationship with them by meeting their creaturely psychological needs: desire to win; need for attention, acceptance/acknowledgement, affiliation and appreciation; and dislike for direct criticism (attack). In order to drive your point home, you might have to use the 'sandwich' technique of strategic communication which involves your starting the message with the most interesting points of the other person's opinion or his most remarkable or unique 'strengths' or 'achievements' so that he feels good and happy followed by your negative comment by putting it indirectly in the style of 'Don't you think…..?' or 'Don't you feel…..?'etc. You end it with a few of the other person's balance positive points, thus giving your whole message the form of a 'sandwich' as shown in Figure 16.2. These behavioural strategies will produce equally good results for you in your family, social as well as work roles.

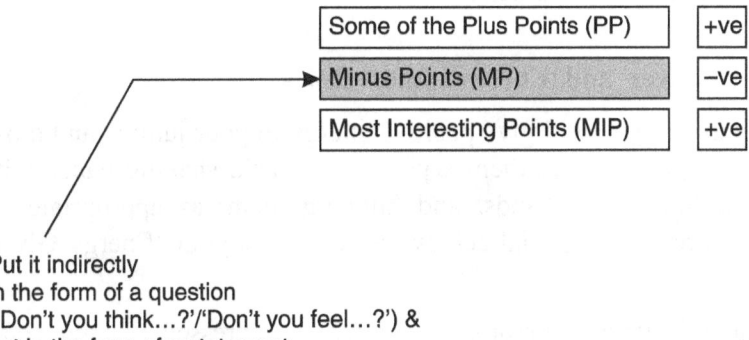

Put it indirectly
in the form of a question
('Don't you think…?'/'Don't you feel…?') &
not in the form of a statement.

Fig. 16.2: The 'Sandwich' Technique of Communication Message Management

Your Mid-day Meal

Your mid-day meal should be light to give you not more than 600 to 750 kcal and you should avoid consuming any rice product because of its *melatonin* (a chemical secreted by the *pineal gland* inside the brain for inducing sleep) content. We certainly need this friendly chemical but not too much of it which would make us sleepy and sloppy. Your diet should be more of vegetables and vegetable proteins like lentil, *chana* (grams), *dahi bada* and *paneer masala*, all cooked lightly.

Your Working Afternoon

Your work-afternoon should include simple and light assignments and this is the time when routine work activities involving your muscular-skeletal system (MBWA activities like taking round of the office, shop floor, plant or project sites) have got to be undertaken and completed. Some time has to be devoted to the preparation of the next day's 'work plan' and 'to do' list.

Being in Touch with the Family

During the working hours, you should always try to be in touch with your family (spouse, children and old ailing parents) from time to time through cell phone/e-mail so that you help them to have a supply, although in small quantity, of the love and trust hormone *oxytocin* which produces softness in our attitude and behaviour.

The 'Energy Giver' and 'Energy Donor' Roles

It is expected that you will give positive energy to your juniors and those reporting to you by giving them a pat on the back, shaking hands with them and holding their hands, and hugging them, as appropriate, to celebrate and rejoice a special achievement. This is your 'Energy Giver' role.

When somebody, your junior or senior or peer, is depressed, you must play your 'Energy Donor' role by cheering him up and donating energy to give a charge of motivation. Make mention, at any depressed moment, of the special past achievements of the person and assure him of the same high level of performance in the future too.

Snacking

You should not consume more than 300 to 400 kcal in the form of a snack. To give you some idea of the kcal value, one 35 to 45 gm packet of potato chips contains 500 to 600 kcal.

EVENING RELAXATION

The whole day's tension can be released in the evening by pursuing a simple relaxation activity. After your light evening snack, find an isolated corner where you will be alone, switch on an Indian classical *raga* tune where the *alap* (beatless) portion is being played on *sarod*. You start deep breathing (in-hold-out cycle) and then once your brain has relaxed and free from the whole day's pressure, you start concentrating on the music and try to enjoy it with all your body and mind. Within 3 to 4 minutes, you feel very light and tension-free as *beta-positive* (or may be *alpha*) electrical wave form has come to be set in your brain.

PREPARATION FOR SOUND SLEEP

Your dinner should be worth 700 to 750 kcal: 3 to 4 *sukha rotis* (or 75 to 100 gm of rice if you want good sleep provided, of course, you do not have any work in the night shift), dal, one vegetable curry, one preparation from vegetable protein (chana, kabuli chana, rajma, whole moong dal, matar or soya bean) and a dessert.

After dinner do not lie down immediately or sit down to watch the TV. Take a short stroll in the room or on the terrace or balcony. Think about all the good incidents that had happened during the day, your achievements, the appreciations you received from others, some new useful learning that you have had, some new acquaintances made and other positive things. Instead of watching the TV, you can listen to some music or even tune yourself to a FM radio station that you like.

After you take a stroll for 15 to 20 minutes, then sit down in an erect posture and listen to the music and enjoy it. After another 40 to 45 minutes, lay your body on the bed. Your mattress should be made from coir instead of foam, topped up with a thin cotton mattress. You should lie in the supine posture (*sabasan*) and start slow deep breathing. If you can retrieve from your memory how you used to feel when your mother used to put you to sleep when you're a little kid. You'll have the love chemical *oxytocin* trickling inside your brain. Now sleep will come.

REFERENCES

[1] 'Babies cost six months' sleep', *Hindustan Times, Kolkata,* 12 July 2010, p. 14.
[2] 'Prolonged bottle-feeding linked to iron deficiency', *Hindustan Times, Kolkata,* 13 July 2010, p. 14.
[3] 'Who can be a bully, a victim or both?' *Hindustan Times, Kolkata,* 12 July 2010, p. 14.
[4] Mukherjee, Pandey, Jhimli and Prithvijit Mitra, 'Kids Driven to Breaking Point: Pushed by Parents to be All-Rounders, the Perform-or-Perish

pressure on Schoolkids is Turning Them into Nervous Wrecks', *The Times of India, Kolkata,* 12 July 2010, p. 2.

KEY TAKE-HOMES

- Achieving a 'work-life balance' would mean we do justice to both our 'life' (which consists of our 'family' and 'social' roles) and 'work' parts of our daily existence in terms of effective time management.
- Hazards of poor work-life balance on the part of the parents do affect them in the form of 'stress' but, more importantly, those take a big toll on the children.
- A wise strategy for achieving a 'work-life balance' would be to do a 24-hour scheduling with every activity being properly recognised and incorporated, starting with the 'sleeping' phase in the previous night.
- Much though you may be a very important and busy workhorse, you have to remain touch with your family through modern tools and techniques like cell phone, text messages, e-mail, voice mail, chatting etc.

CHAPTER 17

Unconscious Motivation and Motivation for Performance in the Work Role

'I always turn to the sports page first. The sports page records people's accomplishments; the front page has nothing but man's failures.'

—*Amitabh Bachchan, actor*
(The Times of India, Kolkata, 11 June, 2010, p. 18)

Bachchan is right. When we are rightly *motivated*, we accomplish; when we are not motivated or wrongly motivated, we fail. Let us see why and how it happens.

WHAT IS MOTIVATION

Needs-Goals-Motive Force

We, humans, like all other living creatures, survive and grow by satisfying a variety of needs. Once a 'need' is very strongly felt and it stimulates our body or brain, waiting to be satisfied, we set a 'goal'. We, then, run towards that goal to reach it with a force which is known as *motive force* and the very existence of this force we describe as *motivation*.

According to the strength of the *motive force*, the *motivation level* in a particular situation may be high, moderate or low.

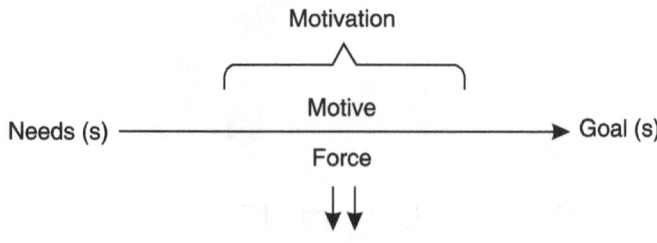

Fig. 17.1: Needs-Goals-Motive Force-Motivation Diagram

'To Motivate': What It Means

'To motivate' someone would mean to make him want to do something, especially something that involves a little more-than-ordinary effort and action.

What is 'Motive'

'Motive' is something (arising out of a need or desire) that causes a person to act. It could also be interpreted as moving or tending to move to action. It also relates to motion or the cause of motion (namely, energy). The word is derived from 'motion' which is an act, process or instance of changing place. 'Motivation' thus represents a desire to move. Movement is involved for satisfaction of basic survival needs such as: hunger, thirst, rest-relaxation-sleep, excretion, recreation-play, procreation, self-defence-safety-security (when the accelerator is pressed hard and there is high-gear movement triggered by the fight-or-flight switch inside the primitive brain).

UNCONSCIOUS MOTIVATION

The Human Brain's Mega-computer Analogy

It will be an underestimation even if we describe our brain as a mega-computer. As a matter of fact, an adult human brain consists approximately of 10,000 million computers as each brain cell—the *neuron*, is equivalent to a computer, it being an 'input → processing → output' device. The soft brain tissue is the *hardware* and the operating systems which control the processing of the inputs in particular ways to produce certain outputs, constitute the *software*.

What Constitutes the Tissue Hardware

We will now see that, barring one or two exceptional situations, most of our *needs* and *motives* arise from the lower primitive structures of our brain, constituting the brain's tissue-based hardware. For brevity's sake, we describe these as the *ground* and the *mezzanine* floors together constituting one storey.

The ground floor consists of the collective soft tissue—the *brainstem*, the bulbous extension of our spinal cord, and the *cerebellum*. This part, known as the *reptilian brain*, evolved 500 million years ago. The mezzanine floor is made of the *primary mammalian brain*—the *limbic system*. (The *limbic system*'s main constituent modules are: the *caudate nucleus,* the *hippocampus* (the memory storage), the *thalamus*, the *hypothalamus*, the *amygdala* and the *putamen*. You need not overload your brain by trying to remember these details, which we have put inside brackets.)

All our basic emotions are generated in the *limbic system*, along with most of the many needs, urges and desires that prompt us to behave in ways that help us to survive. These portions of our brain constitute the source of our inherent, automatic motivational software and thus the 'fountainhead' of our reflex behaviour—physical (like the 'knee jerk'), physiological (like the heart pounding fast, the lungs breathing rapidly and the different hormones being secreted as a consequence of 'stress') and psychological ('pleasure-or-pain'-related behaviour like elation or joy and unhappiness-anger-or-fear).

The *mammalian brain,* our brain's *mezzanine floor*, is much older than the first floor (the *cortex*) in evolutionary terms. The areas below it—the ground floor, the *reptilian brain*, are even more ancient. The *mammalian* and the *reptilian* brains are all *unconscious*. In us, a system of survival mechanisms mainly operates—even in adults—at an *unconscious* level. This system also includes 'unconscious emotions'. 'Conscious emotions' constitute a very small part of the total system [1, 2]. Any motivational situation related to these brain structures would be regarded and shall be described by us as *unconscious motivation.*

Unconscious Acquisition of Software in Infancy and Childhood

Hundreds and thousands, and at times, possibly millions, of stimuli enter into an infant's and, subsequently as it grows, into the child's brain. These may be 'positive' or 'negative' in nature. 'Positive' meaning favourable and 'negative' meaning unfavourable for the child's survival, growth, and comfortable existence in that particular physical, psychological and social environment.

The former category of stimuli would be welcome and thus sought after, whereas the latter category would be unwelcome and thus avoided or resisted. Experiences get converted into 'memories' which store only these specially selected stimuli and their associated experiences rejecting the remaining ones—a whole host of them. These 'memories' come to serve as *unconscious* software. 'Experience is rarely applied objectively or consciously. Rather, experiences are converted into a bundle of knee-jerk responses (fire = pain, so retract; height = danger, so avoid). These 'laws' of response, woven together with thousands of other rules, create conditioning' [3].

However, even in the identification of 'positive' and 'negative' inputs, every child's brain is highly selective as the brain's tissue hardware is endowed with typical genetic propensities—inherited traits. Thus, apart from some very common and general inputs, in a few special cases, what may seem 'positive' to one child would appear, 'negative' for another child's brain according to the child's inherent *'nature'* although both may be placed or brought up (that is, *'nurture'*) in the same environment. For example, one child may love to be touched and hugged, whereas another child may shy away from such gestures; one child may be hungry for people's company, another child may like to remain in isolation, and so on.

The Conscious Brain

Nevertheless, our brain's first floor (the *cortex*), which is *conscious*, is influenced to a great extent by the *unconscious* as it is constantly in touch with the upper structures through close neural connectivity. And being much older in evolutionary age, and having survived millions of years of interaction with the environment, the *unconscious* plays a dominant role by feeding information and automatic responses to the upper floor although the external environment and the lifestyle of us, the modern humans, have changed from those of our primitive and old-world ancestors—in many cases, by almost three hundred and sixty degrees (for example: from 'no language', to writing manually using a language, to typewriting, to word processing using a computer).

Our brain's internal environment (that is, the lower primitive structures) is still ceaselessly hungry to seek out new stimuli as we have to protect ourselves from and safeguard against anything that is hazardous. As a matter of fact, the *unconscious* brain is much better-equipped than the *conscious* brain to deal with such matters. All *unconscious* activities are essential for our survival and they are permanent; all that just do not fade away. 'This greed for information is one of the fundamental properties of the brain and it is reflected in our most basic reactions. People can have their conscious mind totally destroyed, yet their eyes will still scan the room and lock on to and track a moving object. The eye movements are triggered by brainstem and are no more significant of consciousness than the turning of a flower to the sun' [4].

New neuronal connections are made with every incoming stimulus and old connections disappear as memories are lost. Each passing impression is not only received and registered but also recorded for some time in some new shape and form but not stored. However, if it is not stored in memory, the configuration is lost and, along with it, the impression is also lost. It is just like the fact that water falling from a height on top of the hill on a piece of stone down below does not leave a permanent impression unless the event is repetitive and a regular one; or, just like when you stand up the hollow impression of your buttocks on the foam cushion or mattress also disappears unless it experiences the same event regularly.

Stimulus-patterns that come repeatedly establish neuronal connections, trigger activity in other neuronal groups and form associations (that is, memories) or may evolve totally novel concepts. Each time a particular inter-connected group of neurons gets fired together, in theory, we may think that it gives rise to the same thought, feeling or an *unconscious* brain function; but, in practice, since brain is not a rigid but a highly fluid and flexible structure unlike a computer, it never gives rise to any identical pattern of response to the same stimulus. In reality, a somewhat similar but subtly altered response arises. We never really react or respond in the same fashion to two identical stimuli.

The Iceberg Mind: A Soft Analogy

Let us now look at from another angle. Let us bring back here the analogy of an *iceberg* to describe the abstract concept of our mind, the concrete physical existence of which is no doubt in our brain (See Figure 5.1 in chapter 5). During our wakefulness, since we have to keep all our senses (eyes, ears, nose, tongue, skin and the mind) not only awake but also most alert, we may say that our mind is *consciously active*. During such *conscious* activity only a few selective structures of our brain are in action. Being conscious means being in the present, here and now. The *conscious mind* is thus only the top layer—the tip of the iceberg.

Immediately below the *conscious*, is the relatively insignificant *semi-conscious* part of the mind the activities of which are blurred—not clear and distinct at all, and consist of all the stimuli arising in the environment immediately outside you and also outside your attention span as you're not paying any heed to them; they are just happening (like the honking of a car horn on the road outside your room or the crows cawing and the street dogs barking).

A very important part your mind below the *conscious* (representing the 'present') is the *subconscious* which consists of the two extremes on either side of the 'present'—the 'past' and the 'future'. 'Past' means memory of the 'past': both of pleasure and pain, joys and sorrows, achievements and failures, satisfactions and frustrations. 'Future' means hopes and aspirations, dreams and ambitions—both bright and dark. The *subconscious* always remains inadvertently active as it influences most of our *conscious* actions. Our conscious behaviour, at many instances, are guided by our *past* experiences and *future* dreams and goals.

Beneath the *subconscious*, is the deep layer of *unconscious* which is the fountainhead of all the involuntary happenings inside us and all our external behavioural manifestations including our gait or style of walking, our postures, gestures, the inter-personal distance that we maintain, the modulations of our voice and the like over which we do not normally have any control (unless we become conscious) as those are happening spontaneously.

The Creaturely Psychological Needs

Unconscious motivation encompasses all physical and physiological needs as well as a few *creaturely* psychological needs, common to all creatures—birds and animals, which are essential for our survival and growth. The latter comprises: (i) the desire to win by beating others or making others lose (the 'I win, you lose' attitude and behaviour); (ii) the need for 4As: 'attention (look at me, I feel neglected)', 'acceptance (please accept me despite my shortcomings—don't reject me)'/'acknowledgement (do acknowledge my company and contributions)', 'affiliation (please include me in your fraternity)', and 'appreciation (I am hungry for your praise)'; and, (iii) dislike for failure and attack (direct criticism) by others.

PERCEPTION OF 'WORK': HOW IT VARIES

There was a time, and not so many centuries ago, when a man had to be completely self-contained and self-supporting. He had to be a farmer, fisherman, hunter, tailor, carpenter, blacksmith, barber or warrior to satisfy his own needs. Thereafter, the concept of work did undergo many changes with the progress of the human society and civilisation from an agrarian to the industrial and, thereafter, the post-industrial high-tech era. Life is continuous change and it is upon 'movement' that change depends.

We are not concerned here with the motivation to eat, motivation to sleep, or motivation to play cricket. Our focus is on *motivation to work*.

But what denotes *work*? Is it toil for some form of payment? Or, is it any activity that we engage in to achieve a goal?

Briskin (1998) made a distinction between *work* and a *job* by saying that 'when work becomes a job, its intrinsic value vanishes' [5, 6]. According to Fox (1994), a *job* is external, whereas '*work* is the expression of our soul, our inner being... our inner work.' These two expert views on the distinction between *work* and *job* are, no doubt, thought-provoking.

Simply speaking, *work* means different things to different people within different cultures and contexts; although many of them with whom we are concerned may be engaged in the same organisation. For the individual, *work*—at one extreme, may be a primary life interest, at the other, it may be a drudgery leading to *stress* affecting the body and brain powers; or, something in between. Someone may look at *work* as a 'blessing' whereas someone else may look at it as a 'curse'. A third individual may regard *work* as a major activity through which she shapes her ambitions and her talents and, thus, acquires self-knowledge.

Work is both a process of activities (implying expenditure of biological energy) and an outcome. One works for the rewards of doing the work, and toward some end state or result. The outcome or the end-result is a twin feature. One of them is measurable, quantifiable—an adequate economic gain or the financial reward—or its inadequacy or total lack. The other is the physical and mental satisfaction (or gain) or frustration (or loss)—which is apparently not measurable or quantifiable, but can be evaluated with the help of biomedical tools and techniques [7].

Physical and mental satisfactions arise when *'we work to create'*; and, the opposite—dissatisfaction and frustration occur when *'we work to earn money'*. The ideal match is when the *work* that we perform helps us to *create* something and, at the same time, becomes a channel for collecting sufficient compensation, both in cash and kinds.

However, the opportunity to get involved in some work which leads to some *creation* is not a ready possibility for everyone. It can happen only in very rare cases and, in that too, once in a blue moon.

Goldsmith, a leading authority in helping successful leaders achieve positive, lasting change in behaviour for themselves, their people, and their teams, has come up with the novel concept of *MOJO* and its relationship with work. He operationally defines *MOJO* as 'that positive spirit—toward what we are doing now—that starts on the inside and radiates to the outside.' According to him, we experience *MOJO* when we engage in activities that simultaneously provide us with happiness and meaning. *MOJO* is equally relevant for activities at work or outside of work [8, 9].

MOTIVATORS FOR PERFORMANCE IN THE 'WORK ROLE'

Our observations on the work behaviour of employees in Indian business and industry show that prime motivators are:

1. *Learning and Experience-gathering:* Here the prime motive is to *acquire good experience*, which would help in self and professional development and confidence-building for achieving job security and professional growth. [This is directly related to the creaturely psychological need no. (iii); and indirectly to the 4As under (ii)].
2. *Reward and Growth Seeking:* The prime motive here is to work for an organisation which offers *good pay and perks, recognition for good work, fast growth opportunities (horizontally, vertically, or both)*. [This is directly related to the creaturely psychological needs (i) and (ii)].
3. *Comfort/Security-seeking:* Prime motive is to *settle down in a secure job*, which offers generally most of the needs-satisfaction opportunities. [This is directly related to (iii) and indirectly to (ii)].
4. *Record Breaking and Trend-setting:* This motive represents the desire to *break past records*, and set *new performance trends*. [This is also primarily related to the needs under (i) and (ii)].
5. *Power Hunger:* Prime motive here is to be able to *control* substantial resources including manpower. [Related to need (i)].
6. *Social Networking:* Prime motive is to look for *social connectivity* and *contact building* through networking. [This is related the 4As under (ii)].

7. *Brand Hunger:* The prime motive is to be with a *highly well-known organisation* (either in general in the socio-economic scenario like the House of Tatas or Birlas or the Reliance Group, or related to a specific industry like in IT: Infosys, Wipro or TCS, in health care: Apollo, in banking: State Bank of India or the Citi Bank) which helps to enhance and maintain social prestige. [Related to the need group (ii) and need (i)].

REFERENCES

[1] Le Doux, Joseph, *The Emotional Brain,* Simon and Schuster, New York, 1996.
[2] Carter, Rita, *Mapping the Mind*, Phoenix (Orion Books), London, 2000, p. 21.
[3] Krippendorff, Kaihan, *Hide a Dagger behind a Smile*, Adamsmedia, Avon, Mass., 2008, p. xix.
[4] Carter, Rita, *loc. cit.,* pp. 15–16.
[5] Briskin, A., *The Stirring of Soul in the Workplace*, Berrett-Koehler, San Francisco, 1998, p. 143.
[6] Fox, M., *The Reinvention of Work: A New Vision of Livelihood for our Time,* Harper San Francisco, San Francisco, 1994, p. 5.
[7] Ganguli, Siddhartha, *Performance Management: 'First Time Right'*, Platinum Publishers, Kolkata, 2008, pp. 283–286.
[8] Goldsmith, Marshall, *Mojo: How to Get It, How to Keep it, and How to Get It Back If You Lose It,* 2010, www.MojoTheBook.com.
[9] Goldsmith, Marshall, 'Mojo for Learning Professionals', *T&D* (Journal of the American Society for Training and Development), Vol. 64, No. 5, May 2010, pp. 72–73.

KEY TAKE-HOMES

- We are guided by 'needs'. When a 'need' is strong, a 'goal' is set and movement takes place towards the goal with the help of 'motivation' which is an energy supply phenomenon. A highly motivated person has a high level of energy to be expended.
- To 'motivate' someone would mean to make him want to do something—supply him the energy—persuade him to move towards a certain 'goal' which has been set to fulfil some specific 'need'.
- We are *unconsciously* (that is, automatically—without anybody's prompting) 'motivated' to get the *creaturely* physical, physiological and psychological needs (all related to our lower brain) satisfied as those are essential to be met for our survival and physical and emotional security even though the strengths of the different needs may vary from one person to another and in the same person also at different times.
- In modern times, for all of us, the prime motivators for performance in the 'work roles' in Indian business and industry are: learning and experience-gathering; reward and growth-seeking; comfort/security seeking; record-breaking and trend-setting; power hunger; social networking; and, brand hunger. All these needs, interestingly, can be related to our creaturely brain's inherent needs.

CHAPTER 18

Conscious Motivation for Peak Performance

EXTRINSIC AND INTRINSIC MOTIVATORS

All the motivators just described towards the end of chapter 17 are automatic propensities and, therefore, belong to the domain of *unconscious motives*. Try to understand that, in order to satisfy all these *unconscious motives*, the 'inputs' must all come from external sources. Thus we can describe all of them as *extrinsic motivators*.

The 'Unconscious' Motive to 'Create'

Now, there is something very interesting. There is a common saying: 'Necessity is the mother of invention'. When we *invent* something out of mere necessity, the motivation for *invention* is *extrinsic*. Birds, animals and men have all been inventing and using tools, appliances and techniques for achieving the twin needs of survival and stability. The external problematic environmental conditions trigger the internal mechanism to try and find practical solutions to the problem. So, here the *extrinsic* stimulus opens the *internal* fountainhead for *creative problem-solving*. It can be categorised as an *unconscious motive* as birds and animals, which do not possess a *conscious mind*, also indulge in such *creative behaviour*.

For us, humans, physical and mental satisfaction arise when we *'work to create'* and, the opposite—dissatisfaction and frustration occur when we *'work to earn money'*. The ideal match is when the *work* that we perform helps us to *create* something and, at the same time, becomes the channel for collecting adequate compensation—both in cash and kind.

However, the opportunity to get involved in some *work* which leads to some *'creation'* is not a ready possibility for everyone. It can happen only in very rare cases. But, if we look at it from a somewhat different angle, then perhaps it can become possible.

In an organisation, we the organisational members are all involved in some set of work activities which all form integral parts of a large 'activity network system'—a giant wheel of activities, the ultimate outcome of which is some *creation*—some products or services.

If you look at how those products or services 'created' by your organisation are providing satisfaction to its *customers* ('prospects' converted into first-time buyers), helping those *customers* to become *clients* ('repeat buyers'), converting the *clients* into your *advocates* (who plead for your brand), and those *advocates* into *evangelists* (who spread the gospel of your brand through word-of-mouth publicity), then you may feel *motivated* as you certainly have a role to play in the satisfaction-providing and progressive conversion process.

This *motivation*, which is *conscious* (as you had to indulge in deductive logical thinking), may act as a balm to provide you relief from the 'productive toil', repetitive, tedious, and physically and mentally demanding and demeaning labour that drives out the soul and inhibits the human spirit to mere means to a productivity or sustenance-driven end.

Indirect Enjoyment from Your Work

This way, you start enjoying your work *indirectly* as it gives you a sense of fulfilment of some *social responsibility*. 'Needs-satisfaction' of *prospects* (potential buyers) to convert them into *customers* and then succeeding in reaching the progressive goal attainment of *customer* → *client* → *advocate* → *evangelist* is fulfilment of a 'corporate social responsibility' (CSR).

AN EXERCISE

Now, at this stage, take a pause and find out:

(a) What kinds of needs existing in the market environment the products or services 'created' by your organisation are aimed to satisfy? Are they catering to some 'direct demand' (like for consumer products) or any 'derived demand' (e.g. industrial products like sponge iron, iron/steel ingots, EPD services, printing ink required by the printing/publishing industry etc.)?

(b) Can you link your products/services to one or more or all of the broad groups of the human need spectrum? *Basic survival and sustenance*: ordinary food, clothes, shelter, furniture, basic education, training in trade/craft; textbook publication, educational stationeries, health care, pharmaceutical products, basic toiletries, public transportation, electricity, pollution control; *safety and security*: physical, economic (banking/investment/insurance/gold/silver/commodities/jewelleries); *family/social relationships*: gifts, entertainment, hotels/restaurants, shopping malls, amusement parks, clubs and associations, movies, theatres, vehicles; *prestige/status*: high-end products and services; *self-actualisation*: personal talent maximisation; genuine social work; mentoring.
(c) Try to identify what *specific role* you are playing in the fulfilment of this *corporate social responsibility (CSR)*. Write down in a few simple words.

BE CONSCIOUS ABOUT ANOTHER UNCONSCIOUS INTRINSIC MOTIVATOR: THE 'WORKING PERSONALITY PRINCIPLE (WPP)'

However, another *unconscious motive*, which is very special to us—the human beings, has not been touched upon as yet in this chapter. It is what you enjoy doing—how you like to spend your time—what type of activity gives you maximum satisfaction. We have studied this aspect extensively and have proposed the *Working Personality Principle (WPP)* according to which there are three types of work: 'Self-Engagement (SE)'where the upper structures of the brain (the cerebral apparatus) get involved; 'People and Social Engagement (PSE.)' where the speaking and listening accessories (the communicative apparatus) is primarily active and, the 'Physical Engagement (PE)' where the bones, muscles, joints, tendons and ligaments (the muscular-skeletal apparatus) are the main actors. Each individual is born with a typical *Working Personality (WP)*. According to this principle, some people enjoy SE type of work more than PSE and PE; some others enjoy PSE more than SE and PE, whereas a few others enjoy the PE work activities most [1]. Thus, if there is a match between the *work* to be performed and the performer's *working personality*, there is *intrinsic motivation*. *Intrinsic motivator*, therefore, is the 'work itself'.

Each individual has one predominant *WP* and, in some cases, one predominant and a second co-predominant (equally strong as the predominant one) or semi-predominant (that is, slightly lesser or weaker in strength compared to the predominant one). Correspondingly, the second and the third *WP* will be inhibited, or the third one inhibited due to copying error of the DNA codes and uncooperative, selfish genes. A substantial reduction in the error rates and inconspicuous presence of selfish genes would produce a *WP* where all the three *WP* elements, namely, SE, PSE, and PE are present in equal proportions. The result will be a balanced individual with all the powers of the body and the brain being present in the form of potential assets [2].

Movements Involved in Different Types of Work

SE involves cerebral movement—movement in the upper portion of your brain which again could be of different types: mental (logical-analytical-rational), emotional (feelings-related), imaginative-creative-innovative (including pictorial thinking and visualisation), and spiritual (empathic, compassionate-universal, altruistic).

PSE involves communicative movement featuring: kinesic (postures, gestures, sensory), proxemic (inter-personal distance), sonic (involving voice), and linguistic (word-based language).

PE involves physical movements that would include: standing, strolling, walking, jogging, running, stair climbing, ascending-descending a slope or incline and so on.

CONSCIOUS MOTIVATION FOR PEAK PERFORMANCE

Now let us see what *peak performance* is. You achieve *peak performance* whenever you cross the performance standards set, either by your higher management, or by yourself or by mutual involvement and consent. So, if the performance standards set are taken to represent 100, *peak performance* is 100 plus.

Up to a level of 95 to 100 per cent, you can perform without any special *intrinsic motivation*, guided primarily by the *extrinsic motivators* as discussed a little while ago in Chapter 17. For attaining *peak performance*, *intrinsic motivation* is a must.

There are two parameters to be considered in understanding the relationship between *motivation* and *performance*. If we put 'motivation for performance' in the x-axis and 'performance standards set' in the y-axis and put numerical values to each, we get one high-end point where

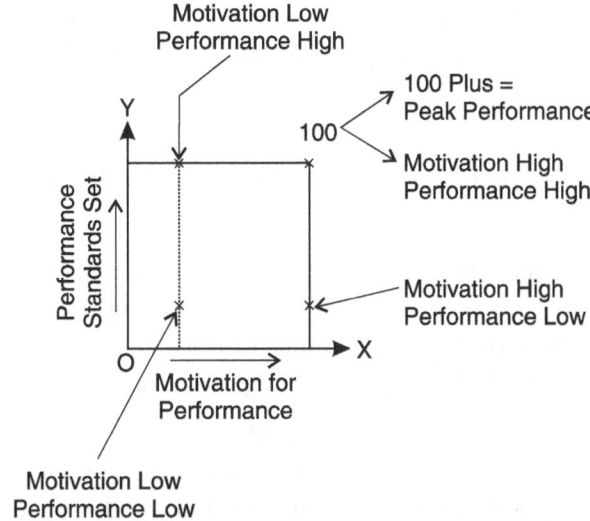

Fig. 18.1: Motivation for Performance and its Relationship with Performance Standards Set

motivation is high and performance is also high; this obviously is the *peak performance* level.

Motivation high, but performance low could be due to: (i) bad leader/bad boss factor and/or (ii) inadequate infrastructure/resources factor.

Motivation low, but performance high is an aggressive leader/boss-driven situation, leading to *stress* in the performer.

Cases where motivation is low, performance is also low, need to be looked into by HRD experts.

We can still get one more point, where motivation is moderate (51–60 per cent) and performance is also moderate (51–60 per cent). This is the 'good' performance level. From here, the journey begins toward the 100 per cent and 100 per cent plus motivation and 100 per cent and 100 per cent plus performance which are 'great' and 'peak' performances respectively. In between, there are: very good (61–70), very very good (71–85) and excellent (86–100) performances.

The 'Work' Itself as an Intrinsic Motivator

We have already discussed the *Working Personality Principle (WPP)* and have seen how the *Work* itself can serve as an 'intrinsic motivator'. Therefore, to attain the level of peak performance, you have to *consciously* choose your 'work contents' to suit your 'working personality' or influence your supervisory person—the controlling manager to follow the *WPP* in work allocation [3, 4].

Intrinsic Motivation by Realising Your 'Value Addition Agent (VAA)' Role

Did you know that every cell of your body and every cell of your brain is an input → processing → output device (or, shall we say, system)? The work activities that you perform are going as *inputs* into the organisational system (the organisation that you are engaged in).

There, these inputs are getting integrated into certain activity compounds which are the *outputs*. With this input → processing → output cycle being carried out right across the length and breadth of the organisation, it is offering certain products and services for consumption in the society.

Did you know that you are engaged in some value addition activities? Your work contribution is *adding value* to your own self. You must analyse how your *work habit* (H) (99 per cent perspiration) is helping you to acquire and master some *Knowledge* (K), transform your *Attitude* (A) (from a negative to a positive one; from an inferior to a superior one; from a lower grade to a higher grade one), develop some new *Skills* or sharpen some existing *Skills* (S) (which at a higher plane represent *Intelligences* or 'I', or, at a still higher plane, are represented by *Talents* or 'T').

Have you reached a level where others regard you as a *Genius* (G)? And, just like the force of gravity (g) pulls you down to our mother planet Earth, your *Genius* (G) pulls all people around you? *Genius* is the *mastery* of something and you are the *maestro*—the great performer, who has been attaining the level of *peak performance* again and again.

Intrinsic Motivation by Pursuing the 'Change Agent (CA)' Role

Would you be considering yourself as a *change-agent* who loves to and takes pride in bringing about some changes?

Try this list.
1. I like to try out new things:
    (i) just for fun;
    (ii) because it is a challenge.

2. I prefer to:
   (i) stay at home
   (ii) travel and see new places
   (iii) investigate new things.
3. (i) I want to please other people as much as possible by any means.
   (ii) I don't care whether other people like me or the way I do things.
   (iii) I take it up as a challenge to influence or convince them by studying them scientifically—by applying practical psychology—their likes, dislikes, strengths, weaknesses, any interesting points or unique features.

If you have chosen the answers 1 (ii), 2 (iii) and 3 (iii), then you have maximum potential to pursue the *CA* role. However, if you have chosen 1 (iii) but 2 (ii) and 3 (i), then the potential in you is only around 33 to 35%; or, 1 (ii) and 2 (iii) but 3 (ii) then although you have 65 to 70% *CA* potential, 3 (ii) will spoil the potential.

Brain and Change Making

Ventral striatum is that part of the brain that is linked with brain's reward system. *Hippocampus* is responsible for specific memory functions, for stored experiences.

While we experience change, bring about change, or make change, the brain cross-checks with the stored memory in the *hippocampus*—which identifies the situation as something new and then finds that the new experience is not stored there and thus newness makes you happy—the reward system in your brain's *ventral striatum* gets stimulated. In change-oriented people, both these centres apparently interact particularly well [5].

Right Livelihood

'…work can be something enjoyable that gives a sense of fulfilment, purpose and social responsibility and may even provide a means to reawakening to a 'higher calling', 'right livelihood' or a spiritual endeavour. The idea of working for a higher calling is common. For example, right livelihood, an Eastern concept attributed to one of the eight Buddhist steps or paths to enlightenment, suggests that work, whether physically tedious or mentally challenging, is 'love made visible'…'

"Right livelihood' implies that work should be accomplished without harming, depriving, or exploiting people, animals, and the environment... 'Right livelihood' doesn't necessarily mean that all people working in the defence industry or in nuclear power plants are evil or subversive. What right livelihood suggests is that one first be aware of and acknowledge the inherent harm their occupation may cause and then seek to *balance* that negative outcome with positive ones...'

'Work, even mundane work, can be the source of an inner awakening that causes us to realise the spiritual relationship between our inner being (soul) and our occupation. When we view work as something providing intrinsic worth we move it beyond its extrinsic value as a simple job and give it transcendent value' [6].

A CASE OF MOTIVATION IN A FAMILY ROLE

Riti Patel, MBA (Rural Management) was working for an upcoming NGO, *'Kalyan'* engaged in rural development work near Delhi. She got married to IT engineer Rakesh Shah who was employed in an IT firm at Gurgaon. Within two years of their marriage, Riti got a beautiful girl child Payal. Riti realised that for effective parenting she has to give lesser priority to her job. She approached the Management Committee of her organisation with a request for converting her whole-time job into a part-time one and her appeal was approved. She was managing both very well with part-time help to take care of Payal while she was away to her office.

Meanwhile, Rakesh got a breakthrough as head of IT in a reputed firm but his posting was at the company's industrial township about 70 km away from Ahmedabad in Gujarat. He had to join immediately so he left his family behind without having any opportunity to think out what they will do. This put Riti into a big dilemma but she soon decided to leave her job in Delhi and join her husband as she was convinced that at such a small age and being the first child, it was important for both the parents to be near Payal for her balanced upbringing.

At Rakesh's industrial township there was no job available for Riti. She even contacted the CSR (Corporate Social Responsibility) wing of his company but nothing was available due to recession. In fact, the department had been downsized only recently. Riti was in the midst of a deep frustration leading to depression. She felt that parenting was her duty but she would have felt more motivated to do something in her own professional field.

Payal joined the township toddlers' school and, soon after her joining, Riti fell ill. Medical investigation diagnosed that she had jaundice so life became most restricted for her. Her depression deepened. She was compelled to keep a full-time maid to take care of everything including Payal's chores. She was lucky to get a good one.

Payal started liking going to her school. It took almost two months for Riti to recover from her illness finally. Now, one day when she visited Payal's school to enquire about her progress, Mrs Varghese, Payal's class teacher caught hold of her. 'Oh! You are Payal's mother? I've been wondering who could it be as I have met the mothers of all the students in my class except for Payal's and she told me that you had not been well. Mrs Shah, I wanted to congratulate you for having brought up such an excellent child. She is sweet, sociable, intelligent, has good leadership quality, interested in studies. In a nutshell, she is superbly balanced. I was really keen to meet the mother of such a grand child. It is your achievement, Mrs Shah. She is definitely going to snatch the best student prize this time.'

Riti got a most unexpected surprise with such profuse compliments from Mrs Varghese. And, with this brief interaction, her attitude took an almost 180 degrees turn. All this while, she was so frustrated having been without a professional job and having had to do whole-time parenting. Now, she had a sudden feeling that her role as a mother was more important and motivating than any other job wherever it could have been. She started feeling very proud that her performance as a mother had perhaps reached a peak level otherwise she would not have been showered with so much praise.

What do you think of this real case study? You should take a fresh at your family role as a spouse and perhaps also as a parent and ensure if you had been performing at the peak level with high positive motivation.

REFERENCES

[1] Ganguli, Siddhartha, *Performance Management: 'First Time Right'*, Platinum Publishers, Kolkata, 2008.
[2] Ridley, Mark, *The Cooperative Gene: How Mendel's Demon Explains the Evolution of Complex Beings*, The Free Press, New York, 2001, First Edition, pp. vi–xii.
[3] Ganguli, Siddhartha, *Performance Management, loc. cit.*
[4] 'Choose a job you love & you'll never have to 'work'' *Hindustan Times, Kolkata*, 30 November 2008, p. 14.

[5] "'Wiring' is key to your innovativeness', *Hindustan Times*, Kolkata, 1 December 2008, p. 13.
[6] Hatcher, Tim, *ethics and HRD*, Perseus Publishing, 2002, pp. 50–52.

KEY TAKE-HOMES

- 'Motivation' is of two types: 'extrinsic' (where the motivational inputs would have to come from outside, generated by the work organisation or some others) and 'intrinsic' (where the motivation comes from within yourself—it is self-generated).
- The ideal match is when the work that we perform helps us to create something and, at the same time, becomes the channel for collecting adequate compensation—both in cash and kind. Can you look at your 'work role' from this angle? Needs-satisfaction of your customers is, in a way, one vital channel for the fulfillment of a 'Corporate Social Responsibility (CSR).
- Striking a balance between one's 'working personality (WP)' and his 'work (W)' will also lead to intrinsic motivation.
- If the highest of the performance standards set are taken to represent 100, the *peak performance* would be '100 plus'. It is possible to reach that level through the 'intrinsic motivation' route.

CHAPTER 19

Unconscious Leadership Styles

THE ERA OF UNCONSCIOUS LEADERSHIP BY THE SELFISH GENES

Leadership in the Pre-language Human Society

In the animal world, *leadership* has always been practiced by physical power and prowess. And animals, as we all know, are not intelligently *conscious*. They are conscious just because they are awake and alert—a state of the brain which is essential for survival. Their behaviours are all spontaneous and thus *unconscious* as they cannot think. The pre-language, primitive human world also witnessed the same practice originating from the *creaturely brain* that has been handed down to us, humans, from our animal ancestors (See Figure 5.2).

Leadership in the Post-language Society

With the advent of language, socialisation and civilisation, the power-centric leadership culture manifested itself into a variety of 'control-oriented' leadership styles in addition to the good old way of leading (*'leading'* in the sense of being in control of others) by physical build and power. These included: leadership by skill, leadership by intimidation, leadership by guilt, leadership by overt example (where the leader openly says 'If I can do this, why can't you? Follow me as your role model.' or 'When I was of your age, I did it with ease—you should be ashamed if you can't do it'), leadership by positional power or status, leadership by 'reward and punishment' authority, and so on.

'Control'-oriented Leadership

From the deep down inner *creaturely* layers of our brain, we have the propensity to lead others by exercising control. This takes place in one-to-one, one-to-a-few and one-to-many situations. This 'control'-oriented leadership style is a manifestation of our creaturely psychological needs.

One of these needs, the 'desire to win by beating others and making others lose' becomes very strong in a control-oriented leader and makes him hungry for 'attention', 'acceptance/acknowledgement', 'affiliation' and 'appreciation' from others. When another person is controlled by you, no doubt you are getting his attention and feeling important; he is accepting and acknowledging you in your leadership role; you're getting affiliated into his orbit of respect and honour; and obtaining his silent appreciation.

Leading by control takes place unconsciously and while it may work with a handful few, most people will rebel against it and react by getting into the aggression ('fight') or avoidance ('flight') mode.

In the immediate pre-industrial and freshly industrialised societies, which for many many years were shrouded under cognitive darkness, these control-oriented leadership styles generally worked because the people under the leader took such styles in the image and spirit of parent-child, teacher-student, *guru-shishya* relationships. For leaders, that was the *era of leadership by their selfish genes.*

A LEADER'S CONCERNS

An effective leader has to have equal concern for three factors: the task *performance* (P-1), the performer of the task—the performing person's *personality* (P-2), and the *potentials* of the performer—his skills, intelligences and talents (P-3). For a truly effective leader, these concerns are conscious. He has to be conscious to strike a healthy balance between all these three.

CONTROL-ORIENTED LEADERS: THE BASIC TWO TYPES [L-1] AND [L-2]

There are variations in the control-oriented leadership style. L-1 is the primitive 'hard' control-oriented leadership style, where the leader has concern only for the task performance and targets (P-1) and there is no concern for the performer (P-2) and his potentials (P-3).

L-2 is the 'soft' control-oriented leadership style, where the leader has concern for P-1 and P-2 only but not for P-3.

The L-1 style can be identified from the leader's typical communication messages: 'I'm telling you to do this!' 'You must complete this task in two hours' time. This is my order.', 'If you don't do this, I will be compelled to take action against you.' and so on. (Undertone: rigid, tight order—no scope for any relaxation).

The L-2 leader's communication would take the following forms: 'Could you please do this in two hours' time?' (Undertone: indirect command.) 'You're a good performer. I'm more than sure that you'll complete this task in two hours' time. However, if two hours is too tough for you, then you can take half an hour more as that would not matter much.' (Undertone: setting a target but keeping it somewhat loose, not that tight.) 'If your colleague Ramesh can do this in two hours, I'm sure you will also be able to do it.' (Undertone: comparison). Although such messages exhibit politeness, there is fervour of command in the leader's tone.

LEADERSHIP BEYOND THE SELFISH GENES [L-3], [L-4] AND [L-5]

The post-industrial society saw a sea change in the exposure and attitude of people in business and industrial organisations. Out of environmental necessity, therefore, other varieties of leadership emerged.

Three examples are: 'democratic' style L-3 which is indirectly control-oriented as the power, although not with an individual, is bestowed upon the majority and concern is only for P-1; the 'bureaucratic' style L-4, where the power is in the rulebook or the system or the standards and the concern is again for P-1 only; and the 'participative-consultative' style L-5, popularised by the Japanese *consensus-building* practice where the power is with the 'consensus principle' and the concerns are for P-1 and P-2. The L-5 process is too slow to be appropriate for competitive business and industrial situations. Power being with the majority, or the rulebook/system/standards, or the 'consensus principle'—all represent dominance of the collective 'self' (or, shall we say the 'Big Ego' in that sense). There was thus a need for smarter styles of leadership beyond the call of the individual or collective selfish genes.

How do you identify the L-3, L-4 and L-5 leadership styles?

In the democratic style of leadership L-3, the leader says: 'If the majority has decided that this task has to be completed in two hours' time, you will have to go by that expectation.'

In the bureaucratic style of leadership L-4, there are standard performance parameters for every task, set by industrial engineering studies, and the leader says: 'According to the rulebook, the task should not take more than two hours; so you have to ensure to complete it within that time.'

In the participative-consultative style L-5, the leader tries his best to convince every member of the team to come to the same decision by adopting whatever communication strategy and style would be most appropriate for the team member and also for the situation.

MOTIVATION-ORIENTED LEADERS: THE 'EXTRINSIC' AND 'INTRINSIC' ROUTES

Motivation, as we know very well by now, is of two types: one is 'extrinsic' where the task performer is guided by what he gets from the external environment by performing an assignment—his pay, perks, and confirmation of employment (job security), special incentive, social acceptance, positional prestige and power, recognition, promotion and so on. The other type of motivation is 'intrinsic' where the task performer enjoys what he does—the act of performance of the task itself—he does not crave much for the extrinsic motivational inputs which, he knows, will eventually automatically come if he puts his whole body and mind into his performance.

MOTIVATION-ORIENTED LEADERSHIP STYLES [L-6], [L-7] AND [L-8]

The very first extrinsic motivation-oriented leadership style L-6 is when the leader says: 'If you can accomplish this task within the prescribed time-frame, you'll get this reward' and he dangles the carrot. This style could be described as the 'trading/give-and-take' or 'We win, you also win (Win-win)' style. For a new entrant or a fresher, a veteran senior may not talk about any financial reward, but may say: 'If you can do this assignment, you'll gain very good experience and the learning will be an asset for your future.' In the latter style, the leader's concern is for P-1 and P-3.

The second extrinsic motivation-oriented leadership style L-7 is used by leaders who honour the performer's creaturely psychological needs. A L-7 leader will establish eye contact and listen to the performer if he wanted to say something, without interrupting him or making him stop. Once the performer has finished conveying his message, the L-7 leader would normally come up with his comments in such a tactful manner that the performer will remain motivated. L-7 leader would also make it a point to: give adequate attention to the performer and make him feel important; accept/acknowledge the performer's good points and admit his own shortcomings, should there be any; affiliate him as an important member of his team; and offer him his appreciation as appropriate. For the performer all these motivational inputs are coming from the leader who is outside him. Therefore, it is a case of extrinsic motivation. The L-7 leader's concern is for P-1 and P-2.

A L-8 leader is one who is a visionary and who tries to motivate his team associates by helping them to appreciate and co-own his vision—either the whole of it or in part or parts depending on the interest level. This is also extrinsic and the leader has concern for P-1 and P-2 only.

THE BEST STYLES L-9 AND L-10

A L-9 leader has concern for P-1, P-2 as well as P-3 as he tries to strike a balance.

The L-9 style represents a 'delegative' attitude and stand on the part of the leader.

It is one such positive 'motivation-oriented' leadership behaviour which works excellently provided it is practiced with regular hard and soft control using the process of sharing positive as well negative feedback with the team members.

Another secret of its success is the leader's intelligent utilisation of the 'Working Personality Principle (WPP)' [1, 2]. According to WPP, there are three types of work and corresponding working personalities: Self-Engagement (SE—cerebral brain-based work); People and Social Engagement (PSE—communication-intensive work—speaking and listening); and Physical Engagement (PE—physical movement-oriented work—indoors/outdoors). The leader goes deep into his own total set of assignments and classifies them into SE, PSE and PE types of activities. He also classifies his team members according to their working personalities. Whatever items of work he would like to keep for himself he keeps, the rest he delegates to his team members according to their working personalities. This strategy has been highlighted as a team-building tool, although a little indirectly, by describing it as the Thinker (T)/SE, Planner (P)/PSE, Doer (D)/PE or T-P-D model [3].

The L-10 style of leadership is one where the leader is absolutely flexible and entirely situational. He does not lead by adopting a fixed and rigid style. He changes his style according to the person or persons to be led and also the situation. Where there is a crisis or time is the main criterion (such as in project management, handling of rejections/rework, or execution of an export order), he adopts any of the control-oriented styles L-1 or L-2. Where time is not so important and some future plan is being formulated, he goes for the participative-consultative style L-5 or the visionary style L-8. If he has to offload some of his assignments to reduce his own pressure, he goes for L-9.

We also hear a lot about the glory of the 'transformational' style of leadership in the B-school corridors. It is represented by charismatic leaders who bring about a positive transformation in people. But, there are three burning questions on this: firstly, how many persons do we come across in business and industry who possess and radiate such charismatic aura; secondly, how long does it take for such a leader to bring in tangible transformation in people; and thirdly and lastly, what is the rate of success of such leaders.

In view of such reservations about the leadership styles currently being highlighted and discussed in management circles, we would like to propose here that the leader must adopt his leadership style and behaviour *consciously*. Because of its 'conscious' nature, we'll call it the *conscious strategic leadership style*. It is going to be elaborated in the next chapter.

REFERENCES

[1] Ganguli, Siddhartha, *Performance Management: First Time Right*, Platinum Publishers, Kolkata, 2008.
[2] Ganguli, Siddhartha, *Live Happily, Work Happily*, Allied Publishers, New Delhi, 2009.
[3] Ganguli, Siddhartha, *Performance Management, loc. cit.*

KEY TAKE-HOMES

- The pre-language, pre-historic human world witnessed the primitive leadership styles, guided by the selfish genes that originated from the *unconscious* 'creaturely' part of our brain. In the post-language society, the same power-centric leadership culture manifested itself into 'control-oriented' leadership styles. These styles generally worked well in the immediate pre-industrial and freshly industrialised societies because it tallied with the 'hidden agenda' of the past parent-child transactions stored in the brains of the people who were being led.
- A leader's three concerns are for: task *performance* P-1, the performer's *personality* P-2 and the *potentials* of the performer P-3. He has to strike a fine balance between the three to be considered as 'effective'.
- The two fundamental 'control-oriented' leadership styles are: 'hard control' and 'soft control'. Later on, these have been joined up by other 'control-oriented' styles, such as, 'democratic', 'bureaucratic' and 'participative-consultative' (where the emphasis is on the principle of consensus-building).
- Among the 'motivation-oriented' leadership styles where the motivational inputs are 'extrinsic', the 'trading (You win, I also win)', the 'creaturely psychological needs satisfaction' and 'visionary' styles are observed in practice.
- The best of the 'motivation-oriented' leadership styles are, however: 'delegative' (where the leader practices empowerment and delegates using the *Working Personality Principle—WPP*, with periodic control to provide guidance and support as necessary); and, 'flexible/situational' where the leader changes his style according to the situation as well as according to the personality profile of the performer/team member so that he can obtain peak performance without stress.

CHAPTER 20

Conscious Strategic Leadership (CSL)

EVALUATION OF LEADERSHIP EFFECTIVENESS

Leadership skill, as a personal quality, cannot be measured and thus leadership effectiveness of an individual in charge of a group of persons cannot be evaluated quantitatively like it is done in the case of brain skills and personality traits like intelligence, calculation power, numerical proficiency and aptitude for system development or command over a particular language.

The reason is simple. *Leadership* is the way you deal with people to keep their motivation and morale high, as a consequence of which they carry out their activities and perform the tasks assigned to them to the best of their abilities by tapping the potentials inherent in their personality. All this leads to the results, meeting and, may be, exceeding the goals and targets that were set.

There is something very interesting to note. Negative leadership styles (forcing people to produce) can also compel people to produce the desired or targeted results. People can be driven hard by coercive *control-oriented behaviour* on the part of the leader. So, the measure of leadership effectiveness should not be the 'results', which in the world of work is actually 'performance'. It has to be evaluated considering two most important factors that produce performance, and these two factors are 'personality' and 'potential'—of the leader himself and also of the members of the team. Good leaders deal with their team members, most consciously and knowingly, in a way that their personal resources (namely, the body and brain powers) are positively utilised and their inherent potentials (some special skills, intelligences or talents that they may have) are optimally tapped. Those leaders deal with their own personality and potentials in the same manner. This is our concept of *Conscious Strategic Leadership (CSL)*.

The concept is being presented diagrammatically below:

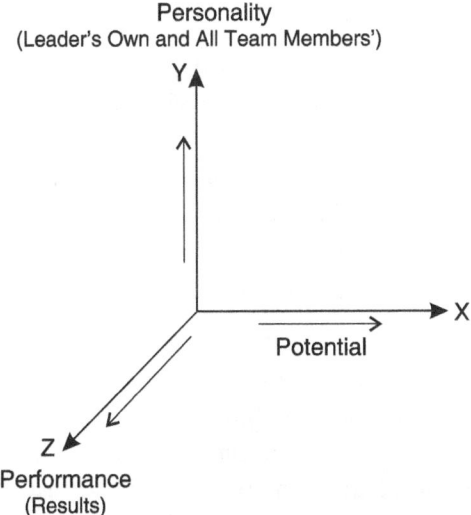

Fig. 20.1: The Conscious Strategic Leadership (CSL) Style

CONSCIOUS STRATEGIC LEADERSHIP (CSL) STYLE: CLEARING THE PERCEPTION

In *conscious strategic leadership*, the leader's steps for leading his people are well chalked out. Which strategy he will adopt with whom and what course(s) of action he will take at what point of time are pre-decided along with a few alternatives thought out, some of which may be taken recourse to if the first attempt failed. Consciously strategic leaders are just like able commanders in the battlefield. Although optimistic and positive-willed, they are prepared for all kinds of consequences. They cannot afford to lose any time by taking a pause to ponder in case one of the moves does not yield the desired results. They are most street smart and situational. Conscious strategic leaders, in today's management, must comply with through their actions, the definition of the term *strategy*, which is the science and art of influencing people to meet the enemy in combat under advantageous or outrightly adverse conditions. The term 'enemy', in the business and industry context, includes the competitors, any internal or external threat and, above all, the leaders' own negative attitudes, feelings and emotions.

In a nutshell, effective strategic leaders always work with a portfolio of strategic options. They endeavour to bring about a painless change in people with non-invasive techniques. They themselves, develop resilience through painstaking habits. They put into practice, certain practically innovative revolutionary ideas.

Jim Collins's *Level 5 Leadership* [1] is uppermost currently in the minds of leadership watchers. The *Level 5 Leadership* is applicable primarily to the top management level (like CEO, COO, CFO, CSO and the like) whereas the *Conscious Strategic Leadership* style that we propose here is applicable at any level including when somebody has only one person reporting to him. It is equally applicable in the family role while leading your spouse or elderly parents and your children.

Secondly, the *Level 5 leadership* calls for the leader's continuity to transform the organisation. Our strategic leadership style does not necessarily demand continuity on the part of the leader. He may leave the organisation, get transferred to another function or location, or move up; but the understanding of the human system is so fast and so thorough in him, that it is relatively easier for him to bring about a painless change—from negative to positive, or from just positive to highly motivated and highly positive with his magical, non-conventional techniques within a short time. Such leaders try to provide positive stimulation to people by providing opportunities for them to enjoy what they do (in other words to 'get engaged') and remain saturated with intrinsic motivation. So by the time he leaves his present organisation to join a new one, those that he was leading would already have undergone an attitudinal change and a value reorientation.

THE UNIQUE BUYING PROPOSITION (UBP) COMMON TO ALL CONSCIOUS STRATEGIC LEADERS

All conscious strategic leaders (CSL in short) possess one common cutting edge in comparison to leaders exhibiting other styles. Their 'Unique Buying Proposition (UBP)', which is something unique or very special to them, is the 4-L *attitude* which has been discussed in Chapter 8. Apart from this, they may possess some other UBPs which would be different for different CSLs but not common like this one [2–4].

A truly CSL's style is firmly supported on four, strong, robust pillars; and these four pillars taken together, constitute his attitude.

The first pillar is the *leader's love for his profession*. Any positive profession, directly on indirectly, is serving the society. An effective strategic leader, like a sincere member of the defence forces, realises this deep inside the heart and takes pride in the profession. In case he does not have much love for his core function, but has love for people, he can look at leadership as his profession because once he is a good leader and has a special knack for it, he will remain a leader all through his forward journey.

The second pillar is the leader's *love for his job*—the work that he does. He loves it because he is performing the leadership role. Since his teens, he had a special knack for leading people as proven by his track records of practical leadership activities. Love for his leadership job supersedes all his other feelings and emotions related to his other work activities.

The third pillar is the *love for his brand—his organisation*. His organisation may have many minus points, many shortcomings; but those do not affect him. He loves it for just one or a limited few most interesting points (for example, it being a learning organisation, or a lean organisation where opportunity for multi-tasking experience can be obtained, or a place where the working environment is excellent etc.)

The fourth pillar is the *love for self*. A strategic leader develops and nurtures love for self by identifying what he is good at in comparison with others. And, this kind of self-discovery is not difficult to make if one is alert and keeps track about what kind of positive feedback or compliments others are offering. There are also others who have developed clarity about his *self-image*; perceptions of own major strengths and critical weaknesses by indulging in introspection and self-audit as a matter of regular habit. Such self-apprising people also qualify to be strategic leaders as, in the process of knowing self, they have set a direction to their life by formulating life's aims and goals. This discipline does also help them to feel positive, proud and confident about themselves as they are far from being confused which most people are.

(There is a simple test that one can try out to determine the level of *self-love*. The human body, including the face, follows the *principle of bilateral asymmetry*. In other words, if the body is divided into two halves through the anterior-posterior or front-back or *sagittal* plane, the left half of the body is not identical with the right side in dimensions. One basic scientific reason is intra-uterine traumatic experience of the foetus during the nine to ten months of pregnancy. An individual whose two halves of the face are symmetrical in all respects is a rare find. A person having self-love is so overwhelmed about self that looking at his own face in the mirror he will have great difficulty in discovering any differences between the two sides. On the other hand, a person who does not love self will have no difficulty in finding out some deviation in the right side from the left side. You can try out this test).

CONSCIOUS STRATEGIC LEADERS 'GIVE' AND 'DONATE'

Those who are full to the brim with 'self-love' are always prepared to 'give'. Energy is ready to flow from their body and brain to others', in contrast with the tendency of stealing energy from others that people normally have or killing others' energy by shouting and screaming while reviewing performance informally or formally.

Strategic leaders belong to the 'giver' category. Their characteristic style is 'You win, I lose'. This propensity does not diminish their energy or effort. On the contrary, they are always filling themselves up with new knowledge, skills and ideas. They are ready to share with those who are willing to receive knowledge, experiences, suggestions, guidance, counsel, physical effort, love, respect and so on.

They also serve as 'donors' as they 'donate' energy to increase the motivation level of the depressed and frustrated.

THE CONSCIOUS STRATEGIC LEADER'S LEADERSHIP STYLES

Conscious strategic leaders know, for certain, that we are all guided by certain 'hungers' and 'thirsts' including the basic ones like for oxygen, food, water and sex. These are essential to be fulfilled for us to survive and reproduce.

Slightly higher order 'hungers' and 'thirsts' are for *stimulus* (physical and emotional strokes without which we get demotivated and depressed); *time structuring* (involving ourselves in activities that we enjoy, without which we get bored and frustrated); and, last but not the least, for *information* (both objective and tangible and subjective and intangible, without which we feel helpless and insecure). Conscious strategic leaders work on people at this level.

PHYSICAL AND EMOTIONAL 'STROKES'

People are provided with physical and emotional *'strokes'* when we satisfy their fundamental 4A creaturely psychological needs: the needs for 'Attention', 'Acceptance/Acknowledgement', 'Affiliation' and 'Appreciation'.

In practical life, satisfaction of these needs takes place through our following behaviours:

- Positive sensory gratification (positive eye-to-eye contact, exchange of smile, greeting gestures including exchange of pleasantries with a soft sonorous voice using sweet and simple words, and occasional caressing body touch like shaking hands, patting or embracing);
- Ensuring emotional security (keeping words and commitments, not comparing with someone else, not managing by intimidation or guilt, not making any deal, not stealing credit rather giving due credit and sharing appreciation);
- Showing concern for the person (expressing interest in his hobbies and pastimes, extending a helping hand in solving personal problems related to family/work-life balance);
- Maintaining internal prestige (by praising in public but criticising in private using the 'sandwich' technique, allowing active participation in decision-making);
- Promptness and timeliness in decisions and actions and putting the right person in the right job—allocating work using the 'Working Personality Principle (WPP)', practicing mentoring and coaching informally and guiding/grooming for personal career growth and so on..

TAKING CARE OF THE TIME-STRUCTURING PROPENSITIES OF PEOPLE

When people are allowed to structure and spend their time in pursuits they enjoy, they feel great; they get fully absorbed and 'engaged' in the literal sense of the term. Their power of concentration reaches its peak and their memory power rises to the maximum level. They also get the advantage of the 'feel good' positive chemicals released and positive electrical waves stimulating the brain cells.

In the field of work, we know by now that there are three types of work in which people can get engaged in, whether at home or outside at the workplace. These are: *Self-Engagement (SE)*, which is working all by one's own self by using the *cerebral apparatus* or the brain; *People and Social Engagement (PSE)*, where the work involves interaction with people and use of the *communicative apparatus* and its various constituents like the eyes, ears, larynx, pharynx, wind pipe, tongue, palate, lips and so on; and *Physical Engagement (PE)*, where the work involves utilisation of the muscles, bones, tendons and ligaments, namely, the *muscular-skeletal apparatus*.

People are generally born with different *working personalities*. Some like SE activities as they are introverted and non-interactive by nature. Amongst them, there are some who are *thinkers* (T); again amongst such 'thinkers', some are logical/analytical/rational thinkers ('Thinkers-Logical'/ 'T-L'), whereas some others are imaginative/creative thinkers ('Thinkers-Imaginative'/ 'T-I'). There may be a few, who combine both logical and imaginative thinking ('Thinkers-Logical-Imaginative'/ 'T-LI').

Several people like PSE activities. They are extroverted by nature. They are very good at interaction and picking others' brains, finally to give shape to some kind of a 'plan'. They are thus *planners* (P). Some of these planners are very good at project/materials/production/procurement/manpower/sales planning—basically the hard side of it, namely, the facts and figures. They may be called 'Planners-Logical (P-L)'. There are others who are very good at planning something with imaginative or visual-spatial inputs (shape of things to come in the physical and temporal space). They may be called 'Planners-Imaginative (P-I)'. There are also the exceptional few who combine both traits (that is, 'Planners-Logical/Imaginative' or 'P-LI').

Some people prefer the PE activities. They are the *doers* (D). Amongst the doers also, there are 'Logical Doers (D-L)', who will implement plans and programmes very systematically, in an absolute step-by-step fashion. There are also 'Imaginative Doers (D-I)' like choreographers, creative dancers, composers, film and drama directors as well as businessmen, industrialists, and managers who contribute imaginative-creative inputs, which enrich their implementation. In the 'doer' category, there are also a few who combine both the traits (namely, 'Doer-Logical-Imaginative' or 'D-LI').

Such people are rare who will like all the three types of work (namely, SE, PSE and PE) equally well and do not perform ineffectively and under stress if the job profile is changed from one type to another. Such versatile (or supernormal) people, if they can manage to maintain a proper balance between the three different traits, go to the top. Otherwise, they become total flops because of not being able to manage the internal conflicts between these three altogether different types of inherent traits. However, it is not difficult to find people who like two types of work (such as, SE and PSE, PSE and PE, or SE and PE) and they do perform both with equal zeal and earnestness.

Conscious strategic leaders distribute work to people according to their working personalities (WP) and use them, in the team situation, according to their T-P-D mix.

LEADING PEOPLE UTILISING THEIR CRAVING FOR INFORMATION

First of all, we have to appreciate that different people have craving for different types of information. They possess innate affinities for different specific types of data. If such data are not available with them, they feel insecure. Conscious strategic leaders are aware about this aspect of human nature, and they utilise people positively using this principle.

Firstly, for any type of work activity such as a project or a problem-solving task, the *thinker* would love to identify and review all the critical factors or parameters that one has to keep track of. The *planner* would love to decide on the priorities and determine who will/can provide what hard/soft data in how much detail and when. He would also love to decide on the specific strategies regarding how to collect all such data/information, and chalk out the structure/format/framework for presentation of the compiled data/information. The *doer* would love to chase people to furnish the data/information, and finally, when the plan is ready, get it implemented in practice by people by taking help from the thinkers and planners.

Secondly, conscious strategic leaders keep people motivated by sharing with them latest figures regarding achievements against planned goals and targets, in which different people are interested specifically—functionally as well as psychologically. They do not share failure data overtly as these are likely to drive joy out of their minds and leave them depressed. Failure data is shared by sandwiching it between two layers of success or achievement data the starting or the bottom layer being made of the most remarkable and unexpected performance achievements (See Figure 16.2 which illustrates the *sandwich technique*).

Thirdly, human brain is selective about information. Not every individual brain is designed to receive and process all types of information. The SE type and thinkers are generally interested in futuristic or long-term information (for example, annual or one full year's results or may be 3 to 4 years' projections). The PSE type and planners are more interested in mid-term information (for example, quarterly/half-yearly results and 2 to 3 years' projections). The PE type and doers are interested mostly in short-term information (namely, daily, hourly, weekly, fortnightly, monthly results and plans and programmes).

ANOTHER UBP THAT MANY CSLs SHARE

Another common UBP that many CSLs share is the people-reading and judging skill. Owing to their passion for people reading and judging, they keep their eyes and ears open for new tools and techniques for human nature study. Several approaches for reading and judging people are discussed in Appendix II. If you are interested you can glance through and if you're not you can just skip as it may seem a little too heavy and serious reading.

REFERENCES

[1] Collins, Jim, *Good To 'Great'*, Random House Business Books, London, 2001, pp. 16–40.
[2] Ganguli, Siddhartha, 'Human Resource Economics: New Insights Into Man's Personal Resources', *Globsyn Management Journal*, Vol. 1, Issue 1, January 2007, pp. 19–27.
[3] Ganguli, Siddhartha, *Performance Management: First Time Right'*, Kolkata: Platinum Publishers, pp. 248–9.
[4] Ganguli, Siddhartha, *Live Happily, Work Happily*, Allied Publishers, New Delhi, 2009, pp. 58–63, 278–290.

KEY TAKE-HOMES

- The evaluation of *leadership effectiveness* should not only be by the result of 'leading'—that is, *performance*. It must also take into serious consideration the *personality* (body and brain powers) and the *potentials* (skills, intelligences and talents) of the leader himself and also of those who are being led by him to perform. Those leaders who attach value and give importance to all these three factors with equal weight are practicing *Conscious Strategic Leadership (CSL)*. This style of leadership would work equally well at any level of the organisational hierarchy as well as in the family role.
- The *conscious strategic leader*, like a real strategist in the battlefield, chalks out alternative *leading plans* in advance. One main UBP that he possesses is his 4L attitude. He is an energy-giver as well as a donor. He consciously satisfies people's hunger for physical and emotional 'strokes' and 'time-structuring', and craving for information. He is also most well-equipped to study people using various scientific (and not just empirical) approaches which other leaders do not even know about.

CHAPTER 21

Conscious Choice of Addiction which will Make You Proud

ADDICTION

Mr Manager, look up a good English dictionary and you will find that 'addiction' is a well-meaning old word signifying commitment, dedication, devotion, inclination, or attachment. In fact, we find a profoundly positive application of the word in *The Bible*: '... they have addicted themselves to the ministry of saints' [1].

Addiction, physically speaking, is like a very strong magnetic 'pull'. When someone is so intimately attached to something—some object, another individual or some activity that he cannot do without it, we say he is *addicted*. Keeping him away from it will make him frustrated and he will suffer from withdrawal symptoms and eventually *stress*. As a result, negative chemicals will flood his brain and body and undesirable vibrations will occupy him, because when he gets what he is addicted to he slips and fits into his 'comfort zone'. There, he is at his high and, outside it, he gets into his lowest ebb and feels terribly insecure. The physiological implications of any addiction, whether it is good or bad, are thus just the same.

ADDICTION IN REAL LIFE

Psychologist Schelling writes: 'People behave sometimes as if they had two selves, one who wants clean lungs and long life and another who adores tobacco...' [2].

Addictions: Bad or Good

In real life, addictions could be bad or good. Bad addictions in real life are far too many to be listed out and we come across some seasoned bad addicts at every other step when we walk. May be you and I are also victims of some bad addictions.

Good Addictions

Good addictions are also of a great variety. Some are addicted to music, others to books, and a few others to physical fitness activities like swimming, body work-out or brisk walking. Some are addicted to a religious faith such as Iscon, Zen Buddhism, Roman Catholicism or Islam; whereas there are others who are attracted to a political philosophy like capitalism, socialism, communism or Maoism. There are also others who are addicted to a 'cause' such as prevention of HIV/Aids, animal rights, fight against racial or gender bias.

There are people who are addicted to another person—may be their mothers, fiancés or spouses or perhaps their coaches and mentors. There are many who are addicted to a habit. Mendicants are addicted to getting up very early in the morning even before the cocks start crooning or to observing a fast periodically.

Creative Persons: Are They Addicted to their Creative Work

We nurture a normal notion that creative people are so addicted to their creative pursuits that they do not need any break. But according to feature writer Kalpana Sharma: 'Many professionals turn off the creative juices once back home' [3]. And she cites as interesting examples the cases of:

- Late painter Manjit Bawa who used to be surrounded by colours at his studio kept the interior walls of his new house in Delhi's Hauz Khas bare.
- Pottery designer Anup Kumar never keeps too many artefacts at home as it blocks his thinking. He believes that it's important for every artist to disconnect from their work in some sphere of their life.
- Fashion designer Ritu Kumar gets tired of looking at a dress she has just designed and keeps it away.
- Interior designer Sachi Gupta chose simplicity for her home instead of the opulence.

- Chef Ritu Dalmia confesses that she hates cooking at home. It gets monotonous.
- Actor Aamir Khan once confessed: 'I don't watch too many films'.

Many creative people certainly love and enjoy their work but they may not be passionately addicted to it. There are some, whose number may be very few, who prefer to live, eat and sleep work—they are called *workaholics*! They are the work addicts. As for others, every working individual looks for a space where he or she is not reminded of work, for a well-deserved break.

As regards *workaholics*, some become glued to their work and continue performing even long after working hours either at the workplace or at home not because of a passion for it, but because they are slow workers and they have to complete assignments within a tight time schedule. There are a few others who pose to be *work addicts* to show to their respective bosses that they are extremely sincere and serious about their jobs. There are still some others who do it out of fear of not getting their confirmation after the probationary period or losing their jobs. A few want to prove their superiority to their colleagues by acting as addicts to their work. These are all cases of fake workaholism. Genuine are only those who are passionately in love with their work and have one-track addiction.

We find instances of truly one-tracked addiction amongst geniuses. Michelangelo and Pablo Picasso were addicted to painting. Einstein and Satyen Bose were addicted to physics. Rabindranath Tagore was addicted to his creative writing and Gandhi to independence for India. Pundit Ravi Shankar is addicted to sitar, Prof. Amartya Sen to economics and Md.Yunus to the concept of micro-credit. Many others, of course, have been and still are equally addicted to their professions, but have not been able to make any significant mark as they lacked extraordinary calibre and talent or perspiration and focused hardworking ability.

ADDICTION: UPS-AND-DOWNS

Those people in whom the intensity of good addiction varies from time to time are lagging behind those others in whom the degree of good addiction follows a certain balanced level or even rises. For instance, addiction to music which is good for you may vary from one period to another. You may be madly addicted to music for a few days, weeks or months; then suddenly your interest may drop. Compared to you an individual who has a sustained or growing interest in music would be considered as being ahead of you.

BAD ADDICTIONS

Addictions to tobacco, alcohol, greasy and spicy food are bad for your health and happiness. The toxic contents of nicotine and alcohol will change the properties of your brain cells and the rich and oily food will make you a victim of hypertension and cardiac-arterial disease.

Human life is always involved with addiction and would be meaningless—perhaps even impossible without addiction. Yet it can be devastated by a badly chosen addiction. A common example today is that of youngsters getting attracted and thereafter, addicted to some cult which gradually unfolds itself into a group of fanatics who are hell-bent to destroy others [4–6].

TWO CASES OF BAD ADDICTION

From the 'Work Role': Nicotine Crazy Suresh Sanwal

Suresh Sanwal, the CEO of a joint sector company having collaboration with a Fortune 500 multinational, is addicted to nicotine. He is simply crazy in his relationship with the toxic chemical as he must have the company of 60 to 70 cigarettes every day. He lights up a cigarette as soon as he wakes up and ends the day with his 60th or 70th one just before he switches off his bed lamp. If one cigarette costs five rupees, he puffs off ₹ 300 to 350 on an average every day. A chest X-ray will reveal only dark shadows instead of what a pair of lungs in healthy condition would look like. But Suresh is afraid of going for an X-ray shooting session. This habit has overtaken him only three years ago when he was promoted to the CEO's post. In spite of his several attempts to give it up, he has not progressed very much. Staying without a puff even for one hour brings headache to him—so acute that he is automatically driven by his addiction reflex to take out a cigarette from the packet that he had put under lock and key.

FROM THE 'FAMILY ROLE'

Love Addict Mriganki Dalmia

Sanjay Dalmia, the working partner of Sabherwal & Singhvi, the top Delhi solicitors' firm and his wife Usha has only one girl child Mriganki who had a passion for design since her high school days. She finished her architecture course from a reputed institute in Mumbai, specialising in interior design. Towards the end of her final year in college, she had entered in one international and one national interior design competition and in both, she topped. Her achievements got good coverage in the media and by the time she finished her course and qualified, she already had a few good assignments to set up her private practice in New Delhi.

Introverted by nature, she was never close to any young man. But, there was a sudden development only about six months ago. She made an acquaintance with Nayan Agarwal, an IT engineer who works for an Indian multinational IT giant in the US. The two seemed to have not only liked each other, but have decided to tie the knot. Strangely enough, Nayan does not want to disclose anything about his family background even to Mriganki, so her parents are totally at a loss how it will work out and what is to be done. Nayan also would not like to come to India for a visit so that they can meet each other. Instead, he is insisting on Mriganki going to the US for higher studies. They could meet there and get married eventually. Mriganki has become so much of Nayan's love addict that she cannot stay even for an hour without chatting with him. Her professional work is suffering very badly and she has started losing some of her best clients. In fact, she has already arranged for her admission in a post-graduate course in a New Jersey university for the coming Fall Semester.

To Sanjay and Usha, the affair does not seem to be very transparent and straight and they also do not want their only child to go away to the US. Meanwhile, however, Mriganki has got so much infatuated to Nayan that she is determined to go to the US even if it means the closing down of her interior business.

DETOXIFICATION OF BAD ADDICTION: IS IT POSSIBLE

Let us first examine what is the current status of techniques to help nicotine addicts to quit smoking. A recent press report says: 'Smokers who have found it difficult to kick the habit may now be shaken out of their craving thanks to a vibratory-cum-acupressure technique likely to be tried out in two Delhi government hospitals and its tobacco cessation clinics. A German-made bio-resonance (vibration therapy) device works with the body's own electrical signals to eliminate nicotine craving... Nicotine craving is based not only on psychological but biological factors. All you have to do is to place your hands on the machine. Vibrations from the machine will lead to body vibrations and the resultant nerve impulses will reduce the craving to smoke' [7]. At least an attempt is on the anvil for helping smokers to give up smoking.

Let us hear what the wellness experts say regarding another addiction—alcoholism, which is as common as smoking. In a recent article called 'Tips to quit alcohol', the writer states: 'Introduce many other drinks like coconut water, lemon juice, buttermilk, mango and other fruit juices etc. in the person's diet so that the craving for alcohol is reduced' [8]. Does he ever claim that the addiction is totally eradicated? In fact, can anyone first claim and then prove it?

Now let us come to the second case. Is the infatuation that Mriganki possesses towards Nayan not some kind of addiction? Is it the *conscious* or the *unconscious* part of her brain which is involved here? Is there a way out? Could there be any handy technique available for detoxification of such brains and eradication of the overpowering addictions?

We'll certainly try to find answer to these pertinent questions which are burning in the minds of millions of people all over the world.

However, first of all, you must upgrade your knowledge about your and others' brain's electro-chemical activities a little more than your present level to develop a better and clearer understanding of the processes. Let us attempt that now.

READ YOUR BRAIN LIKE A BOOK

You are Made of *Cells*

Cells are the bricks that the physical you are made of. Your body and brain are composed of trillions of cells. If these cells were really like bricks, then all those that you are constructed of could have been utilised to build up a complete township. But unlike bricks, your each living cell has its own *consciousness*—a mind of its own.

Your Mind is Made of *Neurons*

What we refer to as 'mind' in general—in common parlance is located in your brain and your brain tissue is composed of cells called *neurons*. There are around 100 billion *neurons* in a single adult human brain. Every *neuron*, infinitesimally small and microscopic in size, has a cell body or *soma* (derived from Greek for 'body') measuring some forty-thousandths of a millimetre in diameter. The *soma* can come in round, oval, triangular or even fusiform (like an old-fashioned spindle) shapes. The *soma* contains the life-support system for the *neuron*.

Each Neuron is Like the Cross-section of a Tree Trunk with Fibrous Micro-branches Coming Out

Tiny branches, tapering at the ends, known as *dendrites* (named after the Greek for 'tree') come out of the *soma* of each *neuron* all around it giving the whole structure a star-like appearance; or they can sprout from its one or both ends. The *dendrites* of a single *neuron* can receive signals from the *axons* of thousands of different *neurons*.

Apart from these mini-branches, most of the neurons have a single, long, extremely thin (so thin that it is hard to see even under a powerful microscope) fibre—*axon*, coming out of the cell body. An *axon* such as one running down the human spinal cord can be up to a metre long. It is your *neuron's* transmitter arm, which makes contact with other adjacent *neurons* to convey 'messages'.

A *neuron* thus looks like the cross-section of a tree trunk, in a real mini-microscopic scale, with relatively stubby micro-branches (*dendrites*) protruding out and one long, hyper-thin hair-like strand (*axon*) jutting out. This object, when alive—can you imagine is the building block of your personality, hopes and fears?

BRAIN'S INTER-CELLULAR COMMUNICATION SYSTEM

Brain's Internal Power Generation System

Your *neurons* can generate electricity, or electrical signals, measured by means of *electroencephalogram (EEG)* in terms of brain waves for the purpose of inter-cellular communication.

To trace the background of the existence of electricity in living tissue, we have to travel back into the scientific journeys of the 18th century experimentalists. During a thunderstorm, Italian investigator Luigi Galvani (1737–1798) laid out a dead frog's legs, separated from the body, on a metal plate. As thunder and lightning appeared suddenly from time to time and the frog's legs twitched in harmony, Galvani's scientist mind concluded that all electricity lay in living tissue. However, later on, British physicist Michael Faraday established that nerves were indeed a source of electricity, but with no particular monopoly.

Dendrites—Receiving Stations: Axons—Transmitting Stations

Talking about your brain's electricity, as a matter of fact, the *dendrites* of one of your brain's *neurons* act as the receiving station for the electrical message signals generated by its own host *neuron*. If these signals are sufficiently strong then a new electrical signal (a product) will be generated. Then the *axons* belonging to the same cell will conduct this new signal on toward the next target *neuron* in the circuit.

The Role of Chemicals in Neuronal Communication

You are aware that chemicals play a very vital role in your life as the food that you eat, the beverages, the drinks and the water that you drink are all chemicals. But, I presume you did not know that some specific chemicals also play a very important part in neuronal communication.

The Communication Process

For a *neuron* to send an electrical signal, positively charged sodium ions (ions are *sub-normal* atoms either backing an electron or possessing an extra one—sodium, potassium, chloride, or calcium ions are distributed either inside or outside of the *neuron*) are briefly able to enter the cells, thus making the potential difference temporarily more positive inside than the outside (depolarisation). You can clearly visualise that the electrical and the chemical processes inside your brain are intertwined and inter-dependent.

However, as soon as this voltage (that is, the difference in potential) becomes positive, say + 20 millivolts, positively charged potassium ions then leave the cell, actually making the voltage temporarily more negative than normal (hyper-polarisation). Hence, when the *neuron* is activated in this way, there is a brief and characteristic change in the potential difference, a positive pulse, followed by a negative overshoot. This transient positive-negative wave usually lasts for about one or two thousandths of a second and is known as *action potential*. The action potential is distinguished from the *voltage* (the resting potential) that is normally generated all the time when the cell is not sending a signal.

THE GAMES THAT THE BRAIN CHEMICALS PLAY

The Role of the Neurotransmitters

There is a minute gap, a *synapse*, between *neurons*. *Neurons* send messages to each other across the *synapse*, between the sending *axon* in the transmitting neuron and the receiving *dendrite* in the receptor neuron. They make synaptic contact with each other with the aid of the transmitter brain chemicals (called *neurotransmitters*) which get diffused on the surface of the receiving *neuron*'s body.

Dendrites can form a *synapse* with other *dendrites*, *axons* with other *axons*, and *axons* can make contact directly with the cell body of the target cell. The most common form of *synapse* occurs when the outgoing part of the cell, the *axon*, reaches out so that its end point, the *axon* terminal, makes a *synapse* with the *dendrite* of the target cell.

The concept of *synapse* immediately presents a problem. Just imagine that a signal—an electrical impulse—travelling at some 220 miles or 354 km per hour, arrives at the end of the *axon*, and hence at the *synapse*. The *axon* end or the *axon* terminal gets excited and develops positive potential. But, then being a gap—the *synapse* between it and the neighbouring *neuron*, how it can cross over to the next *neuron* and serve it as a signal?

What happens is this. As soon as the action potential, the electrical signal, invades the end of the *axon*, it creates the right conditions by which *acetylcholine* (an important and active neurotransmitter) is released into the *synapse*.

Electrical-to-Chemical Conversion

In this way, the original electrical signal is converted faithfully into a chemical one: the higher the frequency of action potentials, the more *acetylcholine* is released. The small chemical molecules cross the synaptic gap within thousandths of a second. They are received by the protein receptors, tailor-made for a specific neurotransmitter chemical, as precisely as a key is made for a lock.

The interlocking of the transmitter molecule within the receptive protein on the target cell creates a potential difference in the target cell which turns into an electrical signal toward the target cell body. There is a net change in voltage in the target cell. If the net change in voltage is sufficiently marked, the target cell will itself be sending a signal to become one of thousands impinging on yet the next target cell. This way, there would be a repeating chain of electrical and chemical events.

There being some 100 billion neurons in an adult human brain, it is virtually impossible to imagine on a macroscopic scale the amount/extent of chemical and electrical activity, even if only 10 per cent of these massive neuronal power were signalling at any one moment. *Neurons* separated from each other by *synapses* take a few milliseconds for the synaptic transmission. However, where some *neurons* are fused together and chemical *synapses* do not exist there electrical transmission takes place directly and much more rapidly. But such cases are few and far between.

Brain Quality: Difference between Individuals: Why

Chemical transmission therefore involves some unnecessary expenditure of time and energy and is responsible for the difference between individuals—from one person to another, as far as the speed of brainpower utilisation is concerned. Compared to chemical transmission, electrical transmission, though fast and economical, will be far less variable and diverse. Chemical transmission endow the brain with enormous versatility: different chemicals have different actions to different extents at different times.

Your brain, therefore, is fundamentally a chemical system—even the electricity it generates comes from chemicals.

Sometimes, neuronal signalling is biased. Known as *neuro-modulation*, it can bias how the target cell eventually responds to an incoming message, even though it does not pass on a message.

BEHAVIOUR OF THE NEUROTRANSMITTERS

The Unique Lock-and-Key Relationship

A message can be sent only if the *axon*'s neurotransmitter (key) fits into the highly specific receptor site (lock) on the *dendrite* as a 'key' fits into a lock. This lock-and-key relationship, unique for each separate neurotransmitter in the brain has been the central discovery of *neuroscience* over the last two decades [9].

Foolproof System

Some neurotransmitters are relatively widespread in your brain while others are more localised. Most *synapses* contain more than one 'neurotransmitter' (key) and more than one type of 'reception site' (lock). Throughout the long process of evolution, the behaviour of the neurotransmitters inside the human brain has evolved in such a manner that they would not like to take a chance in responding to an external or an internal stimulus. The system has evolved as an almost fool-proof one. If one key or one lock is inactive or partially active, the chemical would ensure its entry, release and flow through some other site. However, most unfortunately, some addictive substances, which cause harm to our brain, mimic the effects of some neurotransmitters which cannot be spotted by the receptor sites as you would see in the case of *nicotine* a little later on in this chapter itself.

Neurons: 'Excitatory' and 'Inhibitory' Roles

Neurons primarily serve either 'excitatory' or 'inhibitory' roles in the brain. 'Excitation' or 'stimulation' and 'inhibition' are, in fact, two opposite sides of the same coin. The nervous system works as a balance of 'inhibitory' and 'stimulant' forces.

Neurotransmitters *vis-à-vis* Hormones

What is the difference between *neurotransmitters* and *hormones?* *Neurotransmitters* are local messengers, moving from one *neuron* to another across a single synapse to produce their effects inside the brain only. *Hormones* are long-distance messengers that are carried by the blood to act at distant sites in the body on organs other than the brain.

The Master Hormonal Gland: Pituitary

Your brain's master gland, the *pituitary*, is located in the *midbrain*. It sends out *hormones* to different parts of the body to manage vital body functions such as metabolism, sex and reaction to stress through their effects on the thyroid, sex and adrenal glands. This gland is where 'pleasure' and 'pain' are handled, where hormones are managed and where the brain controls all behaviour.

The Pleasure Chemical: *Dopamine*

Specific nuclei in the brain and their principal pathways are often served primarily by specific neurotransmitters. For example, the neurotransmitter *dopamine* is particularly important in the production of *pleasure*. Central grey areas (neuron cell bodies, often dark grey in colour, making the brain's so-called *grey matter*) at the base of the brain that manage the experience of pleasure are the *nucleus accumbens* and the *ventral tegmental* area as they are connected by pathways responding to the neurotransmitter *dopamine*. The pleasure centres are closely connected to the pathways and the nuclei that manage pain, memory, and emotions as well as appetite, sex, fear, and anger. They are part of the brain's control centre that manage movement from and to the *frontal cortex*, the part of the brain that manages 'conscious thoughts'.

When a person is highly motivated, the rewarding sensations are produced due to a rise in the *dopamine* level in the *nucleus accumbens* and the *ventral tegmental* area.

Brief About Brain Chemicals

A list of your brain's main *neurotransmitter chemicals* are:

Endorphin: It is a 'feel good' chemical which is your brain's natural pain-killer or pain-inhibitor. It appears with the onset of *stress* to provide relief. It is different from closely related *Norepinephrine (NE)* and *Dopamine (DA)* which are small chemicals called *amines*. A search for the natural neurotransmitter 'key' that fits the opiate receptor 'lock' in the *synapses* of the pleasure centres in the brain and elsewhere in the body revealed that it is not a simple chemical like *NE* and *DA,* but a series of relatively long chains of protein building blocks, or 'peptides'. This family of natural neurotransmitters is now known collectively as endogenous opioid peptides, or *endorphins*. The *endorphin* brain system moderates pain, promotes pleasure, and manages reactions to stress. Today, more than a dozen natural *endorphins* are known. *Endorphins* act not only as *neurotransmitters* but also as *neurohormones* (affecting nerve functioning at more distant brain sites to which they are carried by the blood) and as *neuromodulators* (natural chemicals modifying the workings of other neurotransmitters). Endorphin receptors are found not only in the brain but also in other parts of the body as well. Such receptors are prominent in the intestine to help the gut to become happy and remain quiet.

Recent research has shown that co-operating as a group boosts the rush of *endorphins* [10]. Team players, it has been observed, can tolerate as much pain as those who work alone. Researchers at Oxford University found that members of its rowing team had a greater pain threshold after training together than when they dance together, play team sports, or take part in religious rituals.

Serotonin: Its normal level inside your brain will bring happiness and its depletion will lead to depression.

Dopamine (DA): It is a very interesting chemical. On the one hand, it is the messenger for *pleasure* including in eating and in sex. It plays a role in the control of appetite and sex; it brings gusto to the brain. On the other hand, its general depletion throughout the brain leads to *depression*. Its extreme depletion affects the midbrain nucleus controlling fine movements and muscle tone and may eventually lead to *Parkinson's disease* unless tackled timely. And, the presence of excessive *DA* in certain brain areas would lead to *schizophrenia*.

Adrenalin: This hormone is secreted from your *adrenalin glands* at the onset of *stress* and prepares you with the usual reflexive *'fight-or-flight'* strategy for coping with the stressful situation. Another name for *adrenalin* is *epinephrine*.

Noradrenalin (NA): It is a hormone, present with *adrenalin* in your *adrenal gland*. It has an intense vasoconstriction action. Also called *norepinephrine (NE)*, it is a messenger for 'anger' and 'fear'—the 'fight-or-flight' response to *stress*. *NE* deficiency may lead to depression. *NA/NE* governs the *sympathetic nervous system*, which is composed of nerves not subject to voluntary control. These nerves manage the 'fight-or-flight' response associated with the feelings of anger and fear. With the 'fight-or-flight' switch being on, the heart rate increases, the blood pressure gets elevated, blood supply to the intestines is shut down so that blood becomes available to the muscles preparing for emergency action. The *NE* neurotransmitter system is not found in all parts of the brain but in only 1 per cent of the brain's *synapses*. More than half of the *NA/NE* system is concentrated in two small areas associated with the alarm function of the brain, including the *locus coeruleus*, the central grey matter associated with panic attacks in *agoraphobia*. Depression is associated with *NA/NE* deficiency.

A little raised level of *NA/NE* in the *synapse* is essential for result-oriented action and success, in other words, for *achievement motivation*.

Acetylcholine: It is the prototype of many diverse chemical substances that can be released from diverse nerves and neurons in the brain as the all important link in the neuronal signalling process.

Cortisol: It is *hydrocortisone* hormone, an adrenal cortical steroid essential in life. *Cortisol*, usually produced in higher amounts at times of *stress*, is actually thought to help people to keep a lid on their temper and any violent impulses. It has an excitement or arousal suppressing effect. It 'glues' memories into the brain so that unpleasant memories do not prompt the victim to become aggressive or defensive. However, a recent research study has revealed that in delinquent youths, the levels of *cortisol* tend not to rise when they are put in a high pressure or aggressive environment [11].

Fibroblast Growth Factor 2 (FGF 2): Low levels of a brain chemical called *Fibroblast Growth Factor 2 (FGF 2)* lead to 'anxiety' in people. Javier Perez of the University of Michigan, whose study appeared in the *Journal of Neuroscience*, observed in a study of severely depressed people before they died, that the gene that makes *FGF2* was producing very low levels of the growth factor, which is known primarily for organising the brain during development and repairing it after injury [12].

THE SCIENCE BEHIND ADDICTION

Nicotine Addiction: An Example

Of the many drugs and addictive substances that people take to change how they feel, for reducing their tension or any other negative state of mind, perhaps the most common is *nicotine*. *Nicotine* reaches the brain within 10 seconds of the first puff on a cigarette and it is possible to see immediate changes in the smoker's *electroencephalogram (EEG)*, which becomes desynchronised, indicating a less relaxed 'fight-or-flight' action mode.

Nicotine works on a brain cell receptor that is normally reserved for the brain chemical, action-oriented neurotransmitter *acetylcholine*. It mimics the effects of the neurotransmitter but causes harm.

Firstly, the amount of stimulation of the receptor is far greater than would normally be the case for *acetylcholine* itself. With such repeated and stronger stimulation, the stimulators tend to lose their fine sensitivity. Eventually, they cannot function normally with normal amounts of *acetylcholine*; as such, it will need stimulation by *nicotine* again and again. This is the chemical basis of addiction.

Secondly, while *acetylcholine* acts on several different types of receptors, to have more balanced actions, *nicotine* works on only one receptor type; again resulting in rather one-sided effects. These unbalanced effects will also occur in a more global way outside the brain: *nicotine* puts the body into a 'war' mode, ready for 'fighting' or 'fleeing'. Heart rate and blood pressure increase.

Perhaps the feedback to the brain that the smoker is in a fight-or-flight situation is in itself exciting or pleasurable. Most usually, however, smokers will light up simply because their brain is signalling that its respective receptors need more stimulation.

The same relationship exists between the drug *morphine* and its variance *heroin* and your brain's *endorphin*.

ADDICTION TO THE TYPE OF WORK THAT YOU ENJOY (TASK-TALENT MATCHING)

Initial exposure to some kind of work may not make you enjoy so much because you are alien to it and just starting up. But, once you do it repeatedly and don't feel bored and, in fact, start enjoying it, you'll have *dopamine* secretions taking place. The brain's *pleasure centres* take some time to learn to fix or set its response to particular stimuli.

Our *Working Personality Principle (WPP)* is based on this scientific phenomenon [13, 14].

One effective way of detoxification of any bad addiction is by replacing it by a good addiction. It would thus involve diversion of the mind towards some creative or constructive activity that the addict enjoys. Suresh Sanwal can get rid of his addiction to nicotine by finding some really absorbing and interesting work in his work role (either from the 'Technical' or the 'Trans-Technical' side or both) and some good hobby as his pastime. Mriganki Dalmia can reduce her infatuation towards Nayan Agarwal by restoring her keen interest in interior design, by taking up some challenging assignments and participating in some design competitions.

Mr Manager, you have now got a choice of a whole lot of good addictions. Which one or which few you will choose for yourself? The best one, in our opinion, would be for you to choose the type of work you *enjoy* performing. And, if you *enjoy* all the three types, *SE, PSE* and *PE*, then you are at the top of the world. You have the potential to be a peak performer. You should also choose for each of your team members the type of work that he or she enjoys. Then, you have a balanced team. In your family management also, try to distribute the various household tasks according to the likes of the family members and guide the youngsters to direct themselves towards careers and professions which will give them the best satisfaction and happiness.

Now, I'm sure you understand why I called this concluding chapter of *CONSCIOUS MANAGEMENT, Conscious Choice of Addictions which will Make You Proud.*

Wishing you and your team and family a really GREAT future!

REFERENCES

[1] *The Bible*, 1, cor. XVI 15, 1611.
[2] Schelling, Thomas C., *Choice and consequence*. Harvard University Press, Cambridge, Mass, 1984.
[3] Sharma, Kalpana, 'Cut out the creativity', *Sunday Times of India, Times Life Supplement, Kolkata,* 1 August 2010, p. 3.
[4] Schaler, Jeffrey, A., *Addiction is a Choice,* Open Court, Chicago, 2000.
[5] Pettus, Mark, C., *It's All in Your Head*, Macmillan India, Delhi, Indian Reprint, 2008.
[6] Ganguli, Siddhartha, *Live Happily, Work Happily*, Allied Publishers, New Delhi, 2009.
[7] 'Can't quit smoking? Shake it off.' *The Statesman,* Kolkata, 7 June 2010, p. 3.
[8] 'Tips to quit alcohol', *The Times of India,* Kolkata, 11 June 2010, p. 5.
[9] Du Pont, Robert L., *The Selfish Brain: Learning from Addiction*, American Psychiatric Press, Washington D.C., Inc., 1997, pp. 96–97.
[10] Sample, Ian, 'Working in teams reduces human pain', *Hindustan Times,* Kolkata, 17 September 2009, p. 13.
[11] 'Now Bad Boys Can Blame Their Hormones', *The Statesman,* Kolkata, 2 October 2008, p. 5.
[12] 'Brain chemical may play a key role in anxiety', *Hindustan Times,* Kolkata, 14 May 2009, p. 14.
[13] Ganguli, Siddhartha, *Performance Management: 'First Time Right'*, Platinum Publishers, Kolkata, 2008.
[14] Ganguli, Siddhartha, *Live Happily, Work Happily, loc. cit.*

KEY TAKE-HOMES

- Addiction signifies a strong attraction and attachment.
- Addictions could be good or bad. Bad addictions are really harmful whereas good addictions would make the addicts healthy and happy.
- The mechanism of addiction has to do with the activities of some brain chemicals.
- A bad addiction can be detoxified by replacing it with a stronger and over-powering good addiction.
- The best addiction is towards some work activities which you enjoy performing and the act of performing makes you highly motivated and happy.
- You must get addicted to your work and also choose such work for others which they enjoy and the outcomes will make you and them really proud.

Appendix I

10 Key Result Factors (KRFs) for Self-Appraisal and Discovery

If your products and services are losing in competition being 'me too' (ordinary or commonplace), it means that there are no *differentiating features*. It is simple logic that unless they have features that *differentiate* them from the competitors' products and services and provide a cutting edge that will attract the prospects they cannot stand in today's turbulent market.

Differentiating features are outcomes of *creativity*. If creative work is not forthcoming, the conditions for a creative life may not be getting fulfilled for creativity depends heavily on personality traits and environmental conditions within the organisation, which would include creativity-nurturing leadership and supportive team activities and encouraging internal supplier-internal customer relationships. However, such ideal conditions are hard to be found in a typical business and industrial organisation.

Therefore, those *creative-minded* people feel that they are too few in number within the organisational culture and thus they behave egoistically. They are ambitious and determined, but cannot face criticism and stick to their guns. These character traits stand in the way of their producing creative outputs. They are 'at risk' for a creative life. On the other hand, those *creatives* who can ignore or digest criticism and feel comfortably a part of a group and who advance in their *domain* with little feeling of pressure are probably headed for creative or innovative roles.

Creative individuals, in general, whatever may be their domain differences, have quite consistent personalities, and that they are typically demanding, self-centred individuals, with whom it is difficult to remain on good terms unless they themselves adjust with their environment.

However, whether you are *creative* or *not creative*, in order to emerge as a *conscious manager*, you will have to follow the 10 *Key Result Factors (or KRFs)* religiously and ensure that all your team members also follow them. These *KRF*s are recommended equally for your organisational and family management applications. You ought to train the youngsters in your family also to integrate these 10 factors in their day-to-day life.

These 10 *KRFs* have been developed after studying a large number of effective organisations run by effective people.

1. *Time:* Realising that time is the only irreplenishable resource and 'time lost is opportunity lost'; punctuality; regularity of attendance; no time wastage (minm. make-ready and get-ready time; no time wastage for others (timeliness and promptness in seeking, getting and giving services, information etc. advance planning and programming); regular time audit for identification and eradication of time wasters, (e.g. slow working, oversleeping, idle gossip, lack of planning), time killers (e.g., nagging or feudalistic boss, inefficient subordinate, non-cooperative colleague from another dept.), time stealers (too many meetings, late arrival or departure of trains/planes, traffic jam, go-slow/strike/*bandh*); inculcating, 'Just In Time (JIT)', 'First Time Right' (FTR), 'time budgeting' and 'prioritisation' habits; meeting internal customers' and suppliers' time-task requirements; specifying time-task requirements to internal suppliers; evaluating every activity in terms of '*return on investment*' (ROI) of time; using a diary/checklist/memory pad/'to do' sheet etc for effective time management; being focused by setting time-bound goals and targets (both personal and functional) and pursuing them for performance management.
2. *Quality:* Your personal quality (namely, personal neatness/cleanliness, health and fitness, positive body language, best of manners and etiquette, no intrusion into others' private mental zone unless spontaneously allowed, power of effective communication following practical psychological guidelines for inter-personal bridge-building, control of negative emotions like depression, anger and fear in your behaviour with others, knowledge management, motto of satisfying internal customers and suppliers, ego management by thinking beyond self, regular habit of self-audit for value-addition to strengths

Appendix I

and remediation of weaknesses); self-organisation; your environmental quality; the quality of your own work and the work activities supervised by you (with a constant 'Zero Defect' or 'ZD' and 'first time right' or 'FTR' attitude for prevention of rework); the quality of your handwriting; habit of following precision in grammar, spelling and other aspects of verbal language expressions; passion for building a superior quality organisation; attitude for continuous quality improvement for internal/external supplier and customer delight.

3. *Quantity and Productivity:* Attaining optimum speed of 'ZD' performance; ensuring adequate time spent on right positive thinking, right decision-making/problem-solving at the right time; identification of opportunities and anticipation of threats; strategic management; innovativeness; approaching seniors with alternative solutions to problems and not with problems only; targeting optimum power of concentration and memory development; endeavouring productive, positive brainpower utilisation for self and all others being supervised by you.

4. *Cost/Economy:* Looking at all activities from the 'cost centre' point of view; economic habits; identification of visible/tangible and invisible/intangible items/elements of cost with the idea of cost control and saving; cost/expenses budgeting and control.

5. *Income/Cash Inflow/Profitibility:* Looking at all activities from the 'business cycle' approach; identification of 'income centres' and focusing on them; identification of activities and factors on which cash inflow depends and laying thrust on them; endeavouring to increase profitability whenever and wherever there is such scope.

6. *Safety:* Identification of visible/tangible and invisible/intangible hazards; taking all precautions and preventive measures to ensure safety; use of safety devices; ensuring safety in the products and their performance; personal and others' safety.

7. *Information:* Identification of all relevant information/data requirements; collection of information/data—compilation, segregation, classification, analysis and interpretation; sharing of information/data whatever and whenever required; information updating including knowledge management.

8. *Positive Thinking and Open-Mindedness:* Not 'cannot do' but 'can do' (or, at least, 'shall try') approach; no resistance to change—rather willingness to learn, develop, change and take manageable risks; taking all steps for confidence development; helping others to think positively and have an open mind.

9. *Positive Attitude and Behaviour with All:* Responding positively to others' negative attitude /behaviour by identifying from beforehand what 'strengths' they have which you do not have; developing respect for others by looking at their plus points rather than forming a prejudice /bias against them by looking only at their minus points; developing constructive/active loyalty and indebtedness towards the organisation, its policies, its products, its plans and people.— translating such loyalty into a sense of dedication and belongingness.
10. *Your Unique Buying Propositions (UBPs):* What are the special skills-intelligences-talents/unique features in you which make(s) you acceptable to others—inside and outside the organisation (if you cannot find any, you have to delve deep into your hidden potential to make a self-discovery through 'achievements audit' or ask your boss, seniors, colleagues, peers and subordinates).

The following scores are just suggestive. You can change them according to your organisational or family priorities.

1. Time

- Time Budgeting : 4
- Time-Keeping : 4
- Time Saving : 2

2. Quality

- Personal Quality Maintenance : 2
- Environmental Quality Maintenance : 2
- Work Performance Quality Maintenance : 2
- Passion for Building a Quality Organisation : 2
- Attitude for Continuous Quality Improvement for Internal/External Supplier and Customer Delight : 2

3. Quantity and Productivity

- Optimum Work Speed : 2
- Positive and Productive Brainpower Utilisation (Memory; Concentration; Right Decision-making; Making Suggestions; Strategic Thinking) : 4
- Continuous Problem-solving : 2
- Building a Culture of Positive and Productive Brainpower Utilisation : 2

Appendix I

4. Cost/Economy

- Economic Habits—Own and Others : 2
- Costs/Expenses Budgeting and Control : 4
- Continuous Endeavour for Cost Control and Saving : 2
- Keeping Cost Data at Finger Tips : 2

5. Income/Cash Inflow/Profitability

- Endeavour to Prompt Revenue Collection/Credit Purchase/Debtor and Creditor Control : 3
- Profit Improvement Activities : 3
- Taking Judicious Decisions Regarding 'Cash Outflows'/Bearing in Mind 'Cash Inflows' from Interest Earnings and Insurance Premium Savings etc : 2
- Business Sense/Acumen-Gut Feeling of the Core Business Process : 2

6. Safety

- Awareness about Accident-prone Situations/Possible Hazards (Both Visible and Invisible) and Adoption of Preventive Measures : 3
- Safety in Work Habits/Safety in the Workplace/Calculated Risk-taking : 3
- Good Health/Fitness/Hygiene Practices : 4

7. Information

- Updating of Information : 3
- Proper Collection, Collation, Storage, Retrieval : 3
- Sharing of Information : 2
- Giving and Taking Regular Feedback and Reports : 2

8. Positive Thinking and Open-Mindedness

- Past Achievements and Future Winning Events Visualisation : 2
- Looking at Everything from the Positive Angle (as 'Opportunities') : 2
- Openness to New Ideas/Challenges : 2

- Clearing up Conflicts, Biases, Prejudices, Complexes : 2
- Stress Management : 2

9. Positive Attitude and Behaviour with All

- Adverse Situations and Criticisms are Taken as Opportunities for Self-correction : 2
- Absorption of Shocks and Tensions : 2
- Looking at Others' Plus Points : 2
- Balanced Team Approach : 2
- Influencing Others to Attain Effectiveness : 2

10. Your Unique Buying Propositions (UBPs)

Check up with your boss, seniors, colleagues, subordinates to make a self-discovery. If they appreciate some unique points in you which are rare, you will get '10', otherwise '0'.

APPENDIX II

Another UBP of Many Conscious Strategic Leaders (CSLs)

(You can sip through or skip, as you like. It is not a 'must' reading for you. Reading chapters 19 and 20 and following those would be good enough for a practical reader. This appendix is specially meant for a theoretician or a researcher.)

Many CSLs keep themselves well-informed about people as they, by nature, like to study people. People or Human Intelligence (P/HI) is one of the most remarkable UBPs some effective CSLs are observed to possess. They always look for and maintain, at their disposal, alternative tools and techniques for finding out the personality profiles of people, particularly of those who constitute their team or different work groups and task forces. These alternative tools represent different alternative approaches of studying and judging people, their skills, intelligences and talents.

A few approaches are being outlined below.

The Constitutional Approach

The 'Self-Engagement (SE)' type is normally the Thinker T, as already indicated, whose height is the most important factor. For Indian males, any height beyond 1.73 M (5' 8") has a very strong SE or T element; and, for Indian females, 1.57 M (5' 2") and above.

Otherwise, normally the SE type is either very lean and thin in constitution or a little plump and chubby with a short height.

The 'People and Social Engagement (PSE)' or the Planner P has a predominance of fatty tissue and round shapes in the body whereas the 'Physical Engagement (PE)' or the Doer D is of an athletic build with a predominance of square to rectangular shapes [1].

The Endocrinological or Hormonal Approach

Right from the early 60's, for nearly twenty years, Donald Broverman and his research associates in the USA devoted themselves to the study of the impact of sex hormones on humans [2, 3]. They found that high-*androgen* (*androgen* is the group of main male sex hormones, the most prominent amongst them being *testosterone*) men having broad shoulders and chest relative to their height—with more body hair, generally exhibited the 'automatisation' cognitive thinking style. The automatised behaviours are those performed with little *conscious* effort because they have been well practiced and over-learned. They thus belong to the category of routine logical 'planners' and 'doers'.

On the contrary, they also observed that low-*androgen* men performed better in finding a simple figure hidden within a much more complex one—an ability which is described as 'perceptual restructuring' power. Such perceptual thinking style is to inhibit routine, repetitive responses to allow perceptual restructuring—some kind of reorganisation of the ideas available. These low-androgen men are lean, thin, slim, slender and taller than the other two categories of people.

Poor performance on such 'perceptual restructuring' tasks have been observed in the case of robust stalky 'doers' as well as individuals with fatty tissue predominance. In the case of the latter group, the deficiency has been associated with dependency on inter-personal relationships, suggestibility, conformity and a lack of self-reliance [2, 3].

If we were to take these observations seriously, then the top jobs would have to be reserved for men, and within the male group, for the tall, slightly built, low-androgen men who do exhibit intellectual quality and play the role of 'thinkers'. But Broverman found just the opposite—that the automatisation style of thinking was more common in older men with high status, occupation and great social success; because these men were less easily distracted and were more aggressive than 'non-automatising' men. Can we, therefore, draw some kind of a conclusion that, in a group or team situation, it is not the 'thinker' T, but those who strike a balance between the 'planner' P and the 'doer' D, will be more effective in the

Appendix II

leadership role? Certainly, more investigation would be necessary before we can make such an observation.

Women are poorer perceptual thinkers than men in general. But, they perform better than men on simple, repetitive tasks. And, like the high-*androgen* men, as for women, the female sex hormone *oestrogen* at high concentration acts as if it were the male sex hormone *testosterone*.

The Cerebral Selectivity Approach

It is common to think of an individual organism as a learning mechanism, be it a human, an animal or even a plant, as life begins with some sort of basic programme encoded in its genes, and that learning (experience) modifies this programme as the organism matures. The programme exists within the organism and the experience that modifies it comes from outside the organism. However, it must be remembered that the modification does not mean a total transformation; rather it takes place as a refinement or reinforcement of the existing inherent propensities.

The genetic programme seems to set certain conditions on what will be learnt, or, to put it in a different way, on what kind of experience will leave their mark on the individual. It thus makes the individual's brain selective. For example, a species with a superior sense of smell will learn more about the odours in the outside world than a species with a poor sense of smell.

Thus, some individuals are more *visual* in learning, whereas there are people who are more *auditory*; and, there are some others who are more *tactile*, *kinaesthetic* and *motor*. Again, amongst the *visual learners*, some are good at catching the overall and broad aspects, whereas some others have more proficient eyes for details. The *visual*, *auditory* and *audio-visual* learners are good as *planners* ('P').

The 'visual' type can visualise when others are giving some inputs or information, or making some suggestions or proposing something. The 'auditory' type can listen patiently and with concentration when others are talking—they have excellent reception power. The 'audio-visual' type is a combination of both the capabilities—he is a two-in-one person and has a high order of *verbal skill*. Quite a few of the planners, being very friendly, sociable and people-oriented, also do have a strong *olfactory* and *gustatory* power. They love to eat (also to be entertained) and to entertain others.

The 'tactile', 'kinaesthetic' and 'motor' person is primarily a '*doer*': Being a person of action he would always love to be engaged in some physical tasks and activities.

The 'thinker' is guided by his *cerebral* power—logic or imagination or both.

While thinking about the cerebral selectivity of people, we can also bring in, for discussion, another very useful tool, and that is, *Neuro-Linguistic Programming* or *'NLP'* [4].

Some guidelines are provided in Table A1.

Even if we tape record an informal spoken message and then analyse it for word usage, it will take us some time before we can identify the NLP characteristic of the person. Is there any other way by which we can roughly make out an individual's NLP type? Yes, there is. The 'visual' type will establish and maintain free and natural eye contact while trying to recollect something. Same will be the behaviour of the 'auditory' type who will keep his ears alert with the help of sustained eye contact with the speaker. The 'audio-visual' type will appreciate music and, while engrossed in classical or emotional music, will keep the eyes shut. Some of them may hum or whistle a tune.

One 'cerebral' type will have reading and analysing habit. Another 'cerebral' type will be imaginative—either drawing or painting from own imagination or composing a poem or writing a story. There could also be a two-in-one cerebral person. Another 'cerebral' type will be very humorous or witty.

The 'doer' will always look for 'doing'/acting opportunities involving physical movement.

The UBP (Unique Buying Proposition) Approach

An individual's UBP has got to be a natural, inherent trait. It can be honed or sharpened but not acquired or developed out of nothing.

But what is UBP? Is it possible to develop a clear perception of UBP?

Let us take an example from a different world altogether—the world of lizards and reptiles. The *basilisk lizard* also known as the *Jesus lizard* has a seemingly miraculous ability to slurry across liquid, apparently contradicting the usual laws of physical sciences. For a few types of spiders and insects, that are light enough to avoid piercing the surface tension of the water, pond skating is a natural activity. But for heavier creatures, it is an impossible task. But the lizard, *basiliscus plumifrons*, is the only living being that can perform this mystifying trick. Hence this power (which is a *skill)* is the UBP for the *basiliscus lizard*. It makes it possible to produce massive sideways force to stay upright [5].

Appendix II

Table A1

	Terms Frequently Used by	Just a Few Examples		
		Noun	Verb	Adjective
(a)	Thinkers Mental Imaginative	Thought, Idea, Decision, Solution, Opinion, Feeling, Imagination	Think, Decide, Brainstorm, Feel, Worry, Imagine, Create, Originate	Happy/Unhappy Joyous/Depressing, Original
(b)	Planners (i) Visual	Sight, Eyes, Scene, Scenery View, Outline	See, Find, Eye, Observe, View, Witness, Draw	Dark, Fair, Colourful, Far, Near, Bright, Square, Linear
		Drawing, Sketch, Photo, Picture	Outline, Point Out, Colour, Fade, Brighten, Darken	Rectangular, Big, Round, Circular, Small, Faded
	(ii) Auditory	Sound, Noise, Voice, Message,	Speak, Talk, Shout, Scream, Whisper, Murmur, Fumble	High/Low, Fast/Slow Loud/Low, Strong, Weak
		Communication, Speech, Talk, Lecture	Sing, Communicate	
	(iii) Olfactory	Smell, Aroma, Odour	Smell	Strong, Sweet, Fragrant, Faint
	(iv) Gustatory	Taste, Mouth, Tongue, Food, Drinks, Beverages	Taste, Eat, Drink, Sip, Chew, Munch	Delicious, Sour, Sweet, Salted, Hot, Cold, Spicy
(c)	Doers Tactile/Kinaesthetic/Motor	Action, Work, Task, Assignment, Grip, Touch	Touch, Move, Do, Push, Pull, Grab, Grasp, Write, Read, Act	Pushing, Dashing, Dynamic, Soft, Hard, Pulling Strong, Loose, Tight.

Animals that run on land with two legs, such as birds and humans, have little force directed out towards the sides the basilisk lizard is very different. It represents a sub-group amongst the lizard species and all the basilisk lizards possess the same skill. Hence walking or running on a liquid surface is a UBP characterising the entire sub-group as such. In the case of humans, the UBP would differ from person to person in the same social environment, that is, the organisation or even in the same family or clan. That means, if A is a member of the XYZ organisation or family or clan and he has some unique trait which none of the others in the same organisation has and if he is utilising his UBP consciously or unconsciously in the interest and for the benefit of his social unit, then he is owning a *performing asset*. On the contrary, if A has a UBP but he does not utilise it to contribute towards the social unit's operations, then his UBP remains as a *non-performing asset*.

For the water-walking *basilisk lizard*, it is a skill endowed to the creature genetically, but when Jesus walked on water, for him, was it a special skill, or intelligence, or a special talent (which would normally be regarded as a supernatural power and the feat as a miracle)?

Let us take the case of the Greek villagers who, once in a year, walk without pain on red-hot coals, to the honour of a local saint and to the considerable yearly curiosity of the German-based Max Planck Institute [6].

Fire walking could be the 'Skill' level UBP—an inherent/inborn capability, honed and sharpened through practice. It could be due to concentrated application of 'intelligence' using the cause-and-effect reasoning power. It might also be a very special 'talent' (which is of the highest level and order) like the young Canadian woman who had no sensitivity to pain at all, leading to—for the lay people, an extraordinary or supernatural power [7].

'Great holy men and powerful medicine men have always been said to work miracles. The Founder of Christianity was no exception.

Apart from psychic healing, there are reports of holy men changing one physical substance into another, of giving life to inanimate objects and of turning living beings to stone, of levitating, of becoming invisible, of projecting visible thought forms, being able to stay alive while buried in the ground, and much else besides.

While, without doubt, some (or even many) of these performances involved skilful conjuring, and the hypnosis or even drugging of audiences, there is equally no doubt that some of the reports are true. We can be quite sure of this, because there are people alive today who can duplicate these

Appendix II

feats. A large majority of these people are professional yogis, fakirs or spiritualists, but probably the most interesting point is that a few of the individuals involved are not religious in the slightest.'

In the business and industrial context, the UBP may be related to the powers of the body. For example, MBWA ('Management By Walking About' or 'Management By Wandering Around') habit is a body-related UBP.

UBP may also be related to the powers of the brain. For example, innovative propensity is a UBP for some. However, such change-seeking or change-bringing propensity may have different fields of application such as: space (art, architecture, sculpture, landscaping, horticulture, town planning, interior decoration, fashion design, furniture design, painting, writing and so on); materials (developing a new material or bringing about beneficial changes in an existing material), machines (inventing a new machine or bringing about some improvement in an existing machine), methods (devising a new technology or system or amending the existing process), money (multiplying money and/or providing security to money), men (bringing about positive changes in people), and self (bringing about positive and productive changes in self).

Another example of UBP would be 'Total Quality Communication (TQC)', which would indicate the ability to influence and convince people using the 'You Win, I Also Win' approach. This goal may be very difficult to achieve without another UBP and, that is, the ability to judge and read people. If it has been acquired over the years through arduous practice, then it is a *skill*. If it is developed using sharp *intelligence*, then it is not skill, rather it is a type of *intelligence*. And, if the person has the ability to read and judge people, instantaneously or within seconds or minutes then, it is, of course, a *talent*—a quality higher than both 'skill' and 'intelligence'.

Let us take the case of Warren Buffet, one of the greatest investors of all times. He is, as well, one of the best leaders of our times. Warren looks for integrity, energy and intelligence in all his managers. If they don't have the first trait, the manager will destroy your (the customer's) investment. He determines the character of his managers from a distance, by reading what they have written.

Looking at People from another Biological Angle

Testosterone is a so-called male sex hormone secreted by the *testes*. *Androgen* are all male sex hormones collectively. Winning a match elevates testosterone levels whereas losing one lowers them. This elevation of testosterone levels in the winner seems to be related to his elated mood because the elevation in testosterone depends on how the winner feels about winning a match. The creaturely psychological need number one, namely, the *'desire to win'* is thus the natural propensity in a male to raise his testosterone level. The rise is lower or does not happen at all in men who do not regard winning the match as important, or if winning was by chance rather than player's own effort [8–10].

Thus women and men, who are highly competitive in nature having a very strong 'winning' motive, are governed by the male sex hormones.

Female sex hormones are *oestrogen* and *progesterone*. Interestingly, both males and females possess both male and female sex hormones and their levels vary from person to person, from age to age, and from situation to situation.

Androgens in women come from two glands: the *ovaries* and the *adrenal glands*. They also secrete *progesterone* from the *adrenal glands*. Receptors for sex hormones are found primarily in the *hypothalamus* located in the lower brain, also in the 'higher' areas of the cerebral hemispheres of the brain, which are involved in complex processing of information. One of the concerned areas is the *hippocampus*, a region of the brain involved in processing spatial information and short-term memory. Despite that there is no sex difference in the distribution of these receptor sites, the fact that steroid hormones concentrate in the higher regions of the brain suggests the possibility that they might influence ways of thinking. This aspect of human differences has already been covered under 'The Endocrinological or Hormonal Approach' earlier in this Appendix.

The typical nature and behavioural characteristics of males and females are given in Table A2 [11–13].

For any male, who displays one or more good feminine attribute(s), absent in other males in the environment, it is a UBP for him. The same principle is equally applicable in the case of female who possesses some typically male positive qualities.

And, any individual who possesses and exhibit both masculine and feminine quality attributes, is a versatile, supernormal or extraordinary person.

Appendix II

Table A2

Males	Females
(Ancient Occupation: Hunters)Takers of actions. Strong visual-spatial skill (eye acuity/goal-directedness high/good power of visualisation)	(Ancient Occupation: Gatherers of Fruits and Vegetables, Roots and Tubers) Communicators; Strong verbal-perceptual skill
Maths ability (visual-spatial)	Maths ability (verbal)
Intuitive in thinking—not capable of much deep thought process	More self-engaged/loner
Ability to calculate distance/find direction/ superior navigational abilities/can manage talking and route finding while driving	Analytical in thinking
Fine motor coordination and finger dexterity/sensitive to touch	Emotionally inclined; sensitive and sophisticated/ possesses ability to read from verbal/visual cues/ maternal feelings—full of affection
More rule-bound; less sensitive to situational variables; more single-minded/more focused/more persevering	Very sensitive to context
Knack for perceiving/manipulating objects in space/better at orienting themselves in space	Special knack for words: fluency/verbal/reasoning/ reading/writing prose/strong verbal memory
Good at solving problems by visualising them in the form of images (thus much more effective in higher maths solution through symbols)	Good at performing repetitive tasks. Good at solving problems by mentally expressing them verbally
Under threat: more inclined to confront and fight	*Under threat:* more inclined to react by withdrawing / becoming quiet and absorbent
Negative propensities: Hyperactive; mania/aggression/obsession	*Negative propensities:* depression/anxiety neurosis/ hysteria

SKILLS-INTELLIGENCE-TALENTS

Those who are guided largely by the *cerebral apparatus* or brain, we have put them under the *Self-Engagement (SE)/Thinker (T)* categories. The Bible of vocational counselling [14] has shown such activities under the 'Data' group. Data-oriented work activities, which require minimum application of mental power and can be developed into 'skills', include: comparing one item/data/statement with another/copying data from one place to another/computing/compiling data. The place of such *'skills'* is therefore, at the lowest level of SE or T type of work. When the work involves 'analysing', then the question of *intelligence* (logical thinking/ rationalising) crops up which is of a higher status than *'skills'* because these involve some specific powers of the upper brain (the *cerebral cortex*). Examples of such data-oriented work include: coordinating and innovating, and synthesizing, which would be regarded as special *'talents'*.

Our *People and Social Engagement (PSE)/Planner (P)* categories of people, guided by their *communicative apparatus* (the cerebral apparatus, of course, being in the background), would normally be engaged in the following activities:

At the Inner/Lower Brain's 'Skill' Level

Exchanging information: talking to, conversing with, and/or signalling people to convey or obtain information, or clarifying and working out details of one assignment, within the framework of well-established procedures; *coaching*: befriending and encouraging individuals on either in a one-to-one or small group situation, and giving instruction, advice, and personal assistances concerning activities of daily living, the use of various institutional services and participation in groups; *persuading*: influencing others in favour of a product, a service, or *point of view* by talks or demonstration; *diverting:* amusing others.

At the Outer/Upper Brain's 'Intelligence' Level

Consulting: Serving as a source of technical/professional information and giving such information and or providing ideas to define, clarify, enlarge upon, or sharpen procedures, capabilities, or product specifications; *instructing*: teaching subject matter to others, or training others through explanation, demonstration, practice, and test; *motivating*: supporting and influencing individuals to accept or cooperate with tailor-made procedures, when necessary.

At the Outer/Upper Brain's 'Talent' Level

Supervising /managing, determining and/or interpreting work procedures for a group of employees, assigning specific duties to them, maintaining harmonious relations amongst them, evaluating performance (both routine/ prescribed and specially contributed/discretionary) and promoting efficiency and other organisational values; making decisions on procedural and technical levels; *negotiating*: exchanging ideas, information, and opinions with others on a formal basis to formulate policies and programmes on an initiating basis and/or arriving at resolutions of problems growing out of administration of existing policies and programmes, usually after a bargaining process; *mentoring:* dealing with individuals in terms of their overall life adjustment behaviour in order to advise, counsel and /or guide them, with regard to problems that may be resolved by legal, scientific, clinical, spiritual and or other professional principles, advising people on implementation of diagnostic or similar categories, courses of action open to deal with a problem , and merits of one strategy over another.

Our *Physical Engagement (PE)/Doer (D) categories* of people, guided by their whole body or parts of the muscular-skeletal apparatus, would normally be engaged in the following types of work activities:

At the Inner/Lower Brain's 'Skill' Level

Attending to some routine manual or even some mental work requiring involvement of the whole body or major body parts; formally responding physically to somebody's request.

At the Outer/Upper Brain's 'Intelligence' Level

Manipulating, operating, controlling, driving, controlling using one's own discretion largely.

At the Outer/Upper Brain's 'Talent' Level

Precision-working; setting up something; creatively utilising the body and body parts spatially (as in creative dancing/acting/aerobics/improvised physical exercises such as *Tai Chi*) [15].

The *skills*, being of a lower level, can be prescribed and measured and demanded of people particularly at the lower hierarchical levels of the organisation. Conversely, the higher traits such as *intelligences* and *talents* can be least prescribed and measured because those call for the fullest use of the special constellation of abilities that are within you. The more *intelligences* and *talents* you possess, the less people you will have to compete with. The higher you climb in utilising your skills, intelligences and talents, the more motivated and self-worthier you feel because of your intrinsic satisfaction. You will then be able to attain the peak position in your 'self-love' factor.

REFERENCES

[1] Ganguli, Siddhartha, *Live Happily, Work Happily,* Allied Publishers, New Delhi, 2009, pp. 70–79.
[2] Broverman, D.M., 'Generality and behavioural correlates of cognitive styles', *Journal of Consulting Psychology*, Vol. 28, 1964, pp. 487–500.
[3] Broverman, D.M., Klaiber, E.L. and Vogel, W., 'Gonadal hormones and cognitive functioning', In: *The Psychobiology of Sex Differences and Sex Roles* (ed. Parsons, J. E.), McGraw-Hill, New York, 1980, pp. 57–80.
[4] Ganguli, Siddhartha, *Business Communication: The S-M-A-R-T Roadmap for Your Career Growth,* Platinum Publishers, Kolkata, 2009, pp. 149–155.
[5] 'Lizard—a Water Walk Mystery', *Hindustan Times,* Kolkata, 26 November 2004, p. 14.
[6] Durden-Smith, Jo and Diane De Simone, *Sex and the Brain: The Separate Inheritance*, Pan Books, London, 1983, p. 42.
[7] Gooch, Stan, *The Secret Life of Humans*, J. M. dent and Sons Ltd., London, 1981, p. 18.
[8] Mazur, A. and Lamb, T.A., 'Testosterone status and mood in human males', *Hormones and Behaviour*, Vol. 14, 1980, pp. 236–246.
[9] Booth, A., Shelley, G., Mazur, A., Throp, G. and Kittock, R., 'Testosterone and winning and losing in competition', *Hormones and Behaviour*, Vol. 23, 1980, pp. 556–571.
[10] McCall, K., Gladue, B. and Joppa, M., 'Winning, losing, mood and testosterone', *Hormones and Behaviour,* Vol. 26, 1992, pp. 486–506.
[11] Walsh, Kevin, *Neuropsychology*, B.I. Churchill Livingstone, New Delhi, 1994.
[12] Durden-Smith *et al., loc. cit.*
[13] Roger, Lesley, *Sexing the Brain*, Pan Books, London, 1999.
[14] *Dictionary of Occupational Titles*, Vol. II, US Govt. Printing Office, Washington, D.C., 1975.
[15] Bolles, Richard Nelson, *What Color is Your Parachute?* Berkeley, Ten Speed Press, California, 1978, pp. 77–103.

www.ingramcontent.com/pod-product-compliance
Lightning Source LLC
Chambersburg PA
CBHW071426150426
43191CB00008B/1053